T0215688

Practical Vaadin

Developing Web Applications in Java

Alejandro Duarte

Apress®

Practical Vaadin: Developing Web Applications in Java

Alejandro Duarte
Turku, Finland

ISBN-13 (pbk): 978-1-4842-7178-0
https://doi.org/10.1007/978-1-4842-7179-7

ISBN-13 (electronic): 978-1-4842-7179-7

Managing Director, Apress Media LLC: Welmoed Spahr
Acquisitions Editor: Jonathan Gennick
Development Editor: Laura Berendson
Coordinating Editor: Jill Balzano

Cover image designed by Freepik (www.freepik.com)

Distributed to the book trade worldwide by Springer Science+Business Media LLC, 1 New York Plaza, Suite 4600, New York, NY 10004. Phone 1-800-SPRINGER, fax (201) 348-4505, e-mail orders-ny@springer-sbm. com, or visit www.springeronline.com. Apress Media, LLC is a California LLC and the sole member (owner) is Springer Science + Business Media Finance Inc (SSBM Finance Inc). SSBM Finance Inc is a **Delaware** corporation.

For information on translations, please e-mail booktranslations@springernature.com; for reprint, paperback, or audio rights, please e-mail bookpermissions@springernature.com.

Apress titles may be purchased in bulk for academic, corporate, or promotional use. eBook versions and licenses are also available for most titles. For more information, reference our Print and eBook Bulk Sales web page at http://www.apress.com/bulk-sales.

Any source code or other supplementary material referenced by the author in this book is available to readers on GitHub via the book's product page, located at www.apress.com/9781484271780. For more detailed information, please visit http://www.apress.com/source-code.

Printed on acid-free paper

To my father. There's no better teacher than a good father.

Table of Contents

About the Author

Alejandro Duarte is a software engineer currently working for Vaadin Ltd as their Developer Relations Manager. This is his third book on Vaadin. Alejandro started to code at age 13 using the BASIC programming language on a black screen with a blinking cursor serving as the IDE. He quickly moved to C and C++—languages he still loves and enjoys—and then to Java during his computer science studies at the National University of Colombia from where he graduated. Alejandro moved to the UK and later to Finland to foster his career in the open source software industry. He became one of the well-known faces in the Vaadin and Java communities, having published articles and videos with hundreds of thousands of views in official Vaadin channels and other content portals, and presented technical topics at international Java conferences and Java User Groups. Alejandro splits his free time between his passion for the electric guitar and the photography world. You can contact him through his personal blog at `www.programmingbrain.com`.

About the Technical Reviewer

Andres Sacco has been working as a developer since 2007 in different languages including Java, PHP, Node. js, and Android. Most of his background is in Java and the libraries or frameworks associated with this language, for example, Spring, Hibernate, JSF, and Quarkus. In most of the companies that he worked for, he researched new technologies in order to improve the performance, stability, and quality of the applications of each company.

Acknowledgments

Writing a book is quite an adventure. Although you have a map, the fine-grained details of the terrain are uncharted. I took on this adventure fully aware of the fantastic people who, in one way or another, would walk the journey with me.

I had an outstanding cartographer—the team at Apress. Jonathan Gennick helped me to make the most out of the journey. Jill Balzano made sure that my gear worked through the ride. Andres Sacco pointed out the immediate dangers and suggested safer pathways.

Writing this book would have been impossible without the almost unconditional support from Vaadin Ltd. This extraordinary company allowed me to use a substantial part of my work time to write the draft. Marcus Hellberg made sure to clear up many of the obstacles I would have never detected by gazing at the map. My teammates, especially Mikael Sukoinen and Luis Gutierrez, watched my back and told inspiring stories every Monday at 5 p.m.

When you take on an adventure like this, the stories that many other adventurers have told you come to mind and inspire you. In every paragraph that forms the chapters of this book, there is a software developer with whom I interacted before. Sami Ekblad, Matti Tahvonen, Leif Åstrand, Petter Hölmström, Jani Laakso, Geovanny Mendoza, Ricardo Cantillo, Camilo Gonzales, Yury Niño, Julien Monnier, Karan Biawat, Alexandros Milaios, Orlando Vásquez, Andrea Bosio, Jet Beray, and many others left a mark in this voyage.

Like in every endeavor that imposes challenges, I was accompanied by those who provide comfort and love when you need to take a break to prepare for the next leg of the journey. My parents and siblings, Mari Vento, Jussi Kalliokorpi, Eva Adolfsson, Noomi Örså, Dora Quintero, José Pabón, Yenny Bermúdez, Camilo Macias, and Erkki Suikki. To all of you, thank you!

Introduction

This book teaches you how to be productive with Java web application development. Java is the number one programming language and runtime environment for high-quality, enterprise-ready software in the industry, and it will remain as such in the years to come. From credit cards (through Java Card) to remote-controlled rovers searching for water and life on Mars, Java has proven to be fast, secure, reliable, and modern.

The rich Java ecosystem provides developers with an army of libraries, frameworks, tools, patterns, and practices to triumph in the software development field. One of the soldiers in the Java ecosystem is Vaadin—an open source web framework that reduces costs by shortening the development time of business web applications. Vaadin is a Finnish word that means "reindeer," and this reindeer's motto is "Fight for Simplicity." Vaadin simplifies web software development by offering the best developer experience in the market to Java developers who prefer to code in Java.

Audience

This book is for software developers with a basic or higher knowledge of the Java programming language who want to build on their Java skills to create web graphical user interfaces. It's tailored to those who want to create web applications without having to code in JavaScript and HTML and, instead, leverage the power of Java and its ecosystem in the presentation layer. It's also a good resource for developers preparing to take and pass the Vaadin certification exams or who want to strengthen their expertise with the framework.

Structure of the Book

A picture is worth a thousand words. And mostly so in a book that explains how to create graphical user interfaces. The book contains more than 140 screenshots and figures that make the topics easier to grasp. The book includes example projects that can be run independently and, in most cases, are formed by independent screens to reduce the need to remember code from previous chapters or even sections.

The book contains 13 chapters grouped into four main parts:

1. Chapters 1 and 2 get you started with web development and Vaadin. You'll learn about the Web platform technologies, web servers, and Java web development.

2. Chapters 3–6 cover the fundamentals of Vaadin—the building blocks that you'll use to create web user interfaces with the framework.

3. Chapters 7–11 cover advanced topics such as Server Push, custom styles, responsive design, and client-side views with TypeScript.

4. Chapters 12 and 13 cover the basics of the Vaadin integrations with Spring and Jakarta EE and SQL database connectivity using these frameworks.

This book doesn't pretend to be a complete reference document about Vaadin. I made a good effort to explain the concepts using an informal, relaxed writing style in contrast to the more reference-like style often required in official product documentation. I'm convinced that the Vaadin documentation and this book are the perfect mix to master Vaadin.

For topics not covered in this book or in the official documentation, I invite you to join the active Vaadin Community on the channels available at `www.vaadin.com`.

PART I

Getting Started

CHAPTER 1

The World of Vaadin

This chapter serves as a general introduction to web development and the technologies around Vaadin. This is one of the few chapters in which you will see HTML and JavaScript code (and even the Python interpreter), I promise.

A CRUD in One Line of Code

When I started my career in web development, I joined a group of developers in the enrollment department of one of the largest universities in South America. The department operation was supported by a web application written in Java with Struts 2 (a Java web framework), Hibernate (a database persistence framework), Spring Framework (the enterprise configuration framework or, as we used to describe it, the glue of the application), and many other libraries.

Many of the web pages in the application shared a common UI (user interface) pattern: they all had a form to search data, a table to present the data, and options to operate on the data. In other words, the application had tons of Create, Read, Update, and Delete (*CRUD*) views. The code of the application included helpers for implementing these kinds of views. However, this involved duplicating code—something I wasn't very happy about.

I started to research Java web frameworks in hopes of finding ideas that helped me solve this problem when I discovered Google Web Toolkit (GWT). GWT included a Java to JavaScript compiler which allowed developers to implement web user interfaces in Java rather than in JavaScript. I enjoyed the innovative approach, and as I learned more about it, I discovered that there was an even more mature web framework that used the same philosophy, except it didn't compile Java code to JavaScript. Its name, *Vaadin*.

After some days playing with Vaadin, I relatively quickly implemented a reusable library to dynamically create CRUD views with one line of Java. Here's an example:

```
GridCrud<User> crud = new GridCrud<>(User.class);
```

© Alejandro Duarte 2021
A. Duarte, *Practical Vaadin*, https://doi.org/10.1007/978-1-4842-7179-7_1

Figure 1-1 shows the type of CRUD views that can be created with this library.

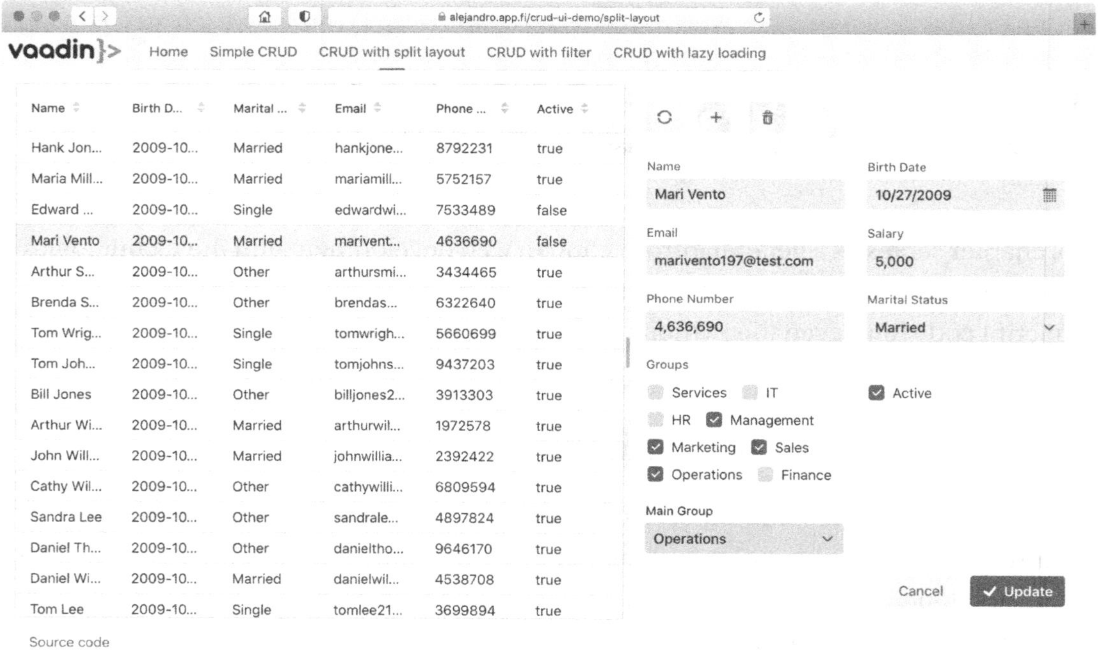

Figure 1-1. *A CRUD view implemented with Vaadin*

The fact that Vaadin allowed me to code the web user interface using Java running on the server side was the main reason I decided to adopt it in many of my future projects. Being able to use the same programming language in all the layers of the application removed the associated efforts in context shifting. Similarly, the learning curve that developers had to go through when they joined a project was almost flat—if they knew Jvava, they were productive with Vaadin almost instantly.

The same will happen to you as you go through this book—you'll quickly be able to implement web UIs for your Java projects as you learn Vaadin. By the end of the book, you'll have the skills to implement and maintain Vaadin applications and, why not, create and publish your own reusable libraries like I did with the CRUD library.

Note   If you are curious, the CRUD library is open source and available for free at `https://vaadin.com/directory/component/crud-ui-add-on`.

The Web platform

Sometimes, developing with Vaadin feels like magic. You type a Java snippet of code that's supposed to show a button on the browser, and the button indeed magically appears there. I want to show you that there's no such thing as magic in software development. If you understand the underlying mechanisms, you'll see there are no tricks, and you'll be in a better position to master any technology.

Beside the Java programming language, the fundamental technologies are those in the *Web platform*. The Web platform is a set of programming languages and API standards developed mainly by the World Wide Web Consortium and implemented by web browsers. This includes HTTP, HTML, ECMAScript (the standard governing JavaScript), DOM Events, XMLHttpRequest, CSS, Web Components, Web Workers, WebSocket, WebAssembly, Geolocation API, Web Storage, and several others.

It can be daunting to master all these technologies, but the reality is that you will mostly use three of them directly in everyday web development: HTML, JavaScript, and CSS. Vaadin abstracts away HTML and JavaScript (alongside related APIs), so you end up using only Java and CSS most of the time. However, it's always good to understand the underlying technologies at least to some degree.

HTML

HTML (Hypertext Markup Language) is what browsers use as the source when they render a web page. Hypertext means text with hyperlinks. You have probably clicked many hyperlinks before when you navigated from one page to another. When you see a web page, you are seeing the rendered version of an HTML document. An HTML document is a file (in memory or in a hard drive) that consists of tags and text and, since HTML5, starts with a *Document Type Declaration*:

```
<!DOCTYPE html>
```

Most tags are used in pairs. For example:

```
<h1>It works!</h1>
```

In this example, `<h1>` is the opening tag, and `</h1>` the closing tag. The text between the tags is the content of the tag and can also contain other HTML tags. In the previous example, the text *The Web platform* is rendered by browsers using a heading style. There are several levels of headings, for example, `<h2>`, `<h3>`, etc.

HTML tags not only format code but render UI controls like buttons and text fields. The following snippet of code renders a button:

```
<button>Time in the client</button>
```

The main parts of an HTML document are structured in three tags:

- `<html>`: The root or top-level element of the document

- `<head>`: Metadata about the document to add resources (images, JavaScript, CSS) or configure things such as the title of the page (using the `<title>` tag)

- `<body>`: The renderable content of the document

Opening tags may include *attributes*. For instance, you can specify the language of the page by using the `lang` attribute of the `<html>` tag:

```
<html lang="en"></html>
```

If we put together the previous snippets of code inside the `<body>` element, we can form a complete and valid HTML document that all browsers can render. Listing 1-1 shows a complete and valid HTML document.

Listing 1-1. A complete HTML document

```
<!DOCTYPE html>
<html lang="en">
<head>
  <title>The Web platform</title>
  <link rel="stylesheet" href="browser-time.css">
</head>
<body>

<h1>It works!</h1>
<button>Time in the client</button>

</body>
</html>
```

> **Note** HTML doesn't care about indentations. Developers do, and some choose to indent the content of the <html> and <body> tags, while others prefer not to do it. I prefer to not indent these since they present in almost all documents, and they just shift everything to the right. However, I do indent the content of the HTML tags inside the <body> tag for readability. In the previous example, none of these tags have other tags as content, so there's nothing to indent inside the <body> tag. Moreover, most IDEs indent with the style I used in the example.

If you use a plain text editor (next chapters cover setting up a development environment) to create a *browser-time.html* file and open this file in a web browser, you'll see something similar to the screenshot in Figure 1-2.

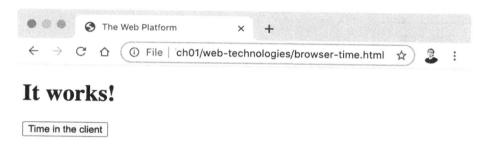

Figure 1-2. *A simple HTML document rendered in a web browser*

I encourage you to try this on your computer and experiment with the code. Try adding tags such as <input> and formatting text with <b>, <i>, and <code>.

> **Note** You can find a comprehensive list of all the tags in HTML on the Mozilla Developer Network (MDN) website at *https://developer.mozilla.org/ en-US/docs/Web/HTML/Element*. In fact, the MDN is an excellent source for learning everything about the technologies of the Web platform.

JavaScript and DOM

JavaScript is a multipurpose, prototype-based (allows the creation of objects without defining classes prior), single-threaded, scripting programming language with first-class functions. Besides its name and the Date object (which is a direct port of Java's java.util.Date class), JavaScript has nothing to do with the Java language itself. However, JavaScript is frequently used in conjunction with Java to develop web applications—Java on the server, JavaScript on the client. JavaScript is the programming language of the web browsers.

The *DOM* (Document Object Model) is a language-independent API that represents an HTML (or more generally, XML) document as a tree. Web browsers implement the DOM as a JavaScript API. Figure 1-3 depicts the DOM hierarchy of the HTML document developed in the previous section.

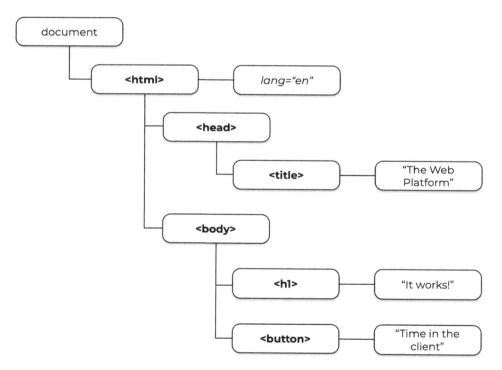

Figure 1-3. *Example of Document Object Model for an HTML document*

With the JavaScript DOM API, developers can add, change, and remove HTML elements and its attributes, enabling the creation of dynamic web pages. To add JavaScript logic to an HTML document, you can use the <script> tag:

```
<!DOCTYPE html>
<html>
...
<body>
...
<script>
   ... JavaScript code goes here ...
</script>

</body>
</html>
```

I like to have the JavaScript code in separate files. An alternative way to add JavaScript is by leaving the content of the <script> tag empty and using the src attribute to specify the location of the file:

```
<script src="time-button.js"></script>
```

Returning to the HTML document of the previous section, the JavaScript logic to make the button work can be placed in the *time-button.js* file (next to the *browser-time. html* file) with the following content:

```
let buttons = document.getElementsByTagName("button");

buttons[0].addEventListener("click", function() {
  let paragraph = document.createElement("p");
  paragraph.textContent = "The time is: " + Date();
  document.body.appendChild(paragraph);
});
```

I tried to write the previous JavaScript code as clear as possible for Java developers. This script gets all the <button> elements in the document as an array and adds a click listener to the first one (incidentally, there's only one button). The click listener is implemented as a function that gets called when the user clicks the button. This listener creates a new <p> element using the DOM API and sets its text content to show the current time. It then appends the newly created element to the end of the <body> element. The result is shown in Figure 1-4.

Figure 1-4. *A simple JavaScript application running in a web browser*

CSS

CSS (Cascading Style Sheets) is a language that allows to configure fonts, colors, spacing, alignment, and other styling features that dictate how an HTML document should be rendered. One easy way to add CSS code to an HTML document is to use a `<style>` tag in the `<head>` element:

```
<!DOCTYPE html>
<html>
<head>
  ...
  <style>
    ... CSS code goes here ...
  </style>
</head>
  ...
</html>
```

As with JavaScript files, I like to have separate files to define CSS styles. This is done by using a `<link>` tag in the `<head>` section:

```
<head>
  <link rel="stylesheet" href="browser-time.css">
<head>
```

> **Tip** `<link>` is one of the tags that doesn't have an end tag (`</link>`). In HTML5, the end tag is not allowed; however, browsers just ignore `</link>` or the cargo cult practice of adding a / before > when rendering a page.

CSS rules apply styles to the HTML document. Each CSS rule is written as a *selector* that targets HTML elements and *declarations* with the styles to apply to those elements. For example, the following CSS rule changes the font of the entire HTML document:

```
html {
  font: 15px Arial;
}
```

The `html` part is the selector. Inside braces are the declarations. There's only one declaration in this rule, but it's possible to define multiple declarations as well. The following CSS rule changes all `<h1>` elements to have a full width (100%), a semi-transparent blue background color, and a padding (space around the element text) of 10 pixels:

```
h1 {
  width: 100%;
  background-color: rgba(22, 118, 243, 0.1);
  padding: 10px;
}
```

Selectors allow targeting by tag name (like in the previous examples), element ID, attribute values, and others. One of the most important selectors is the *class selector*. A class selector allows to target elements that have a specified value in their `class` attribute. The following snippet shows how to add the `time-button` CSS class to the button in the example:

```
<button class="time-button">Time in the client</button>
```

A CSS class selector starts with a period followed by the name of the class to target. To style the button in the previous example, you can use a rule like the following:

```
.time-button {
  font-size: 15px;
  padding: 10px;
  border: 0px;
  border-radius: 4px;
}
```

This rule changes the size of the font to 15 pixels, adds a padding of 10 pixels around the text in the button, removes the border, and makes its corners slightly rounded. Combining these concepts, it's possible to style the full HTML document in a separate *browser-time.css* file:

```
html {
  font: 15px Arial;
}

body {
  margin: 30px;
}

h1 {
  width: 100%;
  background-color: rgba(22, 118, 243, 0.1);
  padding: 10px;
}

.time-button {
  font-size: 15px;
  padding: 10px;
  border: 0px;
  border-radius: 4px;
}
```

Figure 1-5 shows the previous CSS rules applied to the HTML document.

Figure 1-5. An HTML document rendered with custom CSS styles

Web Components

Web Components are a set of technologies that allows creating reusable custom HTML elements. In this section, I'll introduce you to the main technology: *custom elements*. This should be enough for you to understand the key Web platform concepts and see there's no magic really.

A Web Component is a reusable and encapsulated custom tag. The "Time in the client" button of the example is a good candidate for this kind of component. It'd be handy to be able to use the component in multiple HTML documents via a custom tag:

```
<time-button></time-button>
```

Custom elements must have a dash in their names so that browsers (and you) know it's not a standard HTML element. There are two things that are required to be able to use a custom element:

- Implement a class that extends HTMLElement (or a specific element).

- Register the new element using customElements.define(name, constructor).

Here's how:

```
class TimeButtonElement extends HTMLElement {

  constructor() {
    super();
    ...
  }
}

customElements.define("time-button", TimeButtonElement);
```

In the constructor, you can define the content of the element by using `this.innerHTML` or any functionality available in the DOM API:

```
let button = document.createElement("button");
button.textContent = "Time in the client";
button.classList.add("time-button");

button.addEventListener("click", function () {
  let paragraph = document.createElement("p");
  paragraph.textContent = "The time is: " + Date();
  document.body.appendChild(paragraph);
});
```

```
this.appendChild(button);
```

This creates the button programmatically and appends it to the custom element. To make the element more flexible for reuse, it's a good idea to allow specifying values like the text shown in the button instead of hardcoding them (`"Time in the client"`):

```
button.textContent = this.getAttribute("text");
```

With this, the button can be used as follows:

```
<time-button text="Time in the client"></time-button>
```

It's possible to use the component multiple times by just adding more `<time-button>` tags to the document. Listing 1-2 shows a full HTML document that includes two buttons with different texts, and Listing 1-3 shows the companion *time-button.js* file that implements and registers the custom element.

Listing 1-2. An HTML document reusing a custom element

```html
<!DOCTYPE html>
<html lang="en">
<head>
  <title>The Web platform</title>
  <link rel="stylesheet" href="browser-time.css">
</head>
<body>

<h1>It works!</h1>
<time-button text="Time in the client"></time-button>
<time-button text="What time is it?"></time-button>
<script src="time-button.js"></script>

</body>
</html>
```

Listing 1-3. A custom element implemented in JavaScript (time-button.js)

```javascript
class TimeButtonElement extends HTMLElement {

  constructor() {
    super();
    let button = document.createElement("button");
    button.textContent = this.getAttribute("text");
    button.classList.add("time-button");

    button.addEventListener("click", function () {
      let paragraph = document.createElement("p");
      paragraph.textContent = "The time is: " + Date();
      document.body.appendChild(paragraph);
    });

    this.appendChild(button);
  }
}

customElements.define("time-button", TimeButtonElement);
```

You only need a text editor and a browser to try this out. I recommend doing so if you are new to web development. Try creating these files, placing them in the same directory, and opening the HTML file in a web browser. Make sure you understand what's going on before continuing. The client-side step of the journey ends with Figure 1-6 which shows a screenshot of the final pure HTML/JavaScript application developed so far.

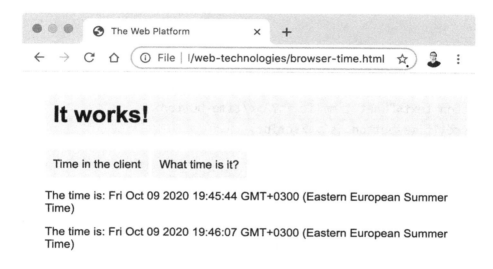

Figure 1-6. *The final pure client-side web application*

Server-Side Technologies

With the fundamentals of the Web platform in place, you can now approach the not-less-exciting server side of the equation. In short, this means understanding what a web server is, how to add custom functionality to a web server, and how to connect the client (browser) with the web server.

Web Servers

The term *web server* is used to refer to both hardware and software entities. In the hardware realm, a web server is a machine that contains web server software and resources such as HTML documents, JavaScript files, CSS files, images, audio, video, and even Java programs. In the software realm, a web server is the software that serves the resources in the host machine (the hardware web server) to clients (web browsers) through HTTP (the protocol that browsers understand). This book uses the software definition of the term web server. Figure 1-7 shows the main components in a client-server architecture and the flow of data through requests and responses over HTTP.

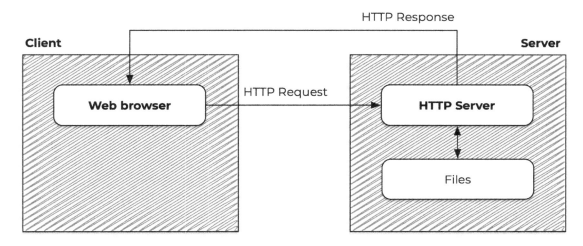

Figure 1-7. *The client-server architecture over HTTP*

Often, web servers are called HTTP servers or application servers, depending on whether the content that is served is static or dynamic. A static web server maps URLs to files in the host and sends them when requested by the browser. A dynamic web server is a static web server, but it offers developers the possibility to process the hosted files before serving them.

A web server is software that you can install and run on your machine. You probably have one (or several) already installed in your computer. In fact, nearly all Unix platforms (Linux, macOs, FreeBSD, and others) come out of the box with Python, which in turn includes a module to easily run an HTTP web server to serve the files in the current directory. On Windows systems, you'll have to install Python or, even better, enable WSL (Windows Subsystem for Linux) and use the Windows store to install a Linux distribution such as Ubuntu which includes Python by default.

Depending on the version of Python, you have to run one of the following commands to start a web server that allows access through HTTP to the files in the current directory:

```
> python -m SimpleHTTPServer 8080
> python3 -m http.server 8080
```

Tip   If you have Node.js installed on your computer, you can alternatively install an HTTP server with `npm install -g http-server` and run it with `http-server -p 8080`.

You can request HTML documents using a URL from any device connected to your network or even the Internet (granted that the firewall and other security mechanisms don't prevent access to your web server). Figure 1-8 shows the example HTML document when I requested it from my phone (the result you get might be slightly different depending on the browser and operating system you use). Notice how I used my IP address to access the file instead of opening it directly in the browser.

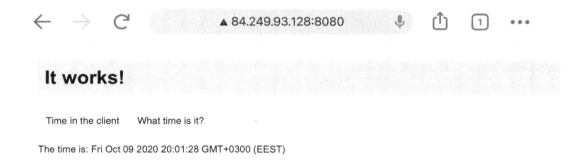

Figure 1-8.   *An HTML document served from a web server*

CGI

CGI (Common Gateway Interface) is one of the simplest ways to serve dynamic content from a web server. I'll avoid the discussion on whether CGI is dead or whether it's good or not. My aim is to make you take one step forward toward server-side technologies, and this technology is easy to understand from a practical point of view.

CGI defines a way to allow web servers to interact with external programs in the server. These programs can be implemented in any programming language. CGI maps URLs to these programs. The external programs communicate with the client using the standard input (`STDIN`) and standard output (`STDOUT`), which in Java are available through the `System.in` and `System.out` objects. The main difference between a standard program and a CGI program is that the output should start with a line containing a Content-Type header. For example, to serve plain text, the output must start with Content-Type: text/html followed by an empty line followed by the content of the file to serve.

The Python HTTP server module includes CGI. To enable it, start the server using the --cgi argument:

```
> python -m SimpleHTTPServer 8080 --cgi
> python3 -m http.server 8080 --cgi
```

With this server, CGI programs should be placed in the *cgi-bin* directory when you are using this server. Other web servers may use different locations and might need the installation of additional modules to make it work.

Let's see how to implement a CGI program in Java. Since version 11, it's possible to create a Java program that can be executed directly from the command line:

```
#!/usr/bin/java --source 11
public class ServerTime {
  public static void main(String[] args) {
    System.out.println("Content-Type: text/plain\n");
    System.out.println("It works!");
  }
}
```

Note   The first line in the preceding example is a shebang—a magic number recognized by Unix-based systems to determine whether a file is a script or an executable binary. Remember to use the full path to the *java* command and make the file executable with *chmod +x server-time*. In Windows systems, you can create a *.bat* file to invoke the *java* program. In this case, you'll need a separate file to place the Java code.

If you name this file *server-time* (don't use the *.java* extension) and place it inside the *cgi-bin* directory (relative to where you started the Python web server), you'll be able to access the program from the browser at *http://localhost:8080/cgi-bin/server-time*. Figure 1-9 shows the result.

Figure 1-9. *Plain text returned by a CGI program written in Java*

The previous example doesn't really create dynamic content—every time you request the page, the browser shows exactly the same. However, it's easy to understand that the Java program can do more than returning a hardcoded string. It could instead read an HTML file and process it to add dynamic content by replacing a placeholder and then sending the result to STDOUT. This is a technique many web frameworks use. Here's a possible implementation:

```
#!/usr/bin/java --source 11

import java.io.IOException;
import java.nio.charset.Charset;
import java.nio.file.Files;
import java.nio.file.Path;
import java.util.Date;

public class ServerTime {
  public static void main(String[] args) throws IOException {
    Path path = Path.of("cgi-bin/template.html");
    String template = Files.readString(path,
        Charset.defaultCharset());

    String content = "Time in the server: " + new Date();
    String output = template.replace("{{placeholder}}", content);

    System.out.println("Content-Type: text/html\n");
    System.out.println(output);
  }
}
```

This program takes the *cgi-bin/template.html* file, reads its content, and replaces `{{placeholder}}` with a string that contains the time calculated in the server. The template file could be something like this:

```
<!DOCTYPE html>
<html lang="en">
<head>
  <title>CGI Example</title>
</head>
<body>

<h1>It works!</h1>
{{placeholder}}

</body>
</html>
```

Figure 1-10 shows the result of invoking the program in the browser. This is now a dynamic page that shows something different every time you request it.

It works!

Time in the server: Sat Oct 10 18:56:48 EEST 2020

Figure 1-10. *Dynamic HTML document generated by a CGI program*

Servlets

Jakarta Servlet (previously known as Java Servlet) is an API specification for Java that allows developers to extend the capabilities of a server using the Java programming language. Although I showed you how to do so with Java in the previous section, CGI has several disadvantages when compared to Java servlets. The main challenges with CGI are related to the fact that the server starts a new process every time the user requests a page (or CGI program in the server). This slows requests to the server, potentially consumes more memory, makes it harder to use in-memory data caches, and makes programs less portable.

Servlets are the Java solution for web development and provide an object-oriented abstraction of request-response protocols such as HTTP through a solid and battle-tested API. A servlet is a Java program (or a class) that you implement and that a software component called *servlet container* manages. A servlet container is a concrete implementation of the Jakarta Servlet API. There are web servers that include a servlet container implementation out of the box. The most popular ones are Apache Tomcat and Eclipse Jetty.

Tip   How to decide between Tomcat and Jetty? I don't have a good answer here but a quick guideline to help you start your own research. Both are production-ready and have been tested by many serious projects. Tomcat is more popular and incorporates latest versions of the specifications quicker. Jetty seems to be used in projects where high performance is key and gives priority to incorporating fixes required by the community over supporting the latest versions of the specifications.

In short, the operating system runs processes. The JVM is run as a process that executes bytecode-compiled programs (written in Java, Kotlin, Scala, Groovy, or other languages for the JVM). Both the Tomcat and Jetty Java servers are implemented in Java (although servlet containers can be implemented in any language as long as they comply with the Jakarta Servlet specification). The Java servers read the files that make up your Java web application, which in turn interacts with the servlet API to handle requests and produce responses. Figure 1-11 shows an overview of this stack.

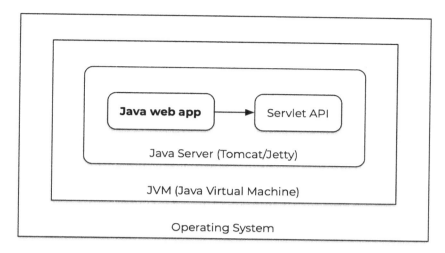

Figure 1-11. *The server-side Java stack*

Here's a simple servlet implementation:

```
import javax.servlet.ServletException;
import javax.servlet.annotation.WebServlet;
import javax.servlet.http.HttpServlet;
import javax.servlet.http.HttpServletRequest;
import javax.servlet.http.HttpServletResponse;
import java.io.IOException;

@WebServlet("/*")
public class ServletExample extends HttpServlet {
  private String replace;

  public void doGet(HttpServletRequest request,
                    HttpServletResponse response) throws
      IOException, ServletException {

    response.setContentType("text/plain");
    response.getWriter().println("It works!");
  }
}
```

This class uses the servlet API to write plain text to the response, similarly to how CGI programs write the response to STDOUT. The @WebServlet annotation configures the URL that the server uses to dispatch requests to this servlet. In this case, all requests to the application will be sent to an instance of the ServletExample class created and managed by the servlet container.

To compile this class, you need to add the servlet API to the JVM class path (the next chapter shows how to do this with Maven). Java servers come with this API. For example, download Apache Tomcat 9.0 as a ZIP and extract its contents. You can download the server at *http://tomcat.apache.org*. You will find a *servlet-api.jar* file which contains the servlet API in the *lib* directory inside your Tomcat installation. Copy the full path to this file and compile the ServletExample class as follows (change the location of your own JAR file):

```
javac ServletExample.java -cp /apache-tomcat/lib/servlet-api.jar
```

Java web applications expect a certain directory structure in order to be used by the Java server. Create a new *java-web-development* directory inside the *webapps* directory of your Tomcat installation. This is the root of your application. Compiled Java class files should be placed in a subdirectory in your application root directory: *WEB-INF/classes*. Create this directory and copy the *ServletExample.class* file to it.

Start the server using the *bin/startup.sh* or *bin/startup.bat* scripts. You might have to make these files executable with, for example, chmod +x *.sh. The servlet can now be invoked at *http://localhost:8080/java-web-development*. Figure 1-12 shows the result.

Figure 1-12. *A text document generated by a Java servlet running on Tomcat*

You can also serve static HTML, CSS, and JavaScript files using the Java server. As an exercise, try copying the example files developed in previous sections to the root directory of your application. You'll need to map the servlet to a different URL to make the files available (e.g., @WebServlet("/example")), recompile, and restart the server. You can stop the server by running *shutdown.sh* or *shutdown.bat*.

Web Development with Vaadin

At this point, it should be clear to you that there's no magic in serving HTML, JavaScript, and CSS files regardless of whether they are generated by a Java program, a Java servlet, or the file system. Most Java web frameworks use these technologies to make web development easier. Vaadin is one of them.

The core of Vaadin includes a Java servlet (`VaadinServlet`) that handles everything (or almost everything) for you. This servlet scans your classes and builds a *component tree* that makes up your web user interface. This component tree is similar (but not the same) to that of the DOM in the browser. You build this tree using a Java API called *Vaadin Flow*.

When a Vaadin application is invoked in the browser, the Vaadin servlet responds with a lightweight client-side JavaScript engine. As the user interacts with the application in the browser, the client-side engine dynamically adds, removes, or modifies elements (implemented as Web Components) in the DOM by sending requests and receiving responses from the Vaadin servlet.

The client-side engine is a set of static resources that include configuration files, Web Components, and HTML documents that are automatically generated by Vaadin when you build the application. These resources are created by a Maven plugin that you will learn about in the next chapter.

Summary

By teaching you the very fundamentals of web development, this chapter put you in a good position to start learning the specifics of Vaadin. You saw how the Web platform allows you to render web pages using HTML documents that can be styled with CSS rules and dynamically modified with JavaScript. You learned what web servers are and how to add functionality to them not only by using CGI programs that can be written in any programming language but also by creating servlets deployed to servlet containers that implement the Jakarta Servlet API. You also got a glimpse of how Vaadin includes a servlet implementation that communicates with a client-side engine to render Web Components in the browser.

The next chapter will teach you how to set up your development environment and how to create and debug Vaadin applications. All this while you learn the key fundamental concepts in the framework.

CHAPTER 2

Setting Up the Development Environment

This chapter explains how to set up all the tools you need to start coding with Java and Vaadin. In short, you need the Java Development Kit and a Java Integrated Development Environment. You'll learn the basics of Vaadin and how to compile, run, and debug your own programs and the examples included with this book.

Installing the JDK

The Java Development Kit (JDK) is a collection of tools and libraries that are required to develop Java applications. This includes the Java compiler which transforms your plain text source code files into binary files that the Java Runtime Environment (JRE) can run. The JRE is required in any device that needs to run compiled Java programs. In the case of Vaadin applications, the device is most likely a Java server. The JRE is what enables the famous and classic "compile once, run anywhere" slogan created when Java appeared in the market years ago. The JDK includes the JRE and additional tools.

There are several high-quality distributions of the JDK. Vaadin recommends *Amazon Corretto*, a free and open source distribution with support provided by Amazon. Amazon Corretto is based on OpenJDK, the reference implementation of the JDK. I personally recommend *AdoptOpenJDK* instead. At the time of writing this book, the project is moving to the Eclipse Foundation under the name of Adoptium, so you might have to look for that name instead of AdoptOpenJDK depending on when you are reading this chapter. The AdoptOpenJDK (or Adoptium) is a high-quality, enterprise-ready build of the OpenJDK, compliant with Oracle's Technology Compatibility Kit (as of the move to the Eclipse Foundation). The project is open source, making all of the build and test scripts available to the community.

© Alejandro Duarte 2021
A. Duarte, *Practical Vaadin*, https://doi.org/10.1007/978-1-4842-7179-7_2

Tip   Think of the JDK as a set of standards developed by a global community of developers through something called the Java Community Process (JCP) for the overall process and Java Specification Requests (JSRs) for specific features or parts of the JDK. Anybody can take these standards and implement them. OpenJDK is an implementation which in practice is source code. A distribution takes the source code and produces the binaries and packages them in an archive that developers can install in their machines.

To install the JDK, go to *https://adoptopenjdk.net* (or *https://adoptium.net*), select OpenJDK 16 (or the latest you find there), and click the big button at the bottom of the page to download the installer. A screenshot of the web page is shown in Figure 2-1.

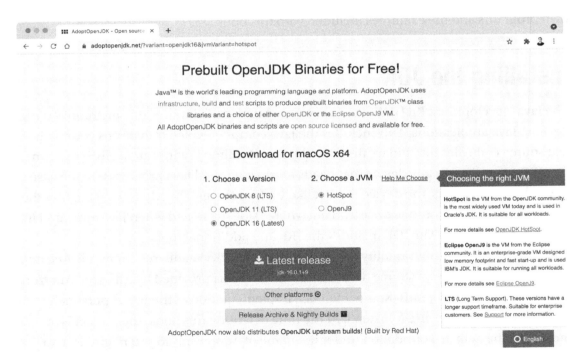

Figure 2-1. *AdoptOpenJDK download page*

Installation packages for Linux, Windows, and macOS are available. You can see all the platforms by clicking the **Other platforms** button. Select the one that matches your machine, run the installer, and follow the steps presented.

To double-check that the JDK is ready to be used, open a terminal or command-line window and run the following to confirm that the version of the compiler matches what you downloaded and installed:

```
> javac -version
javac 16.0.1
```

You can also check that the JVM is ready to be invoked by running java -version in the command line. The command should report the version and distribution of the JDK you just installed. For example:

```
> java -version
openjdk version "16.0.1" 2021-04-20
OpenJDK Runtime Environment AdoptOpenJDK-16.0.1+9 (build 16.0.1+9)
OpenJDK 64-Bit Server VM AdoptOpenJDK-16.0.1+9 (build 16.0.1+9, mixed mode, sharing)
```

Tip   If you have an older version of the JDK installed, you can use a tool like *SDKMAN!* You can learn more about it at *https://sdkman.io*.

Installing the IDE

An Integrated Development Environment (IDE) is an application that includes the tools needed for software development in a single graphical user interface. A good IDE should include a source code editor with syntax highlighting, build tools, and a debugger. The main IDEs for Java are Eclipse IDE, Visual Studio Code, Apache NetBeans, and the one this book uses—the free IntelliJ IDEA Community Edition. You can use any IDE, but the screenshots and instructions in this book are tailored to IntelliJ IDEA since there's not enough space in this chapter to cover all of them. I have actually used Eclipse IDE to develop the examples of this book, but decided to show IntelliJ IDEA since it offers a quick way to run Maven projects (more on this later).

To install IntelliJ IDEA, go to *www.jetbrains.com/idea* and click the download option. A screenshot of the web page is shown in Figure 2-2.

Figure 2-2. IntelliJ IDEA website

Select your operating system, download the free Community Edition installer, and run it. You can use the default configuration options given by the IDE the first time you run it.

Using the Examples of This Book

This book contains multiple independent examples. For convenience, all the examples are aggregated in one single project that you can import into your IDE. Download the code via the book's product page located at *www.apress.com/9781484271780*. On this page, you'll find a link to a Git repository hosted on GitHub where you can download the code as a ZIP file. Extract the contents of the ZIP file anywhere in your hard drive.

Tip   As an alternative, and if you are a Git user, you can use Git to clone the repository.

Importing the Code in the IDE

Once you have downloaded and extracted the source code, run IntelliJ IDEA, and click the *Open or Import* option in the welcome screen shown in Figure 2-3. If you already were an IntelliJ IDEA user and have projects opened, either close all the projects to see the welcome screen or select *File ➤ Open* instead.

Figure 2-3. *The welcome screen of IntelliJ IDEA*

IntelliJ IDEA shows a window to select a project from the files on your hard drive. Go to the directory (or folder) where you extracted the source code and select the *pom. xml* file in this directory as shown in Figure 2-4. Make sure to select the *Open as Project* option when prompted.

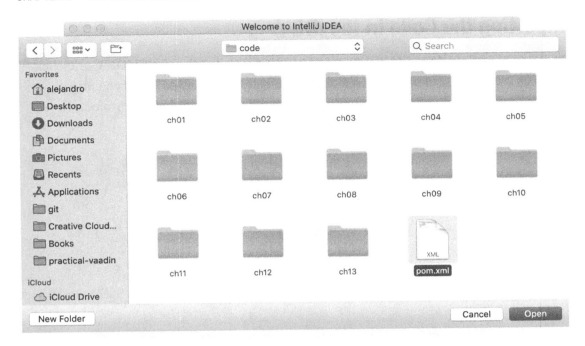

Figure 2-4. *The aggregator project pom.xml file*

Once the project is imported, check that it is associated to the JDK you installed. Select the root (topmost) directory that contains all the other subdirectories in the project view and select *File* ➤ *Project Structure...*. On the left of the *Project Structure* window, click *Project* and make sure that the JDK version 16 or later is selected in the *Project SDK* and *Project language level* sections on the right of the window. Figure 2-5 shows this configuration.

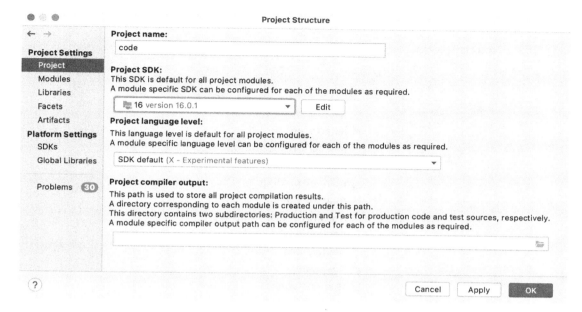

Figure 2-5. *JDK configuration in IntelliJ IDEA*

Running the Examples

Thanks to Maven and the good integration to it provided by IntelliJ IDEA, building and running the examples becomes a breeze. Click *Maven* on the right of the IDE's window or select *View ➤ Tool Windows ➤ Maven* in the menu bar. You'll see all the examples included in the bookmark with a blue "m" icon. All the examples starting from Chapter 2 are available in this view.

Caution   The examples of Chapter 1 aren't based on Maven. You have to follow the instructions in Chapter 1 to build and run these examples.

Start by running the welcome project I've prepared for you. In the *Maven* view, select the *welcome-to-vaadin* project and click the *Run Maven Build* button with a "play" icon on it. See Figure 2-6.

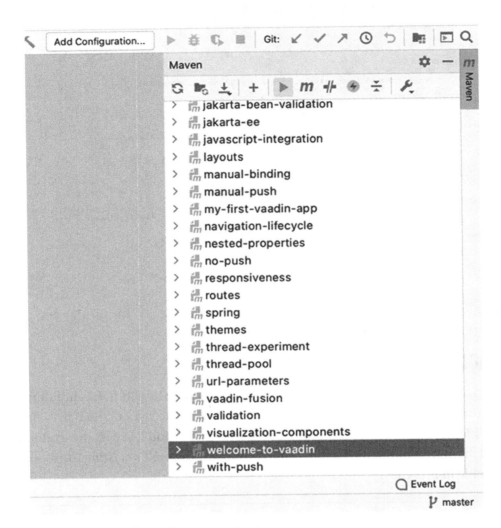

Figure 2-6. *Running the welcome project*

The first time you build a Vaadin (or in general, a Maven) project, it might take longer than you expect. This is because Maven has to download all the dependencies (Java libraries in the form of JAR files) to your local Maven repository. Once these dependencies are in your local repository, running projects becomes quicker.

Caution   Vaadin automatically installs Node.js in the *.vaadin* directory inside your home directory. Node.js is required to download the required client-side dependencies. You don't need to worry about it, except if you have Node.js already installed. If so, check that you are using Node.js version 10 or later.

After running the project, wait for a message in the *Run* window (the log of the application) that reads "Frontend compiled successfully" and go to *http://localhost:8080*. You should see a welcome message and a fun fact about Vaadin that I prepared for you.

Note   Maven is a project management tool. It allows you to manage your projects using a file called *pom.xml*. In this file, you define the dependencies of your Java project (e.g., Vaadin, Spring, Hibernate) and the plugins to help to build your project. IntelliJ IDEA has excellent support for Maven so you rarely have to use the command line to run Maven. Explaining Maven is out of the scope of this book. If you want to learn more about it, visit the official website at *https://maven.apache.org*.

Your First Vaadin Application

There is a variety of ways to create a new Vaadin project. Vaadin suggests using the tool available at *https://start.vaadin.com* for creating new projects. Unfortunately, at the time of writing, this online tool doesn't include an option to create a minimal project without generated views and Spring Boot. This might change when you are reading this book, but for your convenience, I have created a minimal *empty project* that you can use as a template to start coding your applications. You can find this empty project in the *ch02/empty-project/* directory of the source included with this book (see the instructions at *www.apress.com/9781484271780*).

To create a new project, duplicate the *empty-project* directory and its content, and change the name of the directory to whatever you want to use as a name for your new project. For example, if you are on a Linux machine, run the following in the command line:

```
cd ch02
cp -r empty-project ~/my-first-vaadin-app
```

This will place the new project in the home directory, but feel free to use any other location. Import the project in your IDE in the same way you did with the aggregator project that contains the examples of this book and change the artifactID to a more appropriate name in the *pom.xml* file. For example:

```
<project ...>

    <modelVersion>4.0.0</modelVersion>
    <groupId>com.example</groupId>
    <artifactId>my-first-vaadin-app</artifactId>
    <version>1.0-SNAPSHOT</version>
    <packaging>war</packaging>

    ...

<project>
```

The *Project* view should look similar to the screenshot in Figure 2-7.

Figure 2-7. *A minimal Vaadin project structure*

All set to start coding your first Vaadin app!

Note Vaadin allows implementing views in server-side Java or client-side TypeScript. Server-side Java means Java code that runs on your server. You code the views that form the web user graphical interface of your application using Java. Client-side TypeScript means views implemented with the TypeScript programming language. This code is compiled to JavaScript and run in the web browser. This book's focus is on server-side Java views.

Routes and Views

Create a new Java class with the name HelloWorldView in the com.example package by right-clicking the package and selecting *New* ➤ *Java Class*. IntelliJ IDEA will generate the following class:

```
public class HelloWorldView {
}
```

Note Package declarations are omitted in most of the snippets of code you'll see from now on.

You are going to implement the web user interface (UI) of your Java application in this class. This class is called a *view*, and you can have multiple in the same project. Each view should be mapped to a different URL. The full URL for a view is formed by the location of the web server (e.g., *http://localhost:8080/* in a development environment) and a route suffix. To map a suffix to a view, use the @Route annotation. For example:

```
import com.vaadin.flow.router.Route;

@Route("hello-world")
public class HelloWorldView {
}
```

This defines a *route* that allows you to access the view using a URL like *http://localhost:8080/hello-world*. If you specify an empty string (@Route("")), then you would access the view using *http://localhost:8080* instead.

Caution   Make sure you import the correct class from the `com.vaadin` packages by placing the cursor on the class to import and hitting *Ctrl+space*. A common mistake is to import classes from the `java.awt` packages which contain classes with the same names as Vaadin's classes. Be aware of this to avoid compilation errors.

UI Components and Layouts

Vaadin includes a set of UI components . A UI component is a reusable element that you can add to the user interface. For example, you can add buttons and text fields by using the `Button` class and `TextField` class, respectively.

A special kind of UI component is a *layout*. A layout allows you to add other UI components (including other layouts) to it in order to arrange them vertically, horizontally, or in any other way that you need.

Classes annotated with @Route have to be UI components. To make the `HelloWorldView` class a UI component, you have to extend an existing one. Since views typically contain many UI components, it makes sense that views extend some kind of layout class.

Tip   Alternatively, you can extend the `Composite` class which provides a better way to encapsulate the logic in your views. The next chapter shows how to use this class.

You'll get to know many of the available UI components in Vaadin as you read this book and play with the framework. For now, just extend `VerticalLayout`:

```
import com.vaadin.flow.component.orderedlayout.VerticalLayout;
import com.vaadin.flow.router.Route;

@Route("hello-world")
public class HelloWorldView extends VerticalLayout {
}
```

This should already work, but it'd look rather boring in the browser. Implement a constructor that adds a paragraph to the view as follows:

```
public HelloWorldView() {
  add(new Paragraph("Hello, World!"));
}
```

Run the application as explained in the previous sections and point your browser to *http://localhost:8080/hello-world*. The result is shown in Figure 2-8.

Figure 2-8. *A "Hello, World" application implemented with Vaadin*

Congratulations! You have successfully implemented your very first Vaadin application—the classic "Hello, World" application written in Java with Vaadin.

Caution   Make sure you stop previous running applications by clicking the *Stop* button in the toolbar or in the *Run* view in IntelliJ IDEA before running a new one. Otherwise, the server will complain about the unavailability of the port 8080.

Events and Listeners

As you can imagine, Vaadin includes all kinds of UI components that are common in business applications. When you develop Vaadin applications, you combine these UI components to make up more complex views. For example, you add components such as text fields, combo boxes, and buttons into vertical or horizontal layouts to build a form for data input.

The input components use an event programming model that allows you to react to things such as clicks or changes in selected values in the UI. To show you this concept in action, try adding the following class to the project:

```
@Route("greeting")
public class GreetingView extends VerticalLayout {

  public GreetingView() {
    var button = new Button("Hi");
    button.addClickListener(event ->
        Notification.show("Hello!")
    );

    add(button);
  }

}
```

This code creates a button and adds an event listener to react to clicks. The listener is implemented as a lambda expression that shows a notification. Try it out. Compile the project by selecting *Build* ➤ *Build Project* in the IDE and go to *http://localhost:8080/greeting* using your browser.

Debugging

Debugging is the process of finding and fixing defects in software, also called bugs. A debugger is a tool that allows you to pause the execution of a running program to inspect its state. It also allows you to execute arbitrary code and run your program one step at a time (line by line).

Debuggers typically work on applications implemented in a specific programming language. IntelliJ IDEA includes a debugger for Java applications. Web browsers include debuggers for HTML, CSS, and JavaScript code. You must learn early how to use these debuggers to hunt the bugs you encounter and to help you understand how programs work.

Server-Side Debugging

If you want to add breakpoints to the example applications, you have to run them in debug mode. Stop the application, right-click the project in the *Maven* view, and select the *Debug 'my-first-vaadin-app ...'* option in the context menu.

Try adding a breakpoint in your application by clicking just to the right of the line number at the line of code that shows the notification. See Figure 2-9.

```
11        public GreetingView() {
12            var button = new Button( text: "Hi");
13            button.addClickListener(event ->
14  ●             Notification.show("Hello!")
15            );
16
17            add(button);
18        }
```

Figure 2-9. *A breakpoint in IntelliJ IDEA*

Now go to the browser and click the button. The program execution is halted, and the debugger is shown in the *Debug* view. You can see the variables in the current scope and inspect their values. For example, you can see where the click happened on the screen by inspecting the values in the event variable. You can also continue the execution of the program line by line or until another breakpoint is encountered if any. Get familiar with the options in this view. They'll become useful at some point during the development of your projects.

Client-Side Debugging

On the client side, you'll be in situations in which you need to see what's the current state of the DOM in the browser to tweak layout issues. All main web browsers include good tools for developers. In the case of Google Chrome, you activate the tool by pressing F12.

A good way to find the HTML for a specific part of the UI is to right-click the UI component you are interested in and select *Inspect*. Try this with the button of your application. Figure 2-10 shows the Chrome DevTools with the HTML that forms the button in the browser.

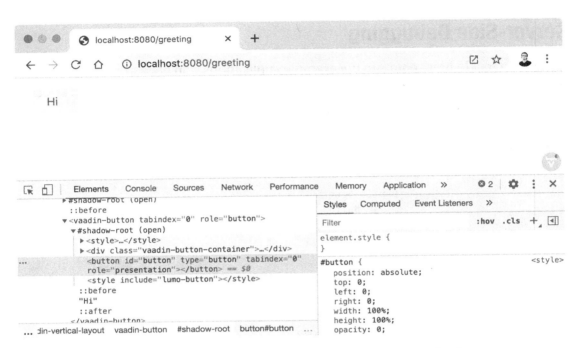

Figure 2-10. *Chrome DevTools after inspecting an element in the browser*

You can modify the HTML and the CSS styles as well, something very handy when you are implementing views and trying to fine-tune the look and feel of the application.

Summary

This chapter enabled you to effectively start using Vaadin. You learned how to install the JDK and a Java IDE. You downloaded and imported the examples included in this book and learned how to run them using IntelliJ IDEA. You also wrote your first Vaadin application and had a first approach at its philosophy of implementing web user interfaces in Java running on the server side. You learned that views can be mapped to URLs using the @Route annotation and understood how Vaadin allows you to compose views by adding UI components into layouts and react to user actions in the browser by implementing event listeners. Last but not least, you took a quick look at the debuggers available on the server and client sides.

The next chapter will present more in depth the concept of layouts. Mastering layouts is key when developing Vaadin applications. You have to make sure you can make the views look the way you want in terms of position and size on the screen.

PART II

The Fundamentals of Vaadin

CHAPTER 3

Layouts

Layouts are the main mechanism to organize UI components on the screen. For example, you might want to create a form with text fields and combo boxes aligned vertically. Or maybe you want a search bar with a text field and a button aligned horizontally. Vaadin includes layouts for these scenarios and more. This chapter teaches you how to use all the layout components included in Vaadin.

Vertical and Horizontal Layouts

Arguably, the most obvious way in which somebody would arrange UI components is from top to bottom or from left to right. The VerticalLayout and HorizontalLayout classes are designed for these scenarios and are the fundamental building blocks in most Vaadin applications.

You use a layout by creating a new instance and adding UI components into it. The layout then takes care of how the contained components are shown on the screen. Take a look at the following example:

```
@Route("vertical-layout")
public class VerticalLayoutView extends VerticalLayout {

  public VerticalLayoutView() {
    add(
        new Paragraph("Paragraph 1"),
        new Paragraph("Paragraph 2"),
        new Button("Button")
    );
  }

}
```

© Alejandro Duarte 2021
A. Duarte, *Practical Vaadin*, https://doi.org/10.1007/978-1-4842-7179-7_3

This view extends VerticalLayout and adds two paragraphs and a button to it. These components are displayed in a vertical fashion forming a column as shown in Figure 3-1.

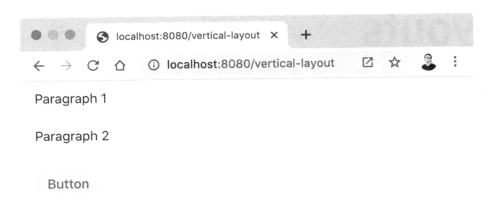

Figure 3-1. *Components arranged in a vertical layout*

By changing the kind of layout that the view extends, you can change how the components are arranged. For example, switching to a HorizontalLayout, the following view arranges the components horizontally like in a row as shown in Figure 3-2:

```
@Route("horizontal-layout")
public class HorizontalLayoutView extends HorizontalLayout {

  public HorizontalLayoutView() {
    add(
        new H1("Horizontal layout"),
        new Paragraph("Paragraph 1"),
        new Paragraph("Paragraph 2"),
        new Button("Button")
    );
  }

}
```

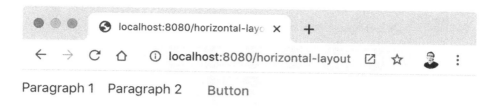

Figure 3-2. *Components arranged in a horizontal layout*

Component Composition

Since layouts are UI components, it's possible to add layouts into layouts. Suppose you want to create a toolbar with buttons in it. You can use a HorizontalLayout for the toolbar and place it in a VerticalLayout where you can also add other components. Here's an example:

```
@Route("composition")
public class CompositionView extends VerticalLayout {

  public CompositionView() {
    var toolbar = new HorizontalLayout(
        new Button("Button 1"),
        new Button("Button 2"),
        new Button("Button 3")
    );
    add(
        toolbar,
        new Paragraph("Paragraph 1"),
        new Paragraph("Paragraph 2"),
        new Paragraph("Paragraph 3")
    );
  }

}
```

You can have as many levels of nesting as needed. Figure 3-3 shows the result.

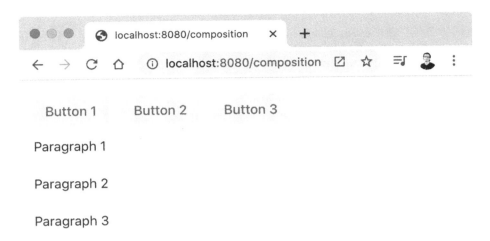

Figure 3-3. *A horizontal layout in a vertical layout*

When you implement a view (or a UI component in general), you are defining a *component tree*. The root of the tree is the view itself. In the previous example, the root is the CompositionView (which is also a VerticalLayout). As direct children, the root contains the toolbar (HorizontalLayout) and three paragraphs. A visual representation of this component tree is shown in Figure 3-4.

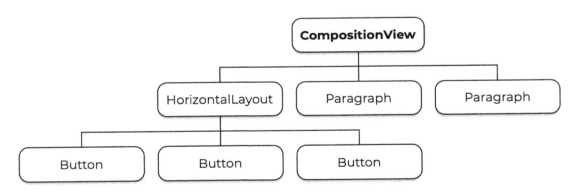

Figure 3-4. *An example of a component tree*

When you request a view, Vaadin uses this component tree to show the corresponding HTML in the browser.

The Composite Class

The CompositionView class of the previous example doesn't hide the fact that it is a VerticalLayout. Clients of the class will know that and will be able to access the methods in VerticalLayout. In practical terms, extending a layout is fine since you rarely directly instantiate views—Vaadin scans classes annotated with @Route and creates instances as needed when the views are invoked in the browser. However, if you want to hide the extended class, you can use the Composite class. Here's a refactor of the previous example that makes use of the Composite class:

```
@Route("composition")
public class CompositionView extends Composite<VerticalLayout> {

  public CompositionView() {
    var toolbar = new HorizontalLayout(
        new Button("Button 1"),
        new Button("Button 2"),
        new Button("Button 3")
    );

    var mainLayout = getContent(); // returns a VerticalLayout
    mainLayout.add(
        toolbar,
        new Paragraph("Paragraph 1"),
        new Paragraph("Paragraph 2"),
        new Paragraph("Paragraph 3")
    );
  }

}
```

Notice how the Composite class takes an argument that specifies the type of component to encapsulate. Since the CompositionView is no longer a VerticalLayout, you cannot call the add method directly. Instead, you should get an instance of VerticalLayout using the getContent() method and then use this instance to build the UI.

Clients of this class won't have direct access to the methods in VerticalLayout either. However, the getContent() method is public, and clients of the CompositionView class could use it to gain access to the underlying VerticalLayout. To solve this, you can replace the argument in the Composite class (VerticalLayout) with Component, override the initContent() method, and move all the logic to build the UI there:

```
@Route("composition")
public class CompositionView extends Composite<Component> {

  @Override
  protected Component initContent() {
    var toolbar = new HorizontalLayout(
        new Button("Button 1"),
        new Button("Button 2"),
        new Button("Button 3")
    );

    return new VerticalLayout(
        toolbar,
        new Paragraph("Paragraph 1"),
        new Paragraph("Paragraph 2"),
        new Paragraph("Paragraph 3")
    );
  }

}
```

The getContent() method is still public, but it returns an object of type Component, not of VerticalLayout. Now you can change the implementation, for example, to use a different kind of layout, without breaking other parts of the application. This is especially useful when you develop reusable components that are not views mapped to URLs (e.g., a form to introduce data about a customer or an order).

Tip   All UI components in Vaadin extend directly or indirectly from Component.

Implementing Reusable UI Components

You can use all the object-oriented techniques to implement UI components using inheritance by extending an existing component and encapsulation and data hiding with the help of the Composite class.

The toolbar of the previous example is the kind of part of a view that you might want to implement as a reusable UI component. Instead of implementing the toolbar in the view itself, you can move the code to a separate class:

```
public class Toolbar extends Composite<Component> {

  @Override
  protected Component initContent() {
    return new HorizontalLayout(
        new Button("Button 1"),
        new Button("Button 2"),
        new Button("Button 3")
    );
  }

}
```

Notice that this class is not annotated with @Route. Most likely, you don't want to show only a toolbar when a certain URL is requested in the browser, right? When you need a toolbar, all you have to do is create a new instance and add it to a layout:

```
var toolbar = new Toolbar();
someLayout.add(toolbar);
```

Tip   You don't have to extend Composite always. There are situations in which extending VerticalLayout, HorizontalLayout, Button, or any other class is a better option. Use the *is-a* relationship test to help you decide. For example, Toolbar *is not a* HorizontalLayout because the layout might be changed to a VerticalLayout maybe even at runtime. On the other hand, a hypothetical SendButton *is a* Button, so it would make sense to extend the Button class in this case.

Accessing the Component Tree

One of the advantages of Vaadin is that it makes it easy to build views dynamically at runtime. For example, a CRUD component could use the Java Reflection API to examine the properties of a given domain class (like User, Order, Customer, etc.) and create the matching UI components according to the type of the Java properties (e.g., text fields for String properties and checkboxes for Booleans). Another example is the logic required to show certain components depending on the privileges that a user has.

When implementing this kind of dynamic UIs, it's useful to be able to modify the component tree in a layout. Let's see some of the methods available in VerticalLayout and HorizontalLayout that will help you to do this.

You can get the components inside a layout as a Java Stream using the getChildren() method:

```
toolbar.getChildren().forEach(component -> {
  ... do something with component ...
});
```

Similarly, you can get the parent component using the getParent() method:

```
toolbar.getParent().ifPresent(component -> {
  CompositionView view = (CompositionView) component;
  ... do something with view ...
});
```

You can remove individual components or all the contained components using the remove(Component...) and removeAll() methods, respectively:

```
var button = new Button();
toolbar.add(button);
toolbar.remove(button); // removes only button
toolbar.removeAll(); // removes all the contained components
```

When building views dynamically, the replace(Component, Component) method could be useful:

```
var button = new Button();
toolbar.add(button);
toolbar.replace(button, new Button("New!"));
```

Padding, Margin, and Spacing

There are three features that you can control regarding space in the area of a layout:

- **Padding:** The space around the border inside the layout

- **Margin:** The space around the border outside the layout

- **Spacing:** The space between the components in the layout

You activate or deactivate these three features using the setPadding(boolean), setMargin(boolean), and setSpacing(boolean) methods. There are corresponding methods that return whether any of these are activated or not. The following view allows you to toggle these values to see the effect it has on the UI:

```
@Route("padding-margin-spacing")
public class PaddingMarginSpacingView extends Composite<Component> {

  @Override
  protected Component initContent() {
    var layout = new HorizontalLayout();
    layout.getStyle().set("border", "1px solid");
    layout.setPadding(false);
    layout.setMargin(false);
    layout.setSpacing(false);
    layout.add(
        new Paragraph("Toggle:"),
        new Button("Padding", e ->
            layout.setPadding(!layout.isPadding())),
        new Button("Margin", e ->
            layout.setMargin(!layout.isMargin())),
        new Button("Spacing", e ->
            layout.setSpacing(!layout.isSpacing()))
    );

    return layout;
  }
}
```

This view creates HorizontalLayout and sets a visible border around it using the getStyle() method which returns an object to set CSS properties.

Tip   You can use the browser's developer tools to inspect the layout and see the borders as you select the HTML elements. I opted for setting the border in the code with CSS so you can see what I'm explaining in the screenshots of the book.

All features are deactivated, and then three buttons are added to the layout. Each button toggles one individual feature. Figure 3-5 shows the view when all the features are deactivated.

Figure 3-5.   A HorizontalLayout with padding, margin, and spacing deactivated

Compare Figure 3-5 with Figure 3-6 where all padding, margin, and spacing are activated.

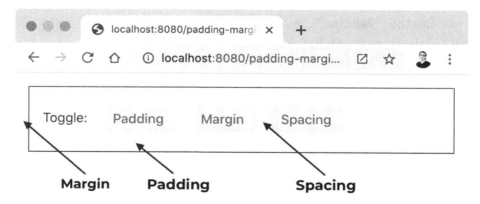

Figure 3-6.   Margin, padding, and spacing activated

Tip   Layouts have sensible defaults for these features. By default, both
`VerticalLayout` and `HorizontalLayout` have spacing activated and margin
deactivated. Additionally, `VerticalLayout` has padding activated while in
`HorizontalLayout` is deactivated.

Sizing

To adjust the size of a UI component, you can use the `setWidth(String)` and
`setHeight(String)` methods and specify a value in CSS absolute or relative length units
(see Table 3-1 for a quick reference on the most common units). For example:

```
button1.setWidth("100%");
button2.setWidth("80%");
button3.setWidth("300px");
```

Table 3-1. *Frequently Used Length Units in CSS*

Unit	Description
cm	Centimeters
mm	Millimeters
in	Inches
px	Pixels
%	Percentage of the parent size
em	Font size of the parent
rem	Size of the root font
lh	Line height

Alternatively, you can separate the length from the unit:

```
button4.setWidth(10, Unit.EM);
```

It's also possible to have an undefined width or height by setting a `null` value. If you want to set undefined size for both width and height, you can use the `setSizeUndefined()` method. Similarly, you can use the `setWidthFull()`, `setHeightFull()`, and `setSizeFull()` methods to set 100% width, height, or both, respectively. An undefined size makes the component shrink to use only the space needed to show its contents. Figure 3-7 shows examples of buttons with different widths.

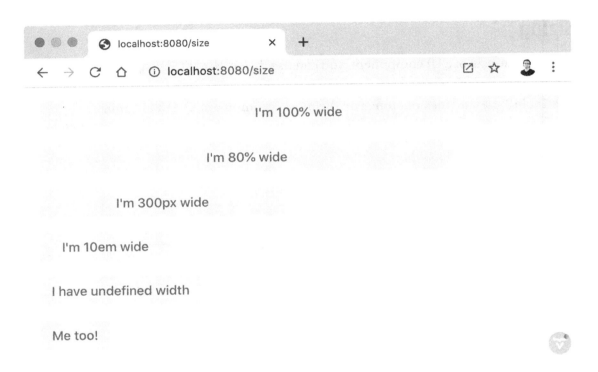

Figure 3-7. *Relative, absolute, and undefined widths*

Components like `Button` have an undefined size by default. The same is true for `HorizontalLayout`; however, `VerticalLayout` has 100% width configured by default.

Tip   You can also configure the maximum and minimum width and height of a component using the `setMaxWidth(String)`, `setMinWidth(String)`, `setMaxHeight(String)`, and `setMinHeight(String)` methods.

Grow

In practice, the grow property determines the size of a component. However, this property is configured in a layout. The grow property sets the proportion of space that a component takes in a layout. You can configure this by calling the setFlexGrow(double, HasElement) method. For example:

```
var layout = new HorizontalLayout(
    button1,
    button2
);
layout.setWidthFull();
layout.setFlexGrow(1, button1);
layout.setFlexGrow(2, button2);
```

In this snippet of code, button1 uses 1 unit of space and button2 uses 2. The layout itself uses 1 + 2 = 3 units. Since it has full width, the layout takes as much space as there is in the window, and this is measured as 3. Figure 3-8 helps to visualize the concept.

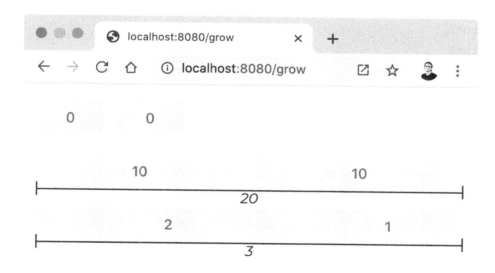

Figure 3-8. *Different grow configurations*

If you set zero (0) as the grow value, the component is not resized and will take the space it needs to accommodate its contents.

Alignment

Think of a VerticalLayout as a column with many rows, and a HorizontalLayout as a row with many columns. In fact, I wish Vaadin had used ColumnLayout and RowLayout instead, but that's another discussion. Alignment means how components are placed in each row of a VerticalLayout or each column of a HorizontalLayout. Kinds of the secondary axis : The x-axis in a VerticalLayout and the y-axis in a HorizontalLayout.

To align components, you use methods in the layout, not in the aligned component. This makes sense if you think that, for instance, a button doesn't really "care" where it's placed—the layout, on the other hand, cares about it so that it can adjust the contained components appropriately. The setAlignSelf(Alignment, Component...) method sets the alignment on the secondary axis of the specified components. For example, say you have a bunch of buttons in a VerticalLayout (a ColumnLayout, I can only wish... maybe I can extend VerticalLayout and use the fancier name instead... no, let's not do that... for now at least... sorry, back to business):

```
var buttons = new VerticalLayout(
    button1,
    button2,
    button3,
    button4
);
```

Then, you can adjust the alignment of each button in the secondary axis (horizontal axis) of the VerticalLayout as follows:

```
buttons.setAlignSelf(FlexComponent.Alignment.CENTER, button1);
buttons.setAlignSelf(FlexComponent.Alignment.START, button2);
buttons.setAlignSelf(FlexComponent.Alignment.END, button3);
```

Figure 3-9 shows the result. Can you see the rows there?

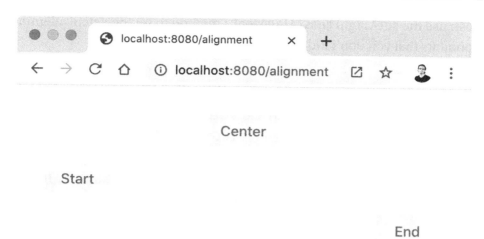

Figure 3-9. *Alignment in the secondary axis (horizontal) of a* `VerticalLayout`

If you change the type of layout to `HorizontalLayout`, set a 100% height for it (you don't need this with `VerticalLayout` since it has 100% width by default), and keep the same alignments, you'll get what you see in Figure 3-10. Can you see the columns there?

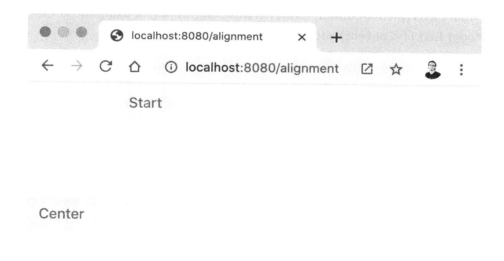

Figure 3-10. *Alignment in the secondary axis (vertical) of a* `HorizontalLayout`

You can use the setAlignItems(Alignment) method to set the default alignment for the components that you don't individually specify an alignment.

Tip   There are easier to remember methods to set the alignment in the secondary axis: With VerticalLayout, you can use setHorizontalComponent Alignment and setDefaultHorizontalComponentAlignment. With HorizontalLayout, you can use setVerticalComponentAlignment and setDefaultHorizontalComponentAlignment. I prefer the shorter names, though, since it makes it easy to change the type layout without breaking the code at least.

Justify-Content Mode

Alignment on the primary axis (y-axis in VerticalLayout and x-axis in HorizontalLayout) is called *justify-content mode*. In the primary axis, you have only one column in a VerticalLayout and one row in a HorizontalLayout. You set the alignment on the primary axis (justify-content mode) of this column or row using the setJustify ContentMode(JustifyContentMode) method. For example:

```
var layout = new HorizontalLayout(
    new Button(justifyContentMode.name())
);
layout.setWidthFull();
layout.getStyle().set("border", "1px solid");
layout.setJustifyContentMode(JustifyContentMode.START);
```

This snippet of code creates a HorizontalLayout, adds a button to it, makes it full width, shows a border, and sets its justify-content mode to START. Figure 3-11 shows three layouts like this with different justify-content modes.

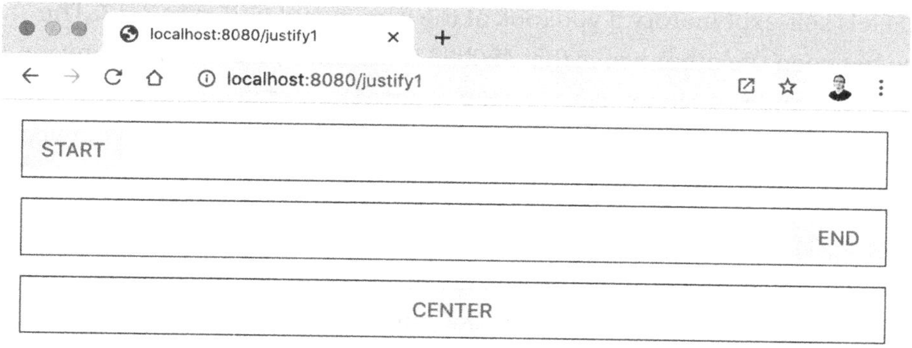

Figure 3-11. *Three VerticalLayouts with different justify-content modes*

In the secondary axis, you saw that there's only one row in a HorizontalLayout. Adding more components doesn't add more rows, but columns. There can be space between these columns (or between rows in a VerticalLayout). You can control how the empty space in a row (or column) is used with three additional justify-content modes: BETWEEN, AROUND, EVENLY. Figure 3-12 shows these modes.

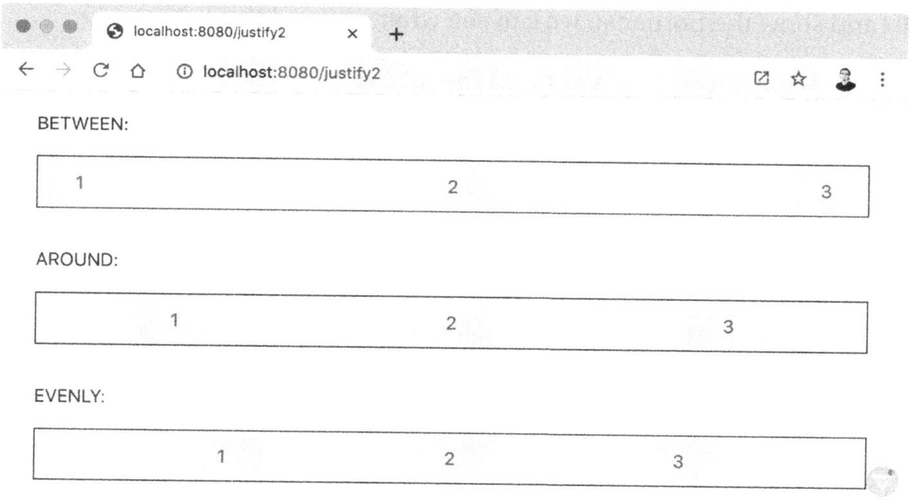

Figure 3-12. *Adjusting the space between components in the primary axis in three different HorizontalLayouts*

BETWEEN is self-explanatory if you look at the screenshot of Figure 3-12. The difference between the other two is that AROUND individually adds space between each component (left and right in the case of a HorizontalLayout) without taking into account if there's already space there, while EVENLY distributes the space between the components to make these spaces have the same size.

Caution   At the time of writing, there's an issue that prevents layouts from working as expected. As a workaround, you have to deactivate spacing in the layout calling setSpacing(false) when you use justify-content modes that affect the space between components. Visit *https://github.com/vaadin/vaadin-ordered-layout/issues/66* for more information on this issue.

Scrolling

Suppose you have a layout with 100 buttons in it, and you want the layout to be 200 pixels tall (and show the border so we can see what we are doing):

```
VerticalLayout layout = new VerticalLayout();
for (int i = 1; i <= 100; i++) {
  layout.add(new Button("Button " + i));
}
layout.setHeight("200px");
layout.getStyle().set("border", "1px solid");
```

When you run this code, you don't quite get what you would expect. See Figure 3-13.

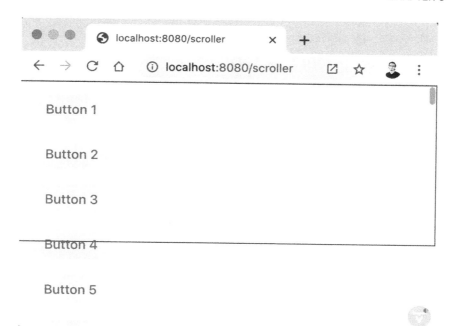

Figure 3-13. Components leaking outside a layout

Moreover, the scroll happens at the page level, not at the layout level. The Scroller component allows you to control how and where scrolling is allowed. You can control the direction (horizontal or vertical) and disable scrolling if you want to. The Scroller component takes the component to be scrolled through the constructor or the setContent(Component) method. For example:

```
VerticalLayout layout = new VerticalLayout();
for (int i = 1; i <= 100; i++) {
  layout.add(new Button("Button " + i));
}
layout.setHeight("200px");

Scroller scroller = new Scroller(layout);
scroller.setHeight("200px");
scroller.getStyle().set("border", "1px solid");
```

Now the scroll bar is shown only for the 200-pixel tall layout. See Figure 3-14.

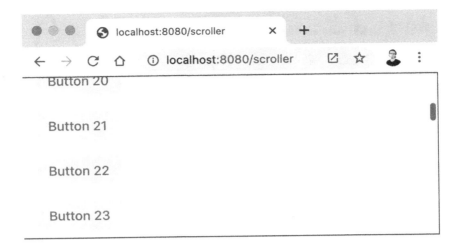

Figure 3-14. The Scroller component

FlexLayout

When VerticalLayout and HorizontalLayout are not enough for your needs, you can access all the features of the CSS flexbox layout by using the FlexLayout class.

Direction

The main feature of the FlexLayout class is that it allows you to set the direction in which the contained components are shown in the primary axis. Use the setFlexDirection (FlexDirection) method and specify one of the following options:

- ROW: The components are arranged in a row from left to right.

- ROW_REVERSE: The components are arranged in a row from right to left.

- COLUMN: The components are arranged in a column from top to bottom.

- COLUMN_REVERSE: The components are arranged in a column from bottom to top.

For example, the following snippet of code uses ROW_REVERSE to show the buttons as depicted in Figure 3-15:

```
var layout = new FlexLayout(
    new Button("1"),
    new Button("2"),
    new Button("3")
);
layout.setFlexDirection(FlexLayout.FlexDirection.ROW_REVERSE);
```

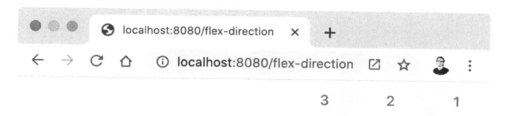

Figure 3-15. *A FlexLayout with ROW_REVERSE direction*

Wrap

By default, components are arranged in a line. You can change this behavior by using the wrap property:

```
layout.setFlexWrap(FlexLayout.FlexWrap.WRAP);
```

A layout with ROW direction and wrap activated is shown in Figure 3-16.

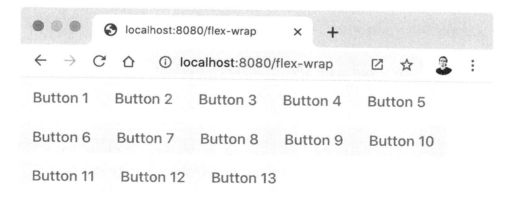

Figure 3-16. *Wrap activated in a FlexLayout*

Alignment

When wrap is activated, you can align the rows or columns (depending on whether the direction is set to ROW or COLUMN) using the setAlignContent(ContentAlignment) method. For example:

```
layout.setAlignContent(
    FlexLayout.ContentAlignment.SPACE_BETWEEN);
layout.setSizeFull();
```

The result is shown in Figure 3-17.

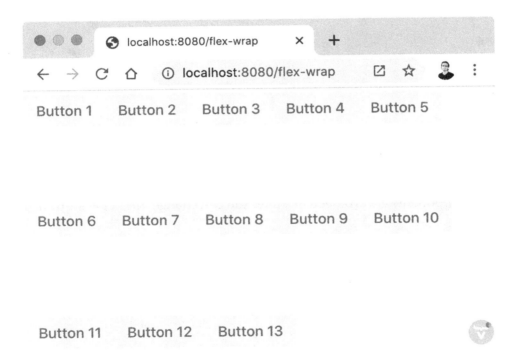

Figure 3-17. *A FlexLayout with SPACE_BETWEEN content alignment*

Shrink

The shrink property is similar to the grow property except that it controls how a component shrinks in the container. You can configure this property as follows:

```
button1.setWidth("200px");
button2.setWidth("200px");
```

```
layout.setWidth("300px");
layout.setFlexShrink(1d, button1);
layout.setFlexShrink(2d, button2);
```

Notice how the combined width of the buttons is 400 pixels, while the layout is only 300 pixels. The combined sum of the shrink values is 1 + 2 = 3 (units), so the whole space is 3. button1 uses 1 unit, while button2 uses 2. Figure 3-18 shows the result.

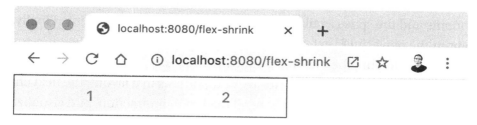

Figure 3-18. *Two buttons with different shrink values*

Tip   Shrink defines how to use the space when there's not enough space for the contained components. Grow defines how to use the space when the container is bigger than the size of the contained components.

Other Layouts

There are more layouts available in Vaadin. We'll see them in action when we cover responsive design later in this book. As a quick introduction, let's briefly mention them: SplitLayout, FormLayout, and AppLayout.

SplitLayout allows you to add components to two resizable areas that the user can adjust in the browser by sliding a split bar. You can set the orientation to show a vertical or a horizontal split.

FormLayout is a responsive layout designed for displaying forms with input components such as text fields, combo boxes, and buttons. The layout reacts to changes in its size showing more or fewer columns depending on the configuration.

AppLayout is a quick way to get a typical application distribution of areas on the screen. It defines a navigation bar on the top, a drawer on the left (suitable for menus, for example), and a content area.

Summary

This chapter was an important step in your Vaadin journey. Understanding how to position and size components is key when you develop UIs. First, you learned how to create UI compositions using the `Composite` class. Then you learned about the `VerticalLayout` and `HorizontalLayout` and how they cover a wide range of use cases by letting you align the components in the primary and secondary axes. You learned how to enable and disable margin, padding, and spacing as well as how to set the size of components and the space available in layouts using the grow property. Finally, you learned about the powerful `FlexLayout` component and its additional features, such as the possibility to configure the direction and wrap modes.

Now that you know how to place and size components in a layout, the next chapter is going to be a lot of fun! You'll learn about all the input, interaction, and visualization components in Vaadin.

CHAPTER 4

UI Components

The word "component" can be a bit overloaded in software development to the point that it might feel like anything can be a component: a class, a module, a JAR, an HTML element, an input field in the user interface... the list goes on and on. However, there's nothing wrong with adopting meanings for this word, and in this book, I use the term "UI component" to refer to a part of the UI that can be encapsulated in a Java class and of which instances can be added to a Vaadin layout. I also use the term "component" to refer to a UI component when the context is clear.

This chapter is all about UI components for data input (fields), action invocation or interaction (buttons and menus), and visualization (icons, images, and such). Vaadin includes a set of UI components that cover most of the needs you'll encounter when developing business applications, so get ready to see the most frequently used UI components in action.

Note There's one UI component you won't see here: the `Grid` component. Worry not. Chapter 6 explores this powerful component in depth.

Input Components

Input components allow users to enter data in several formats (e.g., string, numbers, dates, and even custom types). Most of these components include the `setValue(...)` and `getValue()` methods. With these methods, you can modify and return the value in the component, respectively. They also include a `setLabel(String)` method to set the caption, a `setPlaceholder(String)` method to set a hint text inside the component, the `setWidth(String)`, `setHeight(String)` methods to set size, plus several additional methods to use features specific to each component.

© Alejandro Duarte 2021
A. Duarte, *Practical Vaadin*, https://doi.org/10.1007/978-1-4842-7179-7_4

Tip   There's not enough space in this chapter to cover absolutely every single feature of every component in Vaadin. For an up-to-date list, examples, and API documentation, visit `https://vaadin.com/components`.

Text Input

One of the most frequently used UI components is TextField. Here's a basic usage example:

```
TextField textField = new TextField();
textField.setLabel("Name");
textField.setPlaceholder("enter your full name");
```

Figure 4-1 shows the text field in the browser.

Figure 4-1. *A TextField rendered in the browser*

Most input fields (or simply, field) include functionality to control the data in the field. Take a look at this snippet of code:

```
textField.setAutoselect(true);
textField.setAutofocus(true);
textField.setClearButtonVisible(true);
textField.setValue("John Doe");
```

This code configures the text field to automatically select all the text inside the component when it gains the focus (the cursor is ready to allow typing). It sets the focus on the field so that the user can start typing right away, shows a button to clear the contained value (an X icon inside the field), and presets the text value with a popular name in code examples (at least in my books and talks, especially talks). Figure 4-2 shows the result.

Figure 4-2. *A* TextField *with autoselect, autofocus, clear button, and default value*

Here, there is another set of useful methods:

```
textField.setRequired(true);
textField.setMinLength(2);
textField.setMaxLength(10);
textField.setPattern("^[a-zA-Z\\s]+");
textField.setErrorMessage("Letters only. Min 2 chars");
```

This code activates a visual indicator to let the user know that the field requires a value and cannot be left empty. It also sets a min and max length allowed in the field and a pattern that the value must match. If the pattern doesn't match the regular expression, the component shows an error message.

Note   The Java API for regular expressions was introduced in Java 1.4 and has become a powerful tool to search and manipulate text and data. There are plenty of good resources dedicated to this topic. Oracle's Java Tutorials has an excellent lesson on regular expressions. You can access the lesson at *https:// docs.oracle.com/javase/tutorial/essential/regex*. *Java Regular Expressions* (Apress, 2004) is a classic on teaching Java's regular expression engine. JRebel's cheat sheet (available at *www.jrebel.com/resources/java-regular-expressions-cheat-sheet*) is another resource I consult when I'm working with regular expressions.

Vaadin components interact with the server using event listeners. For example, let's say we want to check the value in the previous example's text field and show a notification when the value is invalid. One way to accomplish this is by adding a *value change listener* to the field:

```
textField.addValueChangeListener(event -> {
    if (textField.isInvalid()) {
        Notification.show("Invalid name");
    }
});
```

The lambda expression is executed when you press ENTER or remove the focus by clicking outside the field or pressing TAB. The lambda expression itself checks if the value in the field is invalid when, for example, there are numbers or less than two characters in the input and then shows a notification if so. See Figure 4-3.

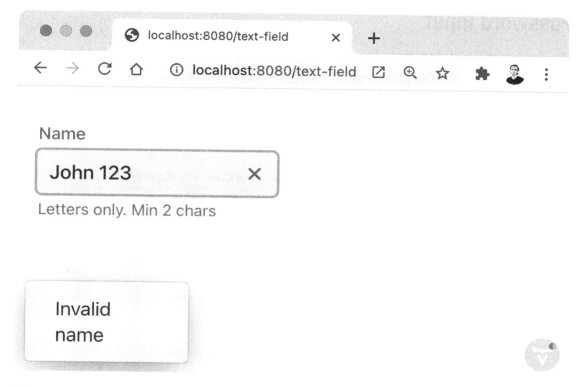

Figure 4-3. *Input validation in a* `TextField`

If you are interested in processing the value every time it changes instead of waiting for the ENTER key or focus loss to happen, you can configure this as follows:

```
textField.setValueChangeMode(ValueChangeMode.EAGER);
```

See the Javadoc of each constant in `ValueChangeMode` to get an idea of all the available configuration options.

Tip   Although most IDEs are able to display Javadoc documentation and source code of external libraries, you can also find it online at *https://vaadin.com/ api*. Consult your IDE's documentation for details on how to display Javadoc or navigate the source code of external libraries.

Password Input

The PasswordField class includes most of the functionality of TextField but provides a convenient way to enable password input. Here's an example:

```
PasswordField passwordField = new PasswordField();
passwordField.setLabel("Password");
passwordField.setRevealButtonVisible(true);
```

In the browser, the input string is shown as a set of dots. See Figure 4-4.

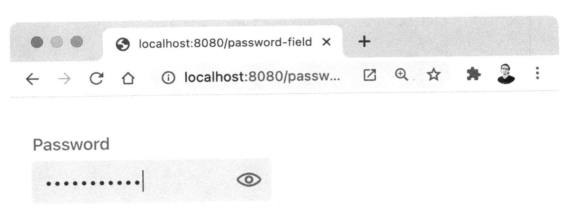

Figure 4-4. A PasswordField

If the reveal button is enabled (like in the preceding example), the user can press the "eye" button to see the entered password. See Figure 4-5.

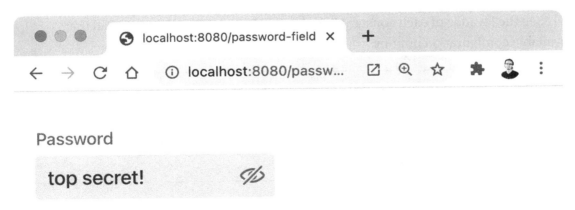

Figure 4-5. A PasswordField with its content revealed

When you get the value by calling the getValue() method, you get the actual text that was introduced in the field (instead of a bunch of dots, obviously):

```
passwordField.addValueChangeListener(event -> {
    String password = passwordField.getValue();
    System.out.println("Password: " + password);
});
```

You can also get the field value from the event parameter so you can decouple the code from the actual field that contains the value:

```
passwordField.addValueChangeListener(event -> {
    String password = event.getValue(); // like this
    System.out.println("Password: " + password);
});
```

This technique works with all the input fields described in this chapter.

Boolean Input

The Checkbox class encapsulates a Boolean value. Here's a basic example:

```
Checkbox checkbox = new Checkbox();
checkbox.setLabelAsHtml("I'm <b>learning</b> Vaadin!");

checkbox.addValueChangeListener(event -> {
    Boolean value = event.getValue();
    Notification.show("Value: " + value);
});
```

This time, the code sets the label using an HTML string. You can still use the regular setLabel(String) method if you don't need to display HTML.

Caution   It's recommended to use plain text whenever possible to avoid cross-site scripting attacks (also known as XSS attacks). Ensure you sanitize strings containing HTML before you pass them to the UI, especially if they come from user input or external services. The Open Web Application Security Project (OWASP) provides a Java library for this. You can learn more at *https://owasp.org/ www-project-java-html-sanitizer*.

Figure 4-6 shows a screenshot of the previous example right after clicking the component.

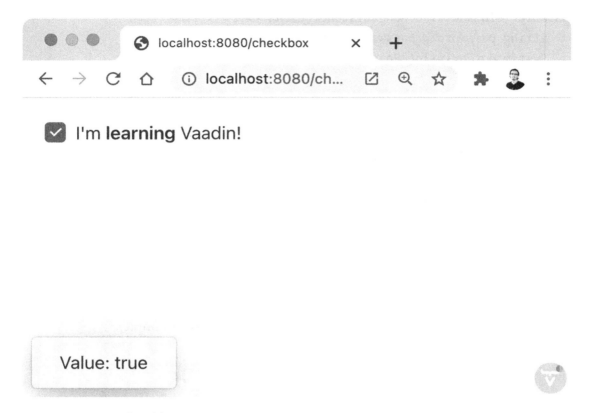

Figure 4-6. *A Checkbox rendered in the browser*

The Checkbox class can take an initial undetermined state to visually hint the user that they haven't clicked the checkbox yet. This doesn't affect the value stored in the checkbox. This is aligned with the HTML5 standard for checkboxes. For example, the following code sets the value to true, activates the undetermined state, and displays the value in a notification:

```
checkbox.setValue(true);
checkbox.setIndeterminate(true);
Boolean initialValue = checkbox.getValue();
Notification.show("Initial value: " + initialValue);
```

Notice how the value shown in Figure 4-7 is true (not null, not false).

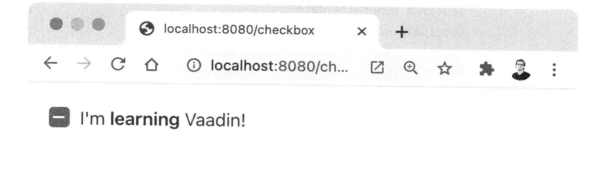

Figure 4-7. A Checkbox with indeterminate state

Since the initial value was true, once you click the checkbox, its value changes to false.

Date and Time Input

The DatePicker class allows you to show an input field for date entry. Instead of using the default constructor (which is available when you need it), let's use one of the several constructors in the class. Study the following example:

```
@Route("datepicker")
public class DatePickerView extends Composite<Component> {

    @Override
    protected Component initContent() {
        DatePicker datePicker = new DatePicker(
```

```
                "Enter a memorable date",
                LocalDate.now(),
                event -> showMessage(event.getValue())
        );

        return new VerticalLayout(datePicker);
    }

    private void showMessage(LocalDate date) {
        Notification.show(
                date + " is great!"
        );
    }
}
```

The constructor accepts a label for the field (equivalent to using the setLabel(String) method), followed by a date value to be shown initially (equivalent to using the setValue(LocalDate) method), and a value change listener (equivalent to using the addValueChangeListener(ValueChangeListener) method). This time, the listener is implemented as a lambda expression that calls a method and gets the value (the date selected by the user) from the event object. Figure 4-8 shows a screenshot of this example.

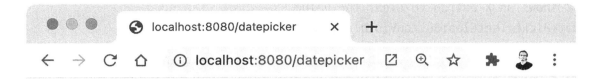

Enter a memorable date

Figure 4-8. *A DatePicker rendered in the browser*

Here are some methods you can use to further configure the date picker:

```
// shows the calendar only when clicking on the calendar icon
// not when clicking the field
datePicker.setAutoOpen(false);
```

```
// shows an X button to clear the value
datePicker.setClearButtonVisible(true);

// sets the date that's visible when the calendar is opened
// * works only when no date value is set
datePicker.setInitialPosition(LocalDate.now().minusMonths(1));

// sets the minimum and maximum dates
datePicker.setMin(LocalDate.now().minusMonths(3));
datePicker.setMax(LocalDate.now().plusMonths(3));
```

A common requirement in web applications is to configure the date format used not only in input components but everywhere a date is shown. The best way to accomplish this is by setting the locale of the component. For example, if the application is meant to be used by a Canadian official or governmental institution, you can set the locale as follows:

```
datePicker.setLocale(Locale.CANADA);
```

When a locale is not set, Vaadin configures the locale reported by the browser when a new session is created.

Caution   At the time of writing this book, there's no method to directly set the date format of a DatePicker. For more information, see the issue at *https:// github.com/vaadin/vaadin-date-picker-flow/issues/156*.

If you need the user to enter a time, you can use the TimePicker class:

```
TimePicker timePicker = new TimePicker("Pick a time");
timePicker.addValueChangeListener(event -> {
    LocalTime value = event.getValue();
    Notification.show("Time: " + value);
});
```

The value stored in the field is of type LocalTime. When you need to get both a date and a time, you can use the DateTimePicker class:

```
DateTimePicker dateTimePicker = new DateTimePicker("When?");
```

Figure 4-9 shows the time components. The DateTimePicker shows a TimePicker next to a DatePicker.

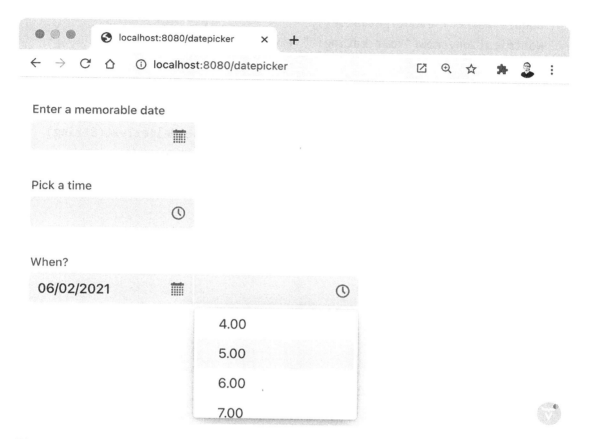

Figure 4-9. *A TimePicker and a DateTimePicker rendered in the browser*

Numeric Input

The NumberField class allows you to get a Double value from the user. Here's an example:

```
NumberField numberField = new NumberField("Rating");
numberField.setHasControls(true);
numberField.setMin(0.0);
numberField.setMax(5.0);
numberField.setStep(0.5);
numberField.setClearButtonVisible(true);
```

```
numberField.setHelperText("From 0.0 to 5.0");

numberField.addValueChangeListener(event -> {
    Double value = event.getValue();
    Notification.show("Your rating: " + value);
});
```

Most of the methods are self-explanatory. You can enable the visualization of controls to allow the user to adjust the numeric value using + and – buttons in the field by increasing or decreasing it according to a step value. The setHelperText(String) method allows you to show hints on how to use the field. See Figure 4-10.

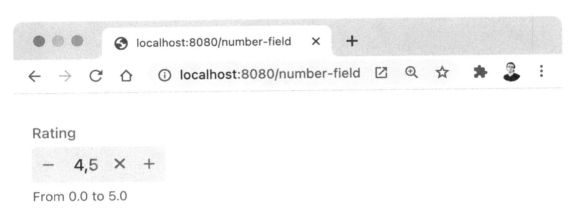

Figure 4-10. *A NumberField rendered in the browser*

If you need Integer input instead of Double, use the IntegerField class instead. It has a similar API.

Single Selection Input

There are several components to get input in the form of a selection between defined values. For example, you can use the ComboBox class to ask the user which department in a company they work for:

```
ComboBox<String> comboBox = new ComboBox<>("Department");
comboBox.setItems("R&D", "Marketing", "Sales", "HR");
```

The result is shown in Figure 4-11.

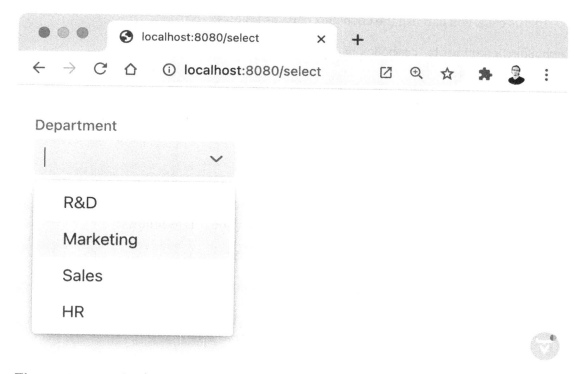

Figure 4-11. *A ComboBox in the browser*

The available values are set using the setItems(T...) method that uses String as a parameter type. You can use any type as a parameter. For example, you might have a class or an enumeration that encapsulates departments instead of having them as strings:

```
public class Department {
    private Integer id;
    private String name;

    public Department(Integer id, String name) {
        this.id = id;
        this.name = name;
    }

    @Override
    public String toString() {
        return name;
    }
}
```

In this case, you can use the ComboBox class as follows:

```
ComboBox<Department> comboBox = new ComboBox<>("Department");
comboBox.setItems(
        new Department(1, "R&D"),
        new Department(2, "Marketing"),
        new Department(3, "Sales")
);
```

Sometimes, you have to configure the string that's shown in the browser per option. By default, the ComboBox class uses the toString() method of the class specified as a parameter (Department in the example). You can override this as follows:

```
comboBox.setItemLabelGenerator(Department::toString);
```

Moreover, you can include any custom logic to produce each string value:

```
comboBox.setItemLabelGenerator(department -> {
    String text = department.getName() + " department";
    return text;
});
```

The result is shown in Figure 4-12.

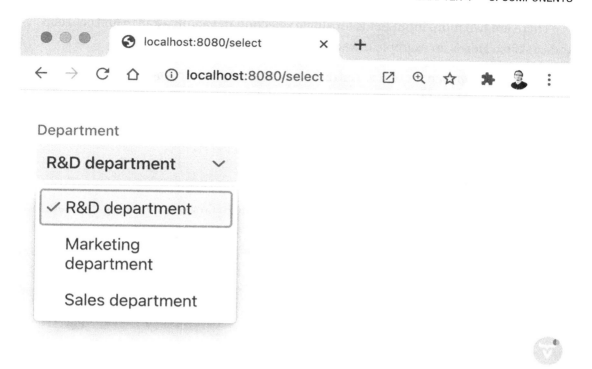

Figure 4-12. *A custom item label generator*

In a previous example, I set the items by creating new instances of the Department class. This was only to show you the idea of using Java beans as items in the input field. In real applications, you would most likely get a Collection of objects that you can pass to one of the versions of the setItems method. For example, if you have a service class, the code could look like this:

```
List<Department> list = service.getDepartments();
ComboBox<Department> comboBox = new ComboBox<>("Department");
comboBox.setItems(list);
```

This possibility is one of the features that makes Vaadin so powerful—you can access your backend directly from the presentation layer in plain Java. The service classes can use technologies such as Hibernate/JPA (Jakarta Persistence API), Spring, CDI (Contexts and Dependency Injection), and many others that are available in the huge and battle-proven Java ecosystem.

There are two more input fields for single selection in Vaadin—`RadioButtonGroup` and `ListBox`. Here's an example of `RadioButtonGroup`:

```
RadioButtonGroup<Department> radio = new RadioButtonGroup<>();
radio.setItems(list);
```

The `ListBox` component works in a similar way:

```
ListBox<Department> listBox = new ListBox<>();
listBox.setItems(list);
```

The APIs of these two classes are similar to the one in `ComboBox`, making them almost entirely interchangeable. Figure 4-13 shows these components in the browser.

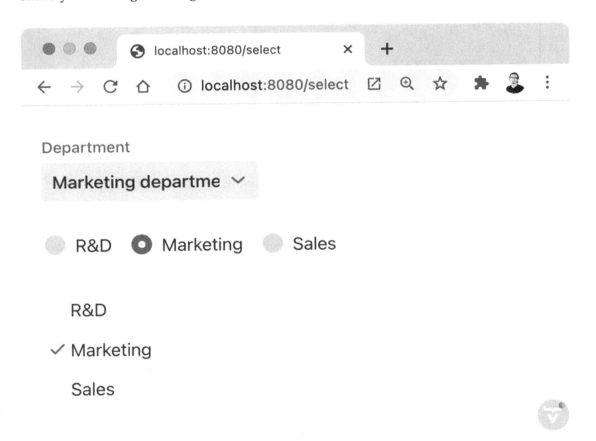

Figure 4-13. *Single selection input fields in Vaadin*

Multiple Selection Input

To allow users to select one or more items from a list, you can use the CheckboxGroup and MultiSelectListBox classes. Here's an example:

```
CheckboxGroup<Department> checkboxes = new CheckboxGroup<>();
checkboxes.setItems(service.getDepartments());

MultiSelectListBox<Department> listBox = new MultiSelectListBox<>();
listBox.setItems(service.getDepartments());
```

Since these components allow the user to select several values, the getValue() method returns a Set with the values that are selected:

```
Set<Department> departments = listBox.getValue();
```

Figure 4-14 shows these components in the browser.

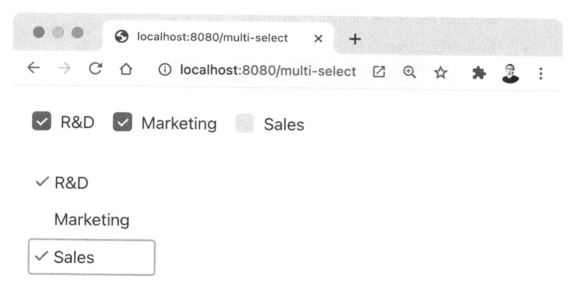

Figure 4-14. *Multiple selection input fields in Vaadin*

File Upload

The Upload class allows you to show an input field to transfer files from the user's machine to the server. It supports single or multiple files and drag and drop from the desktop. Here's the basic usage:

```
MemoryBuffer receiver = new MemoryBuffer();
Upload upload = new Upload(receiver);
upload.addSucceededListener(event -> {
    InputStream in = receiver.getInputStream();
    ... read the data from in ...
});
```

The MemoryBuffer class is an implementation of the Receiver interface. This interface is used to provide the Upload component a way to write the uploaded data. There are several implementations:

- MemoryBuffer: Stores the data in memory

- FileBuffer: Creates a File using the File.createTempFile(String, String) method

- MultiFileMemoryBuffer: Multiple file uploads storing the data in memory

- MultiFileBuffer: Creates multiple Files using the File.createTempFile(String, String) method

Suppose we want to make a program to count the number of times that the letter A appears in a plain text file. This requires limiting the type of the accepted file and processing its content. Let's start with the processing part:

```
upload.addSucceededListener(event -> {
    InputStream in = receiver.getInputStream();
    long count = new Scanner(in).findAll("[Aa]").count();
    Notification.show("A x " + count + " times");
});
```

When the user uploads a file, the listener gets the InputStream from the Receiver and uses a Java Scanner to find all the incidences of the letter A. It then shows the result in a notification. See Figure 4-15.

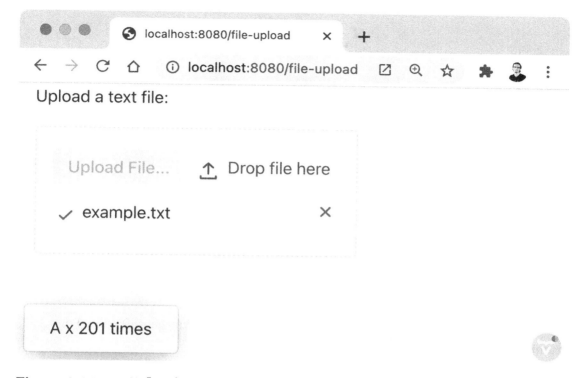

Figure 4-15. *An Upload component rendered in the browser*

When the user clicks the *Upload File...* button, a standard file selector is presented, and the user can navigate through their hard drive to select a file. All the files are permitted by default. To restrict this, you can set the MIME types you want to accept. For example, the MIME type of plain text files is `text/plain`:

```
upload.setAcceptedFileTypes("text/plain");
```

Figure 4-16 shows how an image file (JPG) is disabled (grayed out) for selection on macOS systems.

91

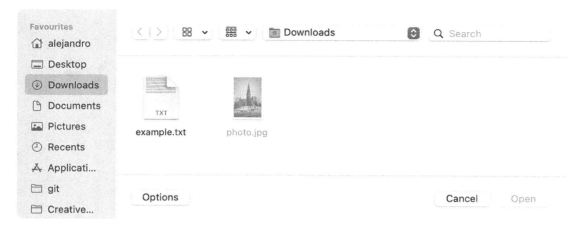

Figure 4-16. *Example of the file selector accepting only text files on macOS*

Interaction Components

Interaction components allow the user to trigger an action in your application. For example, saving data in a form or navigating to another URL.

Buttons

We already saw buttons in the previous chapter, but we didn't really study them. By now, it's very likely that you can guess the basic usage of a button (if I have done my job well, at least, which I truly hope I had). In any case, here it is:

```
Button button = new Button("Time in the server, please");
button.addClickListener(event ->
    Notification.show("Sure: " + LocalTime.now())
);
```

The code is easy to understand. When the button is clicked, the code in the lambda expression is executed in the server. You can add the click listener using a constructor:

```
Button button = new Button("Time in the server", event ->
    Notification.show("Sure: " + LocalTime.now())
);
```

Tip   I prefer to add click listeners, and any other kind of event listeners for that matter, explicitly by using the corresponding method rather than the constructor. In books, tutorials, and presentations, I use the more compact version because I'm there (virtually or in person) to explain the code. However, in real-life projects where the code can grow in size and complexity, I like the clarity of having the code speak for me. Not only to help other developers but also myself. I remember a time in which I was trying to locate the code executed when a certain button was clicked. I searched for "clickListener" in a bunch of source files using my IDE. Luckily, I got only one match. Unluckily, it was the wrong button. The button in question had a caption that came from a database, so I wasn't able to search by that. And the button was probably named "button," "b," or something like that. With a little more work, I found the instance and noticed that the click listener was added using the constructor.

Say you want the application to tell the time only once (per page refresh, to make it simpler). You can hide the button in the click listener using the setEnabled(boolean) method as follows:

```
Button button = new Button("Time in the server", event -> {
    Notification.show("Sure: " + LocalTime.now());
    event.getSource().setVisible(false);
});
```

We cannot use the button instance since it's not defined at that point. Instead, you can get the component on which the event was fired using the getSource() method.

Alternatively, you can call setEnabled(false) to disable the button instead of hiding it altogether to avoid changes in the overall look of the view. And if that's the case, an even better way to disable a button after click is by using the setDisableOnClick(boolean) method:

```
button.setDisableOnClick(true);
```

Figure 4-17 shows the example in the browser.

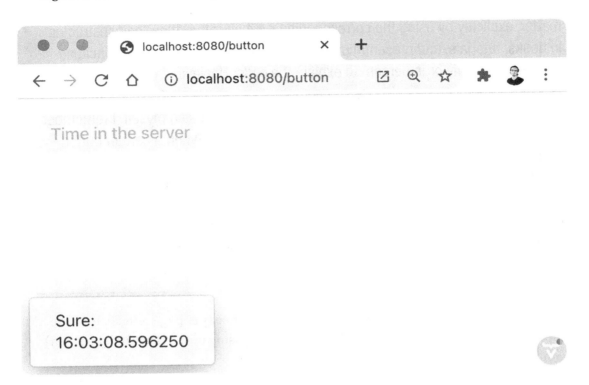

Figure 4-17. *A disabled* `Button` *rendered in the browser*

How Are Events Sent to the Server?

A click listener allows you to run code in the server when the user clicks the component in which the listener is added. In fact, all listeners invoke code in the server when a certain action happens in the browser, for example, a click, a focus gain, a key press, and even when the component is attached to the view. You'll find methods for these events in many UI components in Vaadin.

We know that all interactions with a web application happen through HTTP requests (or WebSocket as we'll see in Chapter 8). If we use the web browser's developer tools, we can see the request that is made when you click a button. Figure 4-18 shows the request that Vaadin sends to the server when you click the button of the previous example.

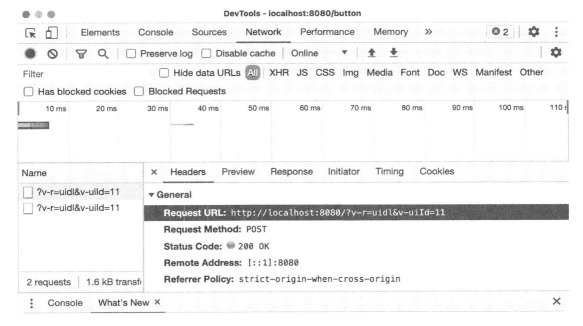

Figure 4-18. *An HTTP request after a click event*

The request URL includes two parameters. You can read these parameters and their values as follows:

- **v-r=uidl:** A **V**aadin **R**equest of type **U**ser **I**nterface **D**efinition **L**anguage. This indicates that the request is intended to process a change in the state of the UI.

- **v-uiId=11:** **V**aadin **U**ser **I**nterface **Id**entifier. This indicates the numeric identifier of the UI that has changed; in this case, the UI was assigned 11 as its identifier. If you open the view in a different browser tab, you should get a different value.

These parameters are directed to the `VaadinServlet` class which in turn delegates to more specialized classes. Vaadin then takes the payload of the request and processes it accordingly. The payload is sent in JSON format as shown in Figure 4-19.

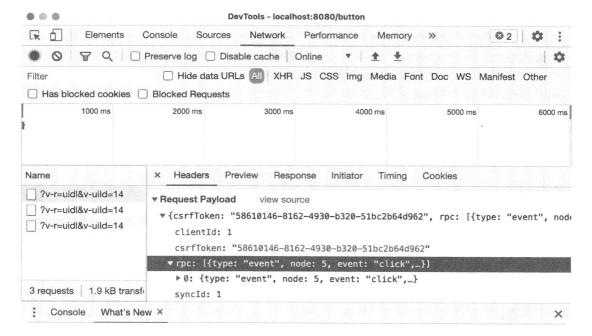

Figure 4-19. *The payload of a uidl request*

The payload includes all the details about the change in the UI. In this case, a click event. It also includes the node (or component) in which the event happened (in the example, the button was assigned the ID 5). With this information, Vaadin can navigate the components tree and find the component with ID 5 and call any click listeners that might have been added to it.

If you inspect the response (in the Response tab shown in Figure 4-19), you'll see something like the following (most of the content has been omitted for clarity and spacing reasons):

```
for (;;);
[{
    "syncId": 2,
    "clientId": 2,
    ...
    "changes": [{
        "node": 5,
        "type": "put",
        "key": "disabled",
```

```
            "feat": 3,
            "value": ""
    },
    ...
    {
            "node": 8,
            "type": "put",
            "key": "innerHTML",
            "feat": 1,
            "value": "Sure: 17:19:17.323399"
    }, {
            "node": 9,
            "type": "attach"
    }, {
            "node": 9,
            "type": "put",
            "key": "tag",
            "feat": 0,
            "value": "vaadin-notification"
    },
    ...
    ],
    "timings": [668, 2]
}]
```

The response, also in JSON format, includes the information about the changes that should be made in the view after the request has been processed. The response states, for example, that the node ID 5 should be disabled (the button) and that a notification with the text "Sure: 17:19:17.323399" should be attached (shown). These are the exact things that we programmed in the click listener in the example of the previous section.

Links

Links (or anchors) allow users to request a different URL. It can be a URL in your application or an external website. Here's an example with a shameless plug:

```
Anchor blogLink = new Anchor("https://www.programmingbrain.com",
        "Visit my technical blog");
```

You can use a UI component instead of a string:

```
Anchor vaadinLink = new Anchor("https://vaadin.com",
        new Button("Visit vaadin.com"));
```

Lastly, you can generate the content at runtime. For example, the following code creates a link to a text file generated in the server at runtime:

```
Anchor textLink = new Anchor(new StreamResource(
        "text.txt",
        () -> {
            String content = "Time: " + LocalTime.now();
            return new StringInputStream(
                    content, Charset.defaultCharset());
        }
), "Server-generated text");
```

When the user clicks this last anchor, a new file with the name *text.txt* is generated and returned to the browser. Chrome downloads this file to the hard drive of the client machine. Figure 4-20 shows the anchors of the previous examples.

Visit my technical blog

Visit vaadin.com

Server-generated text

Figure 4-20. *The Anchor component in the browser*

Menus

Although not that popular in mobile-first applications, menus have a big deal of utility in business applications that often are used on desktop browsers almost exclusively. Even on mobile-first applications, you can find the typical button showing "…" that tells the user there are more options available. Vaadin includes components to show top-level, multilevel, and context menus in your web applications.

Starting at the top level, you build a menu using the following structure:

```
MenuBar > MenuItem > SubMenu > MenuItem > SubMenu > MenuItem > ...
```

This starts to make more sense once you study an example:

```
MenuBar menuBar = new MenuBar();

MenuItem file = menuBar.addItem("File");
file.getSubMenu().addItem("New");
file.getSubMenu().addItem("Open");

MenuItem edit = menuBar.addItem("Edit");
edit.getSubMenu().addItem("Copy");
edit.getSubMenu().addItem("Paste");
```

See the result in Figure 4-21.

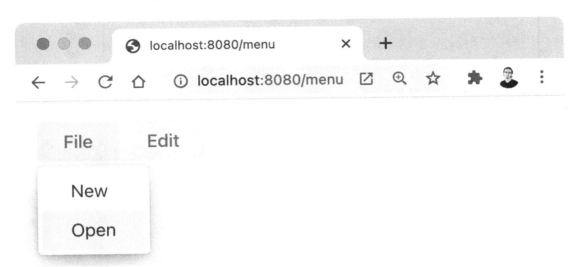

Figure 4-21. *A two-level menu*

Each option with a text in it is a MenuItem. If you want to create more levels, you have to get the SubMenu from a MenuItem and add more MenuItem objects to it. You can have as many levels as required.

Add a click listener to execute code when the user clicks an item using the constructor of MenuItem or the addClickListener(ComponentEventListener) method:

```
edit.getSubMenu().addItem("Copy", event ->
        Notification.show("Copy selected"));

MenuItem paste = edit.getSubMenu().addItem("Paste");
paste.addClickListener(event ->
        Notification.show("Paste selected"));
```

You can also enable or disable items using the setEnable(boolean) method or make them toggable by using the setCheckable(boolean) method.

To add a context menu (a menu shown when the user right-clicks a component), you can use the ContextMenu class and specify a target, usually a layout component, that the user can right-click to see the menu:

```
HorizontalLayout target = new HorizontalLayout(
        new Text("Right click here")
);
ContextMenu contextMenu = new ContextMenu(target);
contextMenu.addItem("Copy");
contextMenu.addItem("Paste");
```

You can add click listeners to the items and have as many levels as required in a context menu. Figure 4-22 shows the context menu in the browser.

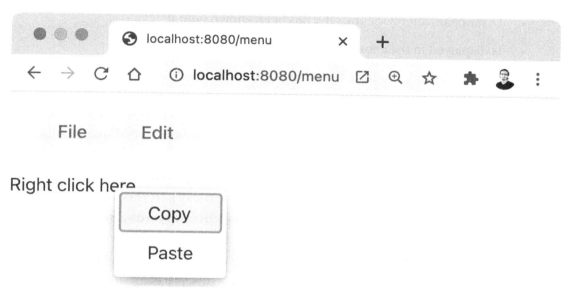

Figure 4-22. *A ContextMenu in the browser*

Visualization Components

The last section of this chapter full of interactive components closes with components that are not as interactive, but that help enriching the way you present data to the users. Let's have a look at them.

Notifications and Dialogs

We have been using the `Notification` class a lot throughout this chapter, but there's more about it than what we have seen so far. To learn more of its features, let's define some requirements. Suppose we have to show a notification that

- Is shown when you click a button in the view

- Remains visible if it's the first time being shown

- Can be closed by clicking a button inside it

- Disappears after 2 seconds if it has been shown before

- Is displayed in the center of the page

The fact is that I think you have the knowledge and experience to implement this. Do you dare to implement it by yourself? Give it a try!

Let me tell you a quick story while you make the decision to try the exercise out. I wrote this on a rainy Saturday night in Turku, Finland. My full-time job didn't let much time during the weekdays to work on the book, so I decided to go all out on Saturday and finish the chapter. The formula was simple—I start with a code example and then transform my abstract thoughts about it into words. The tricky part was to actually start writing the code and paragraphs, but once I start, the ideas and words just flow, and I get things done. Then it's all about practice, and at the end of the day, practice always pays off. Now go and open your IDE and get some practice with Vaadin.

The only excuse I accept to not doing the exercise is that you are reading this on a plane, with no laptop or Internet connection. For that reason, Listing 4-1 shows a possible solution. I hope yours was even better than mine.

Listing 4-1. Some of the features of the `Notification` class

```
import com.vaadin.flow.component.Component;
import com.vaadin.flow.component.Composite;
import com.vaadin.flow.component.Text;
import com.vaadin.flow.component.button.Button;
import com.vaadin.flow.component.notification.Notification;
import com.vaadin.flow.component.orderedlayout.VerticalLayout;
import com.vaadin.flow.router.Route;

@Route("notification")
```

```java
public class NotificationView extends Composite<Component> {

  private boolean firstTime = true;

  @Override
  protected Component initContent() {
    return new VerticalLayout(
        new Button("Notification", event -> {
          Notification notification = new Notification();
          notification.add(new VerticalLayout(
              new Text("Here it is!")));
          notification.setPosition(Notification.Position.MIDDLE);

          if (firstTime) {
            notification.setDuration(0);
            notification.add(new Button("Close", e ->
                notification.close()));
          } else {
            notification.setDuration(2000);
          }

          firstTime = false;
          notification.open();
        })
    );
  }

}
```

Pop-up dialogs are similar to notifications, but they have more functionality. Here's a basic example:

```java
new Dialog(
    new VerticalLayout(
        new H2("Title"),
        new Text("Text!"),
        new Button("Button!!!")
    )
).open();
```

By default, the user can interact with other parts of the application while the dialog is opened. You can change this by making it modal:

```
dialog.setModal(true);
```

If you want to avoid the dialog to disappear when the user clicks outside of it, you can use the following:

```
dialog.setCloseOnOutsideClick(false);
```

In this case, you should probably provide a way to close the dialog. One way to do it is by enabling closing it with the ESC key:

```
dialog.setCloseOnEsc(true);
```

Finally, you can make the dialog draggable as follows:

```
dialog.setDraggable(true);
```

Figure 4-23 shows a dialog in the browser.

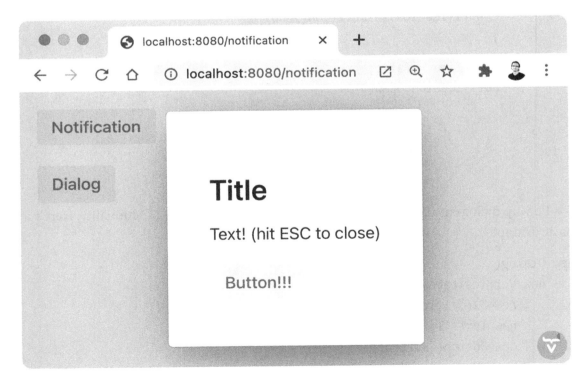

Figure 4-23. *A* `Dialog` *rendered in the browser*

Tabs

Tabs are a good way to allow users move between views that are related to a shared topic. In Vaadin, tabs are simply a way to show a group of "buttons" with a tab style, and it's up to you, the programmer, to react to clicks on those buttons to, most likely, show different layouts in a view when each tab button is clicked (or selected). Here's a basic example:

```
Tab order = new Tab("Order");
Tab delivery = new Tab("Delivery");
Tabs tabs = new Tabs(order, delivery);
```

See the result in Figure 4-24.

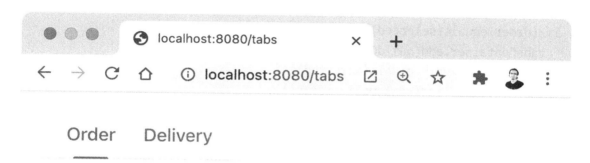

Figure 4-24. *A Tabs component rendered in the browser*

Where's the content of the tabs? Like I mentioned before, the Tabs component doesn't include this functionality. Unfortunately.

Tip   In Vaadin 8 and earlier, the API of the tabs component included a container and all the logic to automatically switch between "pages" when a tab is selected. If you come from these versions of Vaadin and miss this behavior, you might want to take a look at the open source free paged-tabs component available in the Vaadin Directory at *https://vaadin.com/directory/component/paged-tabs* developed and maintained by the author of this book. Ha! Two shameless plugs in a single chapter.

To make the tabs useful, you have to implement the logic to make them work as you wish. Most commonly, this means to show different components when the tabs are selected. This can be implemented using a listener. Here's an example:

```
VerticalLayout tabsContainer = new VerticalLayout();

Tab order = new Tab("Order");
Tab delivery = new Tab("Delivery");
Tabs tabs = new Tabs(order, delivery);

tabs.addSelectedChangeListener(event -> {
  Tab selected = event.getSelectedTab();
  tabsContainer.removeAll();

  if (order.equals(selected)) {
    tabsContainer.add(buildOrderTab());
  } else if (delivery.equals(selected)) {
    tabsContainer.add(buildDeliveryTab());
  }
});
```

The buildOrderTab() and buildDeliveryTab() methods can return any layout containing the components you want to show. The code uses an if else if structure to which you can add more cases as needed. Alternatively, you can use a Map to match tabs with the layouts to show or implement any algorithm you want to switch between layouts. You can find an example at *https://vaadin.com/components/vaadin-tabs/java-examples*.

Caution   The previous example has a bug. When you request the view, the *Order* tab doesn't show its contents. The selection change listener hasn't fired up. Can you solve the bug? Hint: Extract logic to a separate method.

Icons

Vaadin comes with a set of more than 600 ready-to-use icons. You can create an icon and add it to any layout:

```
Icon icon = VaadinIcon.YOUTUBE.create();
layout.add(icon);
```

Like most UI components (including all the ones we have seen in this chapter), you can set its size:

```
icon.setSize("4em");
```

Many UI components include the setIcon(Icon) method. For example, here's how to add an icon to a button:

```
Button button = new Button("Edit");
button.setIcon(VaadinIcon.EDIT.create());
```

You can combine these two lines into one:

```
Button button = new Button("Edit", VaadinIcon.EDIT.create());
```

Figure 4-25 shows a screenshot with these components.

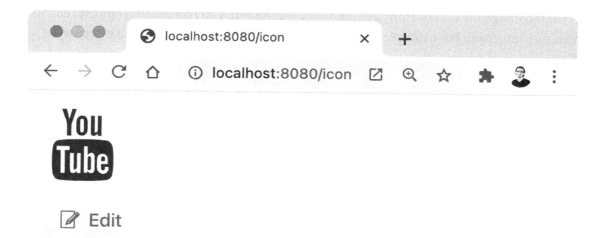

Figure 4-25. *Vaadin icons rendered in the browser*

Tip   You can see all the icons at *https://vaadin.com/components/*
vaadin-icons/java-examples.

Images

There are two ways of showing an image in a Vaadin application. If you have a URL (internal or external) to the image file, you can simply create an image component as follows:

```
Image photo = new Image(
    "https://live.staticflickr.com/65535/50969482201_be1163c6f1_b.jpg",
    "Funny dog"
);
photo.setWidthFull();
```

After the URL in the constructor, you can (and should) pass an alternate text that web browsers can use if the image cannot be displayed. The previous example also sets the width of the image to use as much horizontal space as possible.

If the image file comes from a database or file system, you can use an InputStream to read the data from. For example, if you place a file in the standard *resources* directory of the Maven project, you can create an image as follows:

```
StreamResource source = new StreamResource("logo", () ->
    getClass().getClassLoader()
        .getResourceAsStream("vaadin-logo.png")
);

Image logo = new Image(source, "Logo");
logo.setWidth("20%");
```

You can see the Vaadin logo and the funny dog in Figure 4-26.

Figure 4-26. *Two Image components rendered in the browser*

Summary

This chapter gave you key knowledge on most of the UI components for data input, interaction, and visualization in Vaadin. You learned how input components work, how to get different types of values from the user including strings, dates, files, and others. You got a low-level view of how JSON messages are sent between the client and the server when the user interacts with the application. You also learned how to show notifications, pop-up dialogs, icons, and images, but keep in mind that there are more UI components in Vaadin than what the space in this chapter allows to show. Vaadin is in constant development, so new UI components are added with new versions. You can explore all the components and their API at *https://vaadin.com/components*.

The next chapter will explore a key concept in business applications: data binding—a mechanism to connect values in a Java bean with values in input UI components.

CHAPTER 5

Data Binding

Vaadin is frequently used for implementing the presentation layer of business applications. This kind of applications deals with data typically modeled as a set of domain classes. For example, in an ecommerce application, you might find classes such as Item, Cart, Order, Customer, Payment, and similar. The presentation layer serves as a medium to present data from domain objects and capture data from the user into domain objects that the backend can use to run any business logic.

Data arrives in the application from external services or user interfaces. In the last case, the values in input components need to be set in business objects' properties. For example, the value in a TextField for the customer's name (during the user registration use case) should be set in the name property of the Customer class. As you learned in the previous chapter, you can use the getValue() method to achieve this. The same happens in the opposite direction. For example, to allow the user to update their name, you can read the stored value from a database and present it in a TextField using the setValue(String) method.

Data binding is the process of connecting values in Java properties with values in input components and all the intricacies that might appear in the process. This includes validating input and converting data from formats supported in the presentation layer to forms required in the backend services and back.

Implementing Data Binding Manually

Let's put some of the concepts we have learned so far to implement a simple view to manage products in a hypothetical Point of Sales (POS) software. A central idea in this kind of software is the product. Suppose we are assigned to implement a UI to manage products. The UI should include a list of all products, each one with an option to edit and delete it, as well as a button to create new products.

© Alejandro Duarte 2021
A. Duarte, *Practical Vaadin*, https://doi.org/10.1007/978-1-4842-7179-7_5

Implementing the Domain Model

Let's omit any logic for connecting to a database and use a Set to keep the products in memory. Where would you start? In my case, I would start with the domain model, so to keep it simple, here's an implementation of the domain classes to encapsulate the data we need for the POS software:

```
public class Product {

  private String name;
  private boolean available = true;
  private Manufacturer manufacturer;

  public Product() {
  }

  ... getters and setters ...

}

public class Manufacturer {

  private String name;
  private String phoneNumber;
  private String email;

  public Manufacturer() {
  }

  public Manufacturer(String name, String phoneNumber,
      String email) {
    this.name = name;
    this.phoneNumber = phoneNumber;
    this.email = email;
  }

  ... getters and setters ...

}
```

Implementing the View

What's next? When it comes to the UI, I usually start at the view level—the class that you annotate with @Route. We need a static Set of products, a Set of manufacturers, and a layout to show the products. Static sets because we want to ensure that all the users consume the same data. For simplicity, let's also define all the manufacturers in a static block (this version of the POS software won't include manufacturer management). So, how about the following?

```
public class ProductManagementView extends Composite<Component> {

  private static Set<Product> products = new HashSet<>();
  private static Set<Manufacturer> manufacturers =
      new HashSet<>();
  private VerticalLayout productsLayout = new VerticalLayout();

  static {
    manufacturers.add(new Manufacturer("Unix Beers", "555111",
        "beer@example.com"));
    manufacturers.add(new Manufacturer("Whisky Soft", "555222",
        "whisky@example.com"));
    manufacturers.add(new Manufacturer("Wines Java", "555333",
        "wine@example.com"));
  }

}
```

Before we start coding, let's stop and think for a second. What operations do we need for this class? We need to

- Initialize the content

- Update the list of products anytime the user creates, edits, or deletes one

- Show a form when the user clicks the new button or the update button in a given product

- Save and delete a product

With this in mind, we can add the following methods to the `ProductManagementView` class:

```
@Override
protected Component initContent() {
}

private void updateList() {
}

private void showProductForm(Product product) {
}

private void delete(Product product) {
}

private void save(Product product) {
}
```

Now let's start coding one method at a time. The `initContent()` method should return the layout of the view. It should also update the list of products so that they are visible on page refresh:

```
@Override
protected Component initContent() {
  updateList();
  return new VerticalLayout(
      new Button("New product", VaadinIcon.PLUS.create(),
          event -> showProductForm(new Product())),
      productsLayout
  );
}
```

This will show a button to create a new product (notice how we call the corresponding method passing a new product) and the layout with the list of products (productsLayout). Next is the updateList() method. To "refresh" the list of products, we can rebuild the list by removing all the components in the productsLayout component and add each product at a time:

```
private void updateList() {
  productsLayout.removeAll();
  products.stream()
      .map(product -> new Details(
          product.getName() +
              (product.isAvailable() ? "" : " (not available)"),
          new HorizontalLayout(
              new Button(VaadinIcon.PENCIL.create(),
                  event -> showProductForm(product)),
              new Button(VaadinIcon.TRASH.create(),
                  event -> delete(product))
          )
      ))
      .forEach(productsLayout::add);
}
```

This code uses a Java stream to take each product in the `products` collection and "transform" it into a UI component that we haven't covered yet. Surprise! The `Details` component is an expandable panel for showing and hiding content. In this example, the `HorizontalLayout` with the two `Button`s is hidden until the user clicks the caption (see Figure 5-1). Each product is mapped to a `Details` component with the information about the product and the action buttons and then added into the `productsLayout` instance.

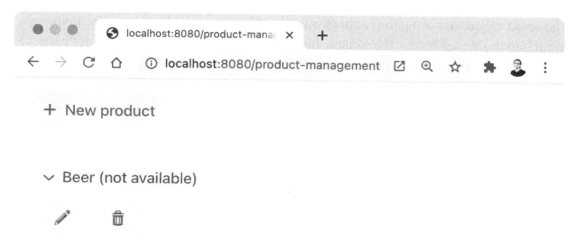

Figure 5-1. *The* `Details` *component. Clicking the title (Beer) shows the buttons*

Let's move on to showing the form. For this, we will delegate the actual implementation of the form to a separate class (ProductForm) that we are going to develop soon. It makes sense to do so since we might want to reuse the form in other parts of the application. Here's the implementation of the showProduct(Product) method:

```
private void showProductForm(Product product) {
  Dialog dialog = new Dialog();
  dialog.setModal(true);
  dialog.open();

  dialog.add(new ProductForm(product, manufacturers, () -> {
    dialog.close();
    save(product);
  }));
}
```

The method starts by creating and configuring a new Dialog and adding an instance of the next-to-be-born ProductForm class. The way I implemented this code was precisely as I'm describing now. I usually tend to write the code that uses a class (the client of that class) before implementing the class itself. That way, I can focus on the API that I need from that class. I figured that the ProductForm class's constructor could accept the product I want to show in the form (a new product or an existing one), the list of available manufacturers, and a callback to execute my code when the user saves the product in the form. So, when the user is done with the form, I can close the dialog and save the product using the callback implemented as a lambda expression. Before we jump into the actual ProductForm class, here's the implementation of the save(Product) and delete(Product) methods:

```
private void save(Product product) {
  products.add(product);
  updateList();
  Notification.show("Product saved: " + product.getName());
}
```

```
private void delete(Product product) {
  products.remove(product);
  updateList();
  Notification.show("Product deleted");
}
```

No surprise components here. These two methods add or remove the product to the static Set, update the list to reflect the change in the UI, and show a notification informing the user that the operation was successfully completed.

Implementing the Form

Let's talk about data binding now as we implement the ProductForm class. This class is connected (bound) to a Product instance (the bean). More specifically, we want to connect the properties of Product with input fields in the form. When we create a ProductForm, the input fields should show the values of the properties in the bean. For example, we need a TextField to introduce or edit the name property in the Product class. Similarly, we need to update the name property when the value in the TextField changes.

Let's start by defining the input components and data that we need. We'll add them as properties in the class because we'll need access to them later:

```
public class ProductForm extends Composite<Component> {

    private final SerializableRunnable saveListener;
    private Product product;

    private TextField name = new TextField("Name");
    private ComboBox<Manufacturer> manufacturer = new ComboBox<>();
    private Checkbox available = new Checkbox("Available");

}
```

The SerializableRunnable is, like the name suggests, a serializable version of Runnable. This allows us to perform a callback to the clients of this class (such as the ProductManagementView class that we developed in the previous section) and give them the opportunity to process the data in the product instance. We also have a TextField for the name, a ComboBox for the manufacturer, and a Checkbox for the availability of the product.

117

> **Tip**   Use `Serializable` classes when you keep references to objects in UI classes. This is required, for example, when you are using session persistence in servers such as Apache Tomcat to allow sessions to be stored in the hard drive across restarts. All the UI components and other helper classes included in Vaadin implement `Serializable`.

In the previous section, we decided that this class should accept a `Product` instance in the constructor (alongside with the listener in the form of a `SerializableRunnable`). In order to implement the binding in the `Product` to input fields' direction, we can set the value of each input field from the corresponding Java property in the `Product` bean in the constructor as follows:

```
public ProductForm(Product product,
    Set<Manufacturer> manufacturers,
    SerializableRunnable saveListener) {
  this.product = product;
  this.saveListener = saveListener;

  manufacturer.setItems(manufacturers);
  manufacturer.setItemLabelGenerator(Manufacturer::getName);

  if (product.getName() != null) {
    name.setValue(product.getName());
    manufacturer.setValue(product.getManufacturer());
    available.setValue(product.isAvailable());
  }
}
```

The first two lines in the constructor assign in the values to the instance fields of the class so we can use them later from other methods. Then, the `ComboBox` is populated and configured to show the name of the manufacturer as each item. Since the `setValue(T)` method in input fields throws a `NullPointerException` if you pass `null`, we have to do a null check before calling it. By setting the values from the bean to the input fields, we have implemented data binding in that direction.

Note   When I talk about *input fields*, I'm referring to UI components for data entry such as TextField and Checkbox. When I speak about fields (or Java fields, or instance fields), I'm referring to member variables in a Java class.

With the input components ready, we can implement the layout of the form as follows:

```
@Override
protected Component initContent() {
  return new VerticalLayout(
      new H1("Product"),
      name,
      manufacturer,
      available,
      new Button("Save", VaadinIcon.CHECK.create(),
          event -> saveClicked())
  );
}
```

This creates a new layout with a header (H1), the input fields (name and available), and a button to allow the user to invoke the save action. In the saveClicked() method, we can implement the data binding in the opposite direction—input fields to Product using the setters of the bean and the getValue() methods of the fields:

```
private void saveClicked() {
  product.setName(name.getValue());
  product.setManufacturer(manufacturer.getValue());
  product.setAvailable(available.getValue());
  saveListener.run();
}
```

We have successfully implemented a form with data binding. The result is illustrated in Figure 5-2.

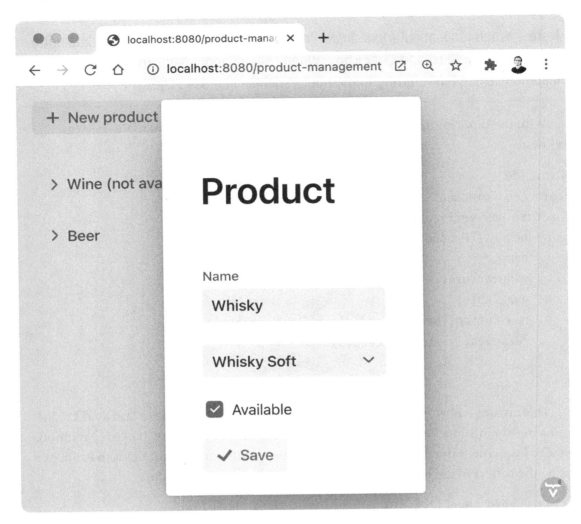

Figure 5-2. *A form with manual data binding*

The Binder Helper Class

Although the technique works, there's a problem with the implementation of data binding in the previous section. As you add properties to the Product class, you have to remember to set input field values in one place (the constructor) and bean property values in another (the saveClicked() method). This makes the code hard to maintain especially as you add more input fields to the form.

Since synchronizing values between data sources (such as domain objects) and input fields is a common task in business applications, Vaadin provides functionality to simplify this process—the Binder class. This class is not a UI component but a helper class that keeps the values synchronized according to a customizable configuration that tells which input field is bound to which bean property.

Defining Bindings Programmatically

Let's modify the ProductForm class to let Vaadin do the data binding for us. Here's the full implementation of the form:

```
public class ProductForm extends Composite<Component> {

  private final SerializableRunnable saveListener;
  private TextField name = new TextField("Name");
  private ComboBox<Manufacturer> manufacturer = new ComboBox<>();
  private Checkbox available = new Checkbox("Available");

  public ProductForm(Product product,
      Set<Manufacturer> manufacturers,
      SerializableRunnable saveListener) {
    this.saveListener = saveListener;

    manufacturer.setItems(manufacturers);
    manufacturerComboBox.setItemLabelGenerator(
        Manufacturer::getName);

    Binder<Product> binder = new Binder<>();
    binder.bind(name, Product::getName, Product::setName);
    binder.bind(manufacturer,
        Product::getManufacturer, Product::setManufacturer);
    binder.bind(available, Product::isAvailable,
        Product::setAvailable);
    binder.setBean(product);
  }
```

```
@Override
protected Component initContent() {
  return new VerticalLayout(
      new H1("Product"),
      name,
      manufacturer,
      available,
      new Button("Save", VaadinIcon.CHECK.create(),
          event -> saveListener.run())
  );
}
}
```

With the help of the `Binder` class, we were able to substantially reduce the amount of code. We no longer need to keep a reference to the `Product` instance since all the data binding logic happens in the constructor. Here, we created a new instance of the `Binder` class parameterized with `Product` because we want to bind the form to a product. We then bound the input fields to their corresponding Java properties in the `Product` class by specifying the input field and the getter and the setter for the Java property in the domain class. The getter is used later by the `Binder` class to get the value from the bean and set it as a value in the input field. The setter is used to set the value in the bean property from the value in the input field. Once we have defined the bindings, we tell the `Binder` class which bean to use by calling the `setBean(BEAN)` method. At this point, the `Binder` class reads the values from the bean and writes them into the matching input fields. And from now on, the `Binder` class will also set the values in the bean from the input fields when the user introduces data in the form.

Note   Internally, the Binder class adds value change listeners to each input field in order to have the chance to write the values back to the bean. No magic. Just the framework doing the job for you.

The `Binder` class offers a lot of versatility. In the previous example, we used method references to specify the getter and setter to use in the bindings. We can also use lambda expressions and include any logic we want. Suppose our client asks us to change the UI to mark products as unavailable instead of as available. That is, the user wants to see a check mark when the product is not available. We don't want to modify the data model because of reasons (e.g., this is the only view in which this requirement makes sense but not in the other 174 views of this hypothetical application). Here's the change that will make our client happy:

```
private Checkbox unavailable = new Checkbox("Unavailable");
...
  binder.bind(unavailable,
      prod -> !prod.isAvailable(),
      (prod, booleanValue) -> prod.setAvailable(!booleanValue));
```

We changed the name of the variable referencing the Checkbox to make the code clear and used lambda expressions to negate the value in the bean (prod, of type Product) and in the input field (unavailable). Simple logic needed in this case, but you get the idea—you can run any business or UI logic (simple or complex) when synchronizing the values between the properties and their corresponding input fields in the UI.

When you need more fine-grained control on when to run the data binding logic, use the readBean(BEAN) and writeBean(BEAN) methods. The first reads the properties and sets the values in the input fields. The second takes the values in the input fields and writes them in the bean's properties. See the Javadoc at *https://vaadin.com/api*.

Defining Bindings Using Property Names

In Java, when you have a field with a matching getter and setter, you can call that variable a *property*. The Binder class allows you to define bindings using the names of the properties in your domain class instead of specifying getter and setter functions. For example, if we want to define the binding for the manufacturer property of the Product class using the name of the property, we have to do two things. The first is to use the Binder(Class) constructor instead of the default constructor to create the instance:

```
Binder<Product> binder = new Binder<>(Product.class);
```

With this change, we can reference the properties by their names as strings to define bindings. For example:

```
binder.bind(manufacturer, "manufacturer");
```

We can also change the name of the input field to make the example clearer:

```
private ComboBox<Manufacturer> comboBox = new ComboBox<>();
```

Now the binding would look like this:

```
binder.bind(comboBox, "manufacturer");
```

Caution   Defining bindings using property names has the advantage that you can use Jakarta Bean Validation. However, your code won't be type-safe anymore, and if later you rename a property in your domain model, you'll have to rename the string that contains the name of the property in your binding logic as well. Failing to do so will produce a runtime error. With method references and lambda expressions, your code is type-safe, and you can use the refactor tools of your IDE to rename a property knowing that the code won't break. Neither approach is right or wrong; you have to decide what's best according to your requirements and design. As discussed in the next section, automatic binding includes a feature that mitigates the risks associated to data bindings by property name.

Using Automatic Binding

We can let Vaadin define the binding for us. This approach can be handy in many scenarios, especially when you want to use Jakarta Bean Validation (covered later in this chapter). Let's see an example of automatic binding:

```
public class AutoBindingProductForm extends Composite<Component> {

    private TextField name = new TextField("Name");
    private ComboBox<Manufacturer> manufacturer = new ComboBox<>();
    private Checkbox available = new Checkbox("Available");
```

```
public AutoBindingProductForm(Product product, ...) {
  ...

  Binder<Product> binder = new Binder<>(Product.class);
  binder.bindInstanceFields(this);
  binder.setBean(product);
}

...

}
```

First of all, notice that I'm using an ellipsis (. . .) to denote extra code we are not interested in at the moment. Second, notice the `Binder` constructor that we used. This is required when using automatic binding since the names of the properties are used to match the input fields with the Java properties in the domain class like we saw in the previous section. Third, see how we replaced the binding definitions with a call to the `bindInstanceFields(Object)` method.

With automatic binding, Vaadin inspects the class that you pass to the `bindInstanceFields(Object)` method to find all the Java fields in that class. If an inspected field is also an instance of `HasValue` (an interface that all Vaadin UI input components implement), then it tries to find a property with the same name as the inspected field in the bean you pass to `setBean(BEAN)` and later use the corresponding getter and setter to perform the data binding.

In the previous example, we have three Java fields that are also of type `HasValue` with matching names in the properties of the `Product` class. So, Vaadin binds

- `AutoBindingProductForm::name` to `Product::name`

- `AutoBindingProductForm::manufacturers` to `Product:manufacturers`

- `AutoBindingProductForm::available` to `Product::available`

To improve maintainability, we can use the `@PropertyId` annotation to override the name convention. This allows us to use any identifier for the input fields in the UI class:

```
@PropertyId("name")
private TextField nameTextField = new TextField("Name");
```

```
@PropertyId("manufacturer")
private ComboBox<Manufacturer> manufacturerComboBox
    = new ComboBox<>();

@PropertyId("available")
private Checkbox availableCheckbox = new Checkbox("Available");
```

See how we can change, for example, the identifier of the Checkbox to
availableCheckbox. We could use any other name we'd like. Without the annotation, the
binding wouldn't happen since the names of the Java fields in the two classes wouldn't
match.

Tip   Always use @PropertyId when using automatic binding to make your code
easier to maintain. You'll have the freedom to change the name of the input fields
without breaking the code. When you rename a property in your domain model, you
can search for @PropertyId("nameOfTheProperty") and replace accordingly.

Defining Bindings for Nested Properties

Suppose that after an online meeting, it's clear that our customer wants to be able to
edit the manufacturers' phone number and email in the same form that they use to edit
products. They claim that this will save a lot of time since the system they currently have
(implemented in Fortran) doesn't have this option.

Note   I've never used Fortran. However, it indirectly motivated me to learn
more about programming as a kid when my father would tell inspiring stories on
using it in university. The closest I have gotten to Fortran is an online text game
implemented in C but based on the original (Adventure) written in Fortran by
Crowther and Woods for the legendary PDP-10 mainframe. You can play the game
at *https://quuxplusone.github.io/Advent*.

The requirements say that we have to show the combo box to select a manufacturer when the user wants to create a new product. However, when they want to edit one, we have to disable the combo box and show two extra text fields for updating the manufacturer's phone number and email. So, we have to add two more fields to the AutoBindingForm class:

```
private TextField phoneNumber = new TextField(
    "Manufacturer phone number");
private TextField email = new TextField("Manufacturer email");
```

These should be added to the layout as well:

```
@Override
protected Component initContent() {
  return new VerticalLayout(
      new H1("Product"),
      name,
      available,
      manufacturer,
      phoneNumber,
      email,
      new Button("Save", VaadinIcon.CHECK.create(),
          event -> saveListener.run())
  );
}
```

The key part of the implementation is in the constructor. We have two scenarios: the form is for a new product or for an existing one. If the product's name is null, it must be a new product. We can use an if...else statement to hide and disable input fields as required. To create the bindings, we can use the "dot notation" to specify the properties we want to bind. Here's the code:

```
Binder<Product> binder = new Binder<>(Product.class);
binder.bindInstanceFields(this);

if (product.getName() == null) {
  phoneNumber.setVisible(false);
  email.setVisible(false);
```

```
} else {
  manufacturer.setEnabled(false);
  binder.bind(phoneNumber, "manufacturer.phoneNumber");
  binder.bind(email, "manufacturer.email");
}
```

```
binder.setBean(product);
```

We are using autobinding to create the bindings to the properties of the Product class. But notice how we create the binding to the nested properties of the Manufacturer class. Unfortunately, at the time of writing, Vaadin doesn't support nested bindings with this notation using the @PropertyId annotation. We can also use type-safe bindings. Since we can use lambda expressions to get and set the values using any Java logic we want, we can opt for something like this:

```
binder.bind(email,
    p -> p.getManufacturer().getEmail(),
    (p, e) -> p.getManufacturer().setEmail(e));
```

Here, p is a Product, and e is a String.

Caution   More complex scenarios might require null checks when creating this type of nested data bindings to avoid NullPointerExceptions.

Figure 5-3 shows the form in edit mode.

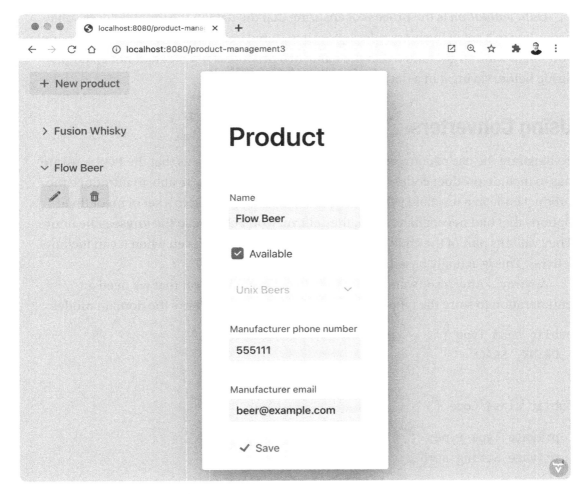

Figure 5-3. *A form with nested data bindings*

Data Conversion and Validation

In order to be effective, a binder tool should include functionality to manage data conversion and validation. Vaadin's `Binder` class includes methods to handle these two aspects in a flexible and robust way.

Data conversion is the process of transforming data from the format supported by an input field (like `String` in `TextField`) to the format in the domain model and back. For example, the number of available items of a certain product might be editable through a `TextField` (although, in this situation, I'd suggest using `NumberField` instead) and stored in an `int` property in the domain model.

Data validation is the process of ensuring that the data in the input fields is valid according to a set of business rules before it is stored in the domain model. For example, you might want to guarantee that the name of a product is not null and not an empty string before saving it in a database.

Using Converters

To illustrate the use of converters, suppose the customer tells us that the POS software has to include product codes. They insisted that they want to be able to introduce the product code in a text field even when part of the code is fixed to a set of predefined options that had never chance and, they affirm, won't change in the foreseeable future. They call this part of the code "type" and the rest "number" (even when it can include letters). This is actually based on a true story.

Anyway... After a software design meeting, it becomes clear that we need an enumeration to store the type and a string for the number. Here's the domain model:

```
public enum Type {
  DRINK, SNACK
}

public class Code {

  private Type type;
  private String number;

  public Code(Type type, String number) {
    this.type = type;
    this.number = number;
  }

  ... getters and setters ...
}

public class Product {
  ...

  private Code code = new Code(Type.DRINK, "");
  ...
}
```

We need a new input field in the form:

```
public class AutoBindingProductForm extends Composite<Component> {

  ...

  private TextField code = new TextField("Code");
  ...
}
```

We of course add the text field to the layout (omitted here). If you try the application with no other changes, you'll get an error message like the following:

```
Property type 'com.apress.practicalvaadin.ch05.Code' doesn't match the
field type 'java.lang.String'. Binding should be configured manually using
converter.
```

This happens because Vaadin doesn't know how to convert a Code instance to a String for the TextField. Although the error message affirms that we need a converter, we could implement the conversion using getter and setter functions accepted when we define a bind:

```
binder.bind(codeTextField,
    (p) -> p.getCode().getType().toString() +
        p.getCode().getNumber(),
    (p, s) -> {
      for (Type t : Type.values()) {
        if (s.startsWith(t.toString())) {
          p.setCode(
            new Code(t, s.substring(t.toString().length()))
          );
          return;
        }
      }
    }
);
```

Here, p is of type Product and s of type String. The first lambda expression is the getter, so we only need to concatenate the type and the number and return the resulting string. The second lambda expression needs to parse the string in the TextField to correctly set the type and the number in the Code instance.

Although this works, you might want to use a converter instead. Here's how:

```
public class StringToCodeConverter
        implements Converter<String, Code> {

  @Override
  public Result<Code> convertToModel(String value,
      ValueContext context) {
    for (Type t : Type.values()) {
      if (value.startsWith(t.toString())) {
        Code code =
            new Code(t, value.substring(t.toString().length()));
        return Result.ok(code);
      }
    }

    return Result.error("Error parsing the code");
  }

  @Override
  public String convertToPresentation(Code code,
      ValueContext context) {
    return code.getType().toString() + code.getNumber();
  }

}
```

This class implements Converter and its two methods. The first takes a String value and creates a new Code instance. Note the use of the Result class to tell Vaadin whether the conversion was successful or not. The second method takes a Code instance and returns the concatenated values as a String. This might seem extra work since it effectively takes more lines of code than the previous approach. However, this is useful when you want to reuse the conversion logic in multiple parts of the application. With a converter, you can bind the property and specify the converter as follows:

```
binder.forField(codeTextField)
    .withConverter(new StringToCodeConverter())
    .bind(Product::getCode, Product::setCode);
```

This time, we are using a different way to define the binding. First, we specify the input field with `forField(HasValue)`, and then we configure the binding by chaining method calls using the fluent API of the `Binder` class.

Vaadin includes converters for the most common data types. Here's a list of them:

- `StringToBooleanConverter`

- `StringToIntegerConverter`

- `StringToLongConverter`

- `StringToFloatConverter`

- `StringToDoubleConverter`

- `StringToBigDecimalConverter`

- `StringToBigIntegerConverter`

- `StringToDateConverter`

- `LocalDateToDateConverter`

- `LocalDateTimeToDateConverter`

- `DateToSqlDateConverter`

- `StringToUuidConverter`

Implementing Validation Rules

Our customer called us and told us that the product form needs to check the following before saving the data:

1. The product's name is required.

2. The product's code is required.

3. The manufacturer's phone number should be more than seven characters.

4. The manufacturer's email should be a correctly formed email address.

To add custom validation logic when using the Binder class, we have to define the bindings programmatically without using automatic binding. So, let's refactor the input fields in the form to the following (no @PropertyId annotations):

```
private TextField name = new TextField("Name");
private TextField code = new TextField("Code");
private ComboBox<Manufacturer> manufacturer = new ComboBox<>();
private Checkbox available = new Checkbox("Available");
private TextField phoneNumber =
    new TextField("Manufacturer phone number");
private TextField email = new TextField("Manufacturer email");
```

Now let's address validation 1 (name is required):

```
Binder<Product> binder = new Binder<>(Product.class);
binder.forField(name)
    .asRequired("The name of the product is required")
```

By calling asRequired(String), we tell Vaadin to visually mark the field as required and show the specified error when the field is left empty. See Figure 5-4.

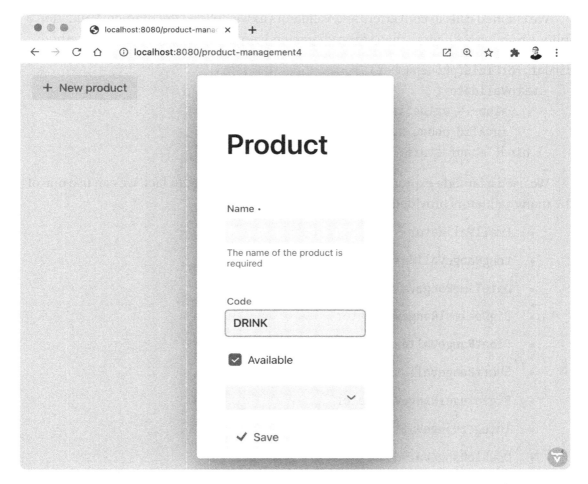

Figure 5-4. *A required field*

Implementing validation 2 (code is required) is pretty similar:

```
binder.forField(code)
    .asRequired("Please introduce a code")
    .withConverter(new StringToCodeConverter())
    .bind(Product::getCode, Product::setCode);
```

We chained calls to converters and validators as we defined the binding. Validation 3 (phone number with more than seven characters) requires a call to a different method:

```
binder.forField(phoneNumber)
    .withValidator(
        value -> value.length() > 7,
        "Invalid phone number"
    ).bind("manufacturer.phoneNumber");
```

We used a lambda expression to implement the validation. In fact, we can use one of the many validators provided by the framework:

- EmailValidator

- LongRangeValidator

- DateTimeRangeValidator

- BigDecimalRangeValidator

- FloatRangeValidator

- ShortRangeValidator

- BigIntegerRangeValidator

- IntegerRangeValidator

- DoubleRangeValidator

- DateRangeValidator

- ByteRangeValidator

- StringLengthValidator

- RangeValidator

- RegexpValidator

Let's use one of them to implement validation 4 (correct email format):

```
binder.forField(email)
    .withValidator(new EmailValidator("Invalid email address"))
    .bind("manufacturer.email");
```

Although the validations run when the value is sent to the server (e.g., when the user edits a field), we should invoke the validations when the save button is clicked. It shouldn't be a surprise that we invoke the validations using the `Binder` class. So first we need to make sure the `binder` object is accessible from the click listener. We can move the definition of the object as follows:

```
public class AutoBindingProductForm extends Composite<Component> {

  ...

  private Binder<Product> binder = new Binder<>(Product.class);
  ...
}
```

Now we can use the binder to first validate the fields to make the errors visible in the UI, and then to check whether there are any errors:

```
new Button("Save", VaadinIcon.CHECK.create(),
    event -> {
      binder.validate();
      if (binder.isValid()) {
        saveListener.run();
      } else {
        Notification.show("Please fix the errors");
      }
    })
```

Using Jakarta Bean Validation

Jakarta Bean Validation is a Java specification defined by the JSR 380. It allows you to express validation rules using annotations in the properties of the domain classes. By switching from the `Binder` to the `BeanValidationBinder` class, we can use annotations instead of manually set validators.

To start using Jakarta Bean Validation, we need to add an implementation of the API. One of the most popular implementations is provided by Hibernate. We can add it into the `<dependencies>` section of the `pom.xml` file:

```
<dependency>
    <groupId>org.hibernate.validator</groupId>
```

```
    <artifactId>hibernate-validator</artifactId>
    <version>6.1.5.Final</version>
</dependency>
<dependency>
    <groupId>org.glassfish</groupId>
    <artifactId>jakarta.el</artifactId>
    <version>    3.0.3</version>
</dependency>
```

Caution   At the time of writing, Vaadin is compatible with Jakarta EE specifications that use the `javax.*` namespace. The latest versions of many of the Jakarta specification implementations, including Hibernate Validator version 7.0.0 and later, use the new `jakarta.*` namespace. This change is known as the "big bang" and is part of the changes required by the move of the Java Enterprise Edition to the Eclipse Foundation. You can learn more about this at *https:// eclipse-foundation.blog/2020/12/08/jakarta-ee-9-delivers-the-big-bang*.

Let's define validation 1 (name is required):

```
public class Product {

    @NotNull
    @NotBlank
    private String name;

    ...

}
```

And now validation 2 (code is required):

```
public class Code {

    ...

    @NotNull
    @NotBlank
```

```
  private String number;
  ...
}
```

Finally, validations 3 (phone number with more than seven characters) and 4 (correct email format):

```
public class Manufacturer {
  ...
  @Size(min = 8)
  private String phoneNumber;

  @Email
  private String email;
  ...
}
```

To make this work, we need to remove all the validators we added when using the binder object and replace its type:

```
private BeanValidationBinder<Product> binder =
    new BeanValidationBinder<>(Product.class);
```

Done. Version 1 of our POS software is complete. Try improving it by adding more validations. For example, the manufacturer should be a required field as well. Experiment and explore the API of the Binder class to learn even more about it.

Note   I wrote a quick tutorial on Jakarta Bean Validation that shows how to add different providers to plain Servlet, Spring, and Jakarta EE applications, how to customize error messages, and what annotations are available. You can find the tutorial at *https://vaadin.com/learn/tutorials/introduction-to-java-bean-validation*. The official website of the Jakarta Bean Validation project at *https://beanvalidation.org* offers multiple resources for learning as well.

Summary

In this chapter, you learned what data binding is and how to define bindings using the `Binder` class either automatically or defining each binding manually. You learned how to use converters to transform data from the format supported by an input field to the format in your domain model. You also learned how to add validators to ensure that values in a form are correct before sending them, for example, to a backend service.

In the next chapter, you'll learn about a powerful component that most business applications use—the `Grid` component.

CHAPTER 6

The Grid Component

Displaying and manipulating tabular data is a cornerstone in most business applications. Vaadin's Grid component is a high-quality UI component for efficiently displaying and manipulating data laid out in rows and columns.

The Grid component resulted from an effort made by the R&D team at Vaadin to overhaul the already powerful Table component in Vaadin 7 and earlier. The component includes features such as filtering, sorting, component rendering, lazy loading, and many others, making it one of the most (if not the most) advanced table components in the industry.

Adding Columns

The Grid component is always parameterized with the domain class you want to present data in each row. For example, if you want to show orders, you use Grid<Order>; if you want to show products, you use Grid<Product>; and so forth. This allows you to directly use your own domain model when adding columns and rows to a Grid component. Adding rows is always done manually (you have to tell the Grid component which rows or data to show). However, with columns, the Grid component supports two modes: automatic or manual column definition. The mode used depends on the Grid constructor you use:

```
// scans Product and automatically adds a column per property
var grid1 = new Grid<>(Product.class);

// no scan, you have to add the columns manually
var grid2 = new Grid<Product>();
```

© Alejandro Duarte 2021
A. Duarte, *Practical Vaadin*, https://doi.org/10.1007/978-1-4842-7179-7_6

Managing Columns by Key

Assume you have the following domain class:

```
public class Book {

  private Integer id;
  private String title;
  private String author;
  private int quantity;

  ... constructors, getters, and setters ...

}
```

You can let Vaadin automatically add columns to show each property in the Book class by passing the class type to the Grid constructor (see Figure 6-1):

```
var grid = new Grid<>(Book.class);
```

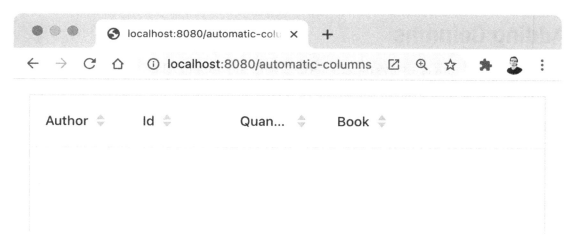

Figure 6-1. *An empty Grid with columns created automatically*

Each column is given a String key that you can use to further configure the column. You do so by using the getColumnByKey(String) method. For example, you can set a header as follows:

```
grid.getColumnByKey("title").setHeader("Book");
```

Moreover, you can chain configurations:

```
grid.getColumnByKey("title")
    .setHeader("Book")
    .setFooter("text here")
    .setAutoWidth(true);
```

The setAutoWidth(boolean) method calculates the width to allow space for the content.

You can add more columns by property name, something useful when you want to show nested properties. For example, if we add a property of, say, type Publisher to the Book class, and you want to show the publisher's name in an additional column, you can add it as follows:

```
grid.removeColumnByKey("publisher");
grid.addColumn("publisher.name");
```

We removed the publisher column that was autogenerated when we used the Grid(Class) constructor. You can also use the column keys to define which properties to show and in what order (see Figure 6-2):

```
grid.setColumns("title", "publisher.name", "author", "quantity");
grid.getColumnByKey("publisher.name").setHeader("Publisher");
```

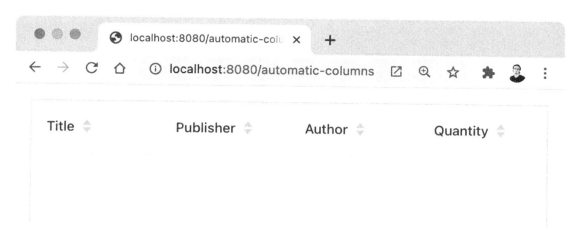

Figure 6-2. *Setting columns' visibility (id is not visible) and order*

Caution   The setColumns(String...) method deletes all the existing columns before adding new columns for the specified properties.

Defining Columns with ValueProvider

We already saw one way to manually define columns by property names when using the Grid(Class) constructor. When you use the default constructor (Grid()), Vaadin doesn't add any columns to the component. Instead, you have to define and configure each column, passing something called ValueProvider. An easy way to implement a ValueProvider is by using method references to the getters in the domain class or lambda expressions to show anything you want to show (e.g., nested properties by navigating through getters). An advantage of this approach over using autogenerated columns is its type-safe nature:

```
var grid = new Grid<Book>(); // default constructor used
grid.addColumn(Book::getTitle)
    .setHeader("Book").setAutoWidth(true);
grid.addColumn(book -> book.getPublisher().getName())
    .setHeader("Publisher");
grid.addColumn(Book::getAuthor).setHeader("Author");
grid.addColumn(Book::getQuantity).setHeader("Quantity");
```

Tip   Use manual column definitions when you want your code to be explicit and type-safe. Automatic columns are suitable in cases in which you prefer shorter code or in advanced scenarios where the Grid is generated at runtime from domain objects you don't know at compile time and that might be provided by third-party libraries.

Adding Rows

Adding rows to Grid components is handled by a number of setItems methods with different signatures. Before we use these methods, let's define a service layer. Typically, web applications consume a backend service that provides the operations over the data. In the case of Vaadin, you can simply call a Java method to run backend logic. For example, we can implement a service class to add any logic to get data without exposing the implementation details to the view layer. The service class can connect to a SQL database, read and write files to the hard drive, connect to an external web service, or even a combination of all of these. For example:

```java
public class BookService {

  ...

  public static List<Book> findAll() {
    ...
  }

}
```

The implementation details are not important here and are omitted. If you want to see the implementation (which merely contains a Java `Collection` to keep the objects in memory), take a look at the code available on GitHub via the book's product page located at *www.apress.com/ISBN*.

In-Memory Data

With a backend service ready, we can start consuming data. To show all the books in a `Grid`, we simply do something like the following:

```java
List<Book> books = BookService.findAll();
grid.setItems(books);
```

It's as simple as that. You can think of this as if each row in the `Grid` has one Book. And the value on each cell depends on what you configured when you defined the column.

Caution   There's no method for removing an item available in the `Grid` class. Instead, you have to pass a new collection or array without the element you want to remove.

The setItems(Collection) method is overloaded with a version that accepts an array or passes individual objects (see Figure 6-3):

```
Book[] booksArray = ...
grid.setItems(booksArray);
gridSetItems(book1, book2, book3, book4);
```

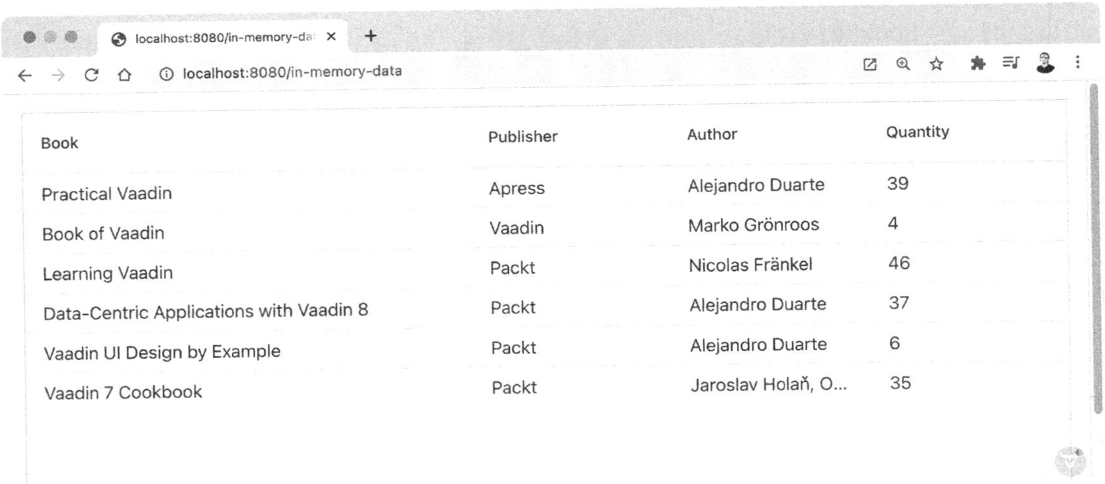

Figure 6-3. *A Grid populated with data*

Once you set the items, the Grid component keeps the objects in memory. Keep this in mind when you are developing your applications. Remember that each user seeing the view will have its own instance of the view in the server and, in turn, an instance of Grid. Each instance of Grid will have its own set of items, that is, its own set of domain objects. This is acceptable only when you are sure that the number of rows in the Grid is not big and won't grow with time. In other cases, you should use lazy loading.

Tip   In your applications, you should consider using Data Transfer Objects (DTOs) to display data in a Grid. Imagine the Book class had 20 more properties. One of them being binary data. When you query the backend, you get a collection with Book instances containing a lot of data you don't really need to show in the Grid. This will consume much more memory than needed. Instead, create a new class to encapsulate the data that your view needs. If you are using a persistence framework, consult the documentation to see how to request only the data you need.

Lazy Loading

What happens if the backend service returns one million books? Let's say the amount of memory required by a Book instance is around 100 bytes. This translates to 100 megabytes of memory to hold the data returned by the backend service. With 1 gigabyte of memory allocated to the JVM, you could handle around ten concurrent users. Probably less since you need memory for other resources. When you are testing your application in your development environment, you might not notice this, since the Grid component is able to handle this amount of data.

Tip   The previous estimation is based on a quick analysis on the number of bytes required to store each field of the class plus a possible overhead added by the JVM. If you need better size estimations in your projects, take a look at the Instrumentation interface available in Java. Consult the API documentation at *https://docs.oracle.com/en/java/javase*.

Although you should review and consider other approaches to showing one million rows in a Grid, if you have to, always use lazy loading. Let's see how to do it.

The backend service should be able to provide data in "slices." If you are familiar with SQL, you probably know the LIMIT and OFFSET clauses, for example:

```
SELECT * FROM book OFFSET 300 LIMIT 100
```

This query skips 300 rows before beginning to return 100 rows. In our example application, we are not dealing with SQL, and we still have all the data in memory. However, the presentation layer doesn't know this, and you should be able to change only the underlying technology to store data with SQL, NoSQL, or any other database solution. In the end, the backend service should include a method like the following:

```
public static List<Book> findAll(int offset, int limit) {
    ...
}
```

The Grid component can use this method as follows:

```
grid.setItems(query -> BookService.findAll(
    query.getOffset(), query.getLimit()).stream()
);
```

A Query object with the offset and limit required by the current state of the Grid (determined particularly by the position of the scroll bar) is provided. We can just pass the values to the backend and convert the Collection to a Stream.

Note   An alternative way to implement lazy loading is by creating numbered pages to show the data in slices. The concept is similar to what we have implemented here but requires you to set up the UI components to show the page numbers (using Button, for example) and add the logic to set the Grid items that make up the selected page.

Sorting

The Grid component allows users to order the rows by clicking the column's headers. When you let Vaadin generate the columns by using the Grid(Class) constructor, all the columns that are mapped to properties that implement Comparable, then the column is made sortable. When you define the columns manually, you can enable sorting as follows:

```
grid.addColumn(Book::getTitle). setSortable(true);
```

You can pass false to setSortable(boolean) to disable sorting. When using column keys, you can enable sorting in multiple columns as follows:

```
grid.setSortableColumns("title", "author");
```

When a property is not Comparable or you want to tweak the comparison logic, you can provide a Comparator:

```
grid.addColumn(Book::getTitle).setComparator(
    (book1, book2) ->
        book1.getTitle().compareToIgnoreCase(book2.getTitle()));
```

The previous example orders the title column ignoring the case. Keep in mind that you can chain calls to multiple methods for configuring a column. For example, you can configure the header and width and add a comparator as follows:

```
grid.addColumn(Book::getTitle)
    .setHeader("Book")
    .setAutoWidth(true)
    .setComparator((book1, book2) ->
        book1.getTitle().compareToIgnoreCase(book2.getTitle())));
```

We are using a lambda expression here, but nothing prevents you from creating a new class to encapsulate the logic when the code is more complex than in this simple example.

Tip   When you are using lazy loading, you can delegate the sorting to the backend. The `Query` class contains the information on how the data should be sorted according to the columns that the user has clicked. The actual implementation of the sorting logic depends on your specific backend. For example, if you are using SQL queries, you can add ORDER BY clauses modified by ASC or DESC according to what `Query::getSorted()` and `Query::getDirection()` return.

Handling Row Selection

Now that we have covered how to show data in a `Grid`, let's explore how to make the component more interactive. And the first thing you might be wondering is how to handle row selection, a feature that enables functionality in areas such as data editing, data drill-down, and in general, data consumption and manipulation.

The `Grid` component has three selection modes that you can configure with the `setSelectionMode(SelectionMode)` method:

- `grid.setSelectionMode(Grid.SelectionMode.NONE)`: No selection allowed.

- `grid.setSelectionMode(Grid.SelectionMode.SINGLE)`: One row can be selected at a time.

- `grid.setSelectionMode(Grid.SelectionMode.MULTI)`: Multiple rows can be selected at the same time.

By default, a `Grid` component allows single selection of rows, so you don't have to configure that option explicitly if you haven't changed it before.

Suppose we need to add a button to increase by one the `quantity` property of the book that is selected in the `Grid`. We want to have the button enabled only when there's a row selected. In the constructor of the view, let's create the button, disable it (since there are no rows selected when the view is built), and add it to the layout (see Figure 6-4):

```
var increaseQuantity = new Button("Increase quantity");
increaseQuantity.setEnabled(false);
...
return new VerticalLayout(increaseQuantity, grid);
```

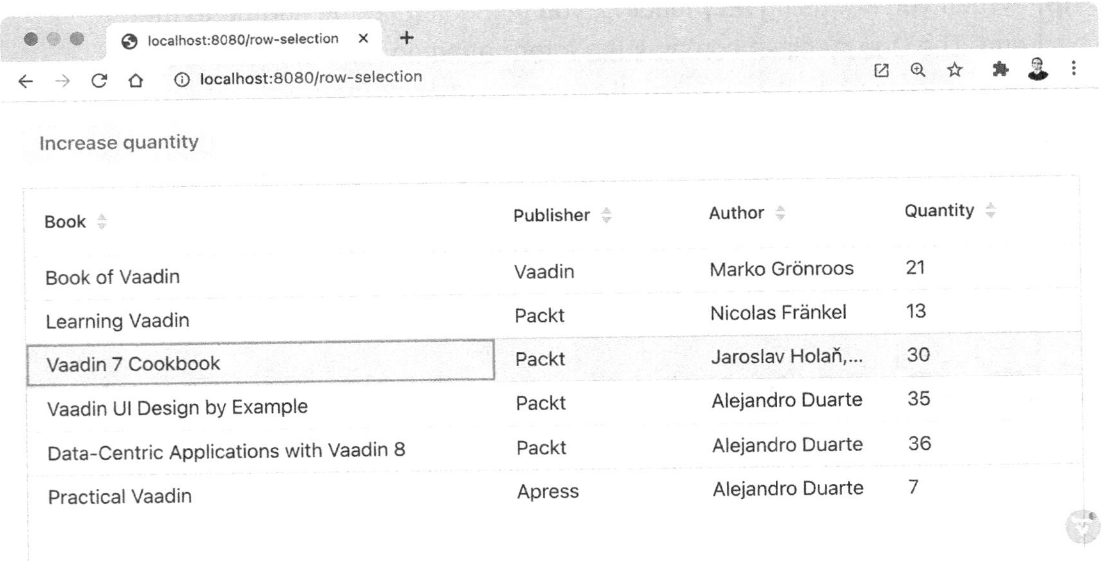

Figure 6-4. *A row selected in a Grid component*

Now we need a listener that is called when a row is selected or deselected:

```
grid.addSelectionListener(event -> {
    ... logic here ...
});
```

As per the logic there, we need to check if there's a row selected. We can get a "single-select" view of the Grid and get the selected value:

```
Book selectedBook = grid.asSingleSelect().getValue();
```

The reference is null when the user deselected a row, so we can use that to enable or disable the button (see Figure 6-5):

```
grid.addSelectionListener(event -> {
  Book selectedBook = grid.asSingleSelect().getValue();
  increaseQuantity.setEnabled(selectedBook != null);
});
```

Or we can use the event object to get the selected book wrapped in an Optional, which is a more elegant solution in my opinion, since it decouples the code inside the block from the grid instance:

```
grid.addSelectionListener(event -> {
  boolean enabled = event.getFirstSelectedItem().isPresent();
  increaseQuantity.setEnabled(enabled);
});
```

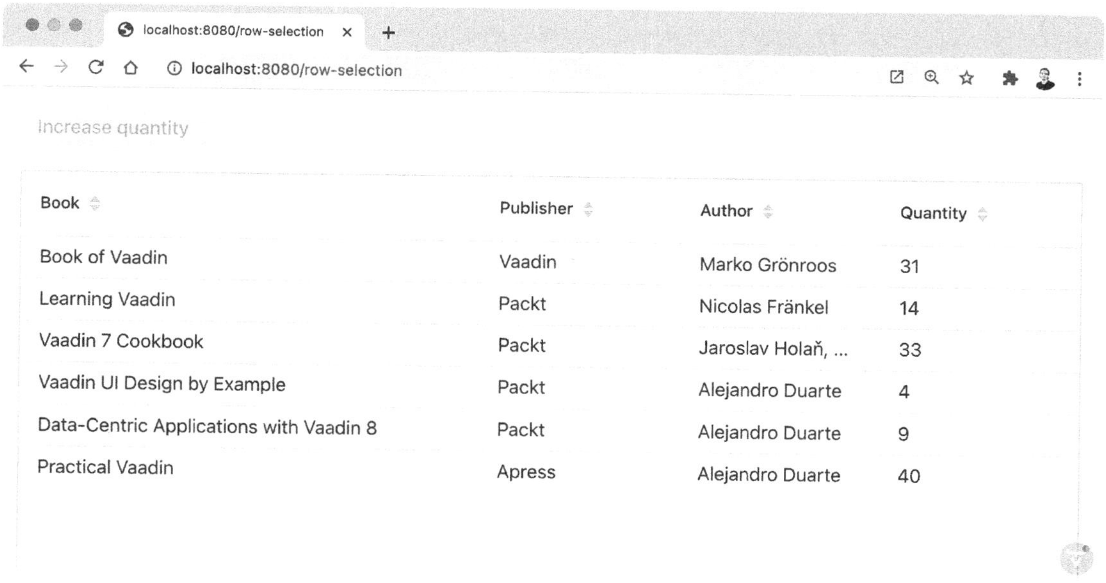

Figure 6-5. *Disabling a button on selection change*

The missing part now is the logic to run when the button is clicked. We need to update the value in the quantity property of the selected Book instance and update the Grid. Since we need to update (populate with data) the Grid from two places (when we create the Grid and when the user clicks the button), it makes sense to create a method for that:

```
private void updateGrid(Grid<Book> grid) {
  List<Book> books = BookService.findAll();
  grid.setItems(books);
}
```

You can either make the grid instance a field in the class or simply pass it to the method. We passed it to the method in the previous snippet of code. With that ready, we can implement the click listener on the button as follows:

```
increaseQuantity.addClickListener(event ->
    grid.asSingleSelect().getOptionalValue().ifPresent(
        book -> {
          BookService.increaseQuantity(book);
          updateGrid(grid);
        }
    )
);
```

We could have just directly updated the quantity property in the listener, but if we were dealing with a real-life application with external services and database connections, you should most likely delegate the logic to the service class. The service method logic is left as an (extremely easy) exercise (adding one to the quantity property of the specified Book).

Notice the use of the getOptionalValue() method instead of getValue() as explained earlier. This is handy since we are only concerned about the presence of a value rather than the value at that point of the execution.

Multiple selection is handled in a similar way, except you can get the selected rows as a Set:

```
Set<Book> selectedBooks = grid.asMultiSelect().getValue();
```

Or from a selection listener:

```
Set<Book> selectedBooks = event.getAllSelectedItems();
```

Adding UI Components to Cells

A feature that highly increases the Grid component's flexibility is the possibility to add other UI components to it. Let's explore the options.

Component Columns

There's a special kind of column that can have components in its cells. Suppose we want to get rid of the button we implemented in the previous section. Instead, we'd like to have one button per book in each row to allow the user to increase the quantity by clicking the corresponding button in the Grid. Here's how:

```
grid.addComponentColumn(
    book -> new Button(VaadinIcon.PLUS.create(), event -> {
      BookService.increaseQuantity(book);
      updateGrid(grid);
    })
);
```

With the addComponentColumn(ValueProvider) method, we can take a Book instance and return a UI component. In the previous example, we returned a Button that runs the logic to increase the book's quantity presented in the row (see Figure 6-6).

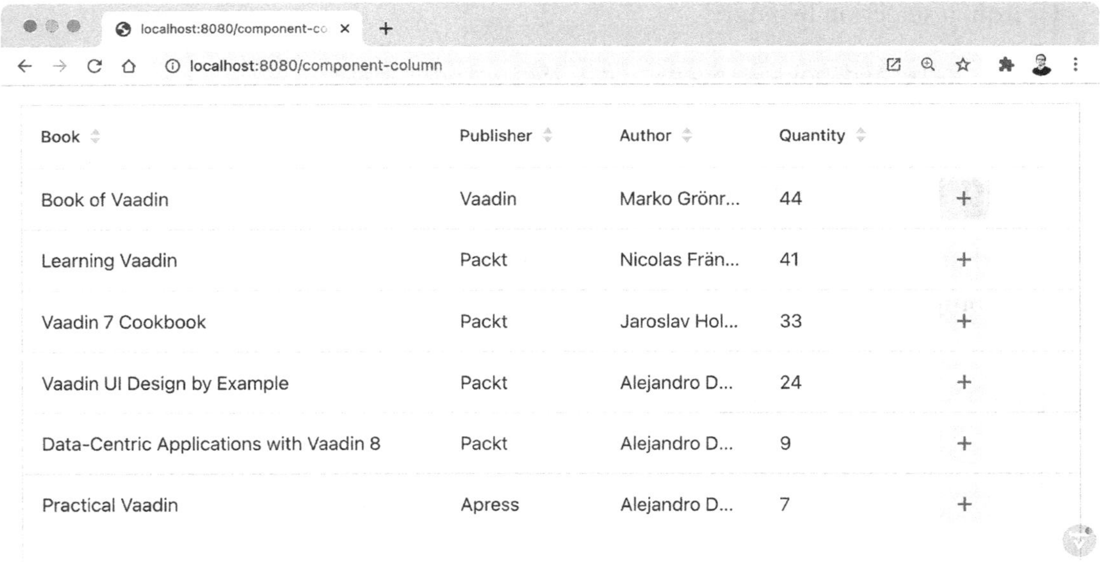

Figure 6-6. *A component column*

We can use the properties in the Book instance when needed. For example, we can replace the numeric value in the *Quantity* column with a progress bar. Let's assume that we can have max 50 copies of each book. Here's how we can configure the column:

```
grid.addComponentColumn(
    book -> new ProgressBar(0, 50, book.getQuantity())
).setHeader("Quantity").setSortable(true);
```

We are also setting a header for the column and making it sortable. However, if you try clicking the header, sorting doesn't work. We need to set a Comparator in this case:

```
.setComparator(Comparator.comparingInt(Book::getQuantity));
```

We are delegating to Java the comparison logic in this implementation. Figure 6-7 shows the result after clicking the header twice to sort in descending order.

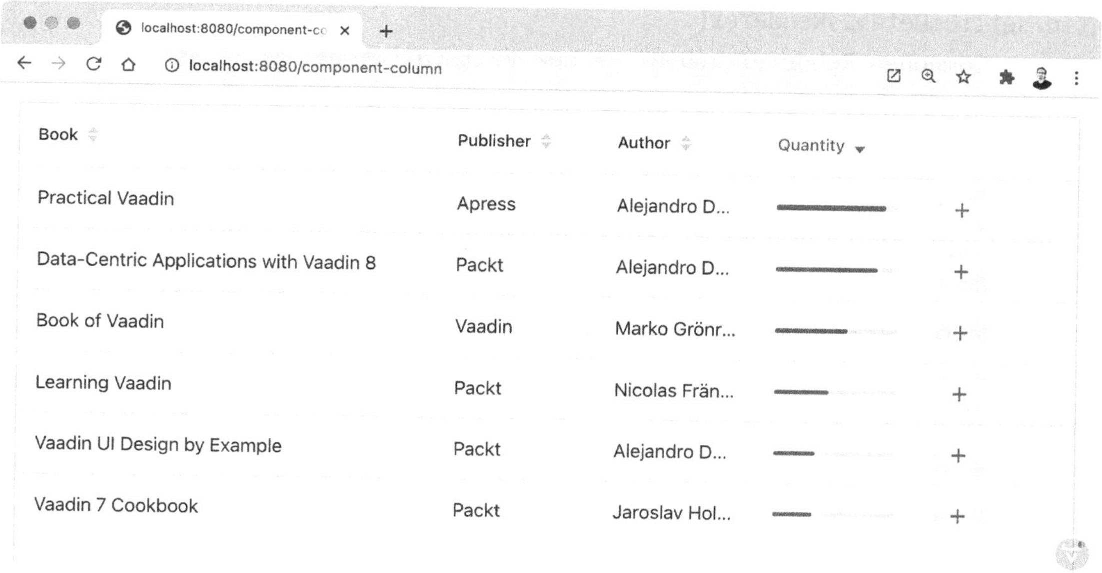

Figure 6-7. *Ordered rows in a* Grid *component*

There is an issue with this implementation. Can you see it? Try clicking one of the buttons many, many times. Investigate the issue. Look at the log of the application in the IDE and try to fix it (the fix is provided in the example of the source code for this book at *www.apress.com/ISBN*). If you feel like coding, try adding another button on each row to decrease the corresponding quantity. You can try adding a new column for the new button or creating a layout that contains two buttons in the same column.

Item Details

Sometimes, a row in a table is not the best place to show all the data related to a domain object. Often, applications include an option to drill down into the details of a row in a table. The Grid component allows you to show more information in a custom component (item details) when the user clicks a row.

Suppose we add a description property to the Book class. The book's descriptions are likely too long to be directly shown in a new column, and a user might want to read the description of the book once they have identified the book in the list. So, let's add the functionality to show the description when the user clicks a row:

```
grid.setItemDetailsRenderer(
    new ComponentRenderer<>(book -> new VerticalLayout(
        new Text(book.getDescription())
    ))
);
```

This code adds a `ComponentRenderer` (an object that takes care of rendering a component in a cell) that uses the specified lambda expression to build a layout with the description of the book associated to the clicked row. Figure 6-8 shows the result.

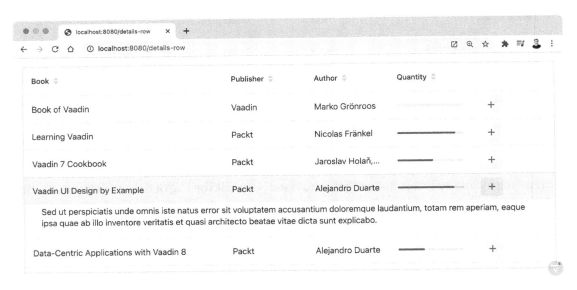

Figure 6-8. *Item details shown when a row is clicked*

We can add any components and layouts to the details section. For example, we add a button to remove or edit a book or even delete the component column we created to increase the quantity and move the button to the details row instead. Let's try moving the button. All we need to do is move the code that creates the `Button` from the component column definition to the `VerticalLayout` in the details section and delete the code that creates the column:

```
grid.setItemDetailsRenderer(
    new ComponentRenderer<>(book -> new VerticalLayout(
        new Text(book.getDescription()),
        new Button(VaadinIcon.PLUS.create(), event -> {
```

```
        BookService.increaseQuantity(book);
        updateGrid(grid);
        grid.select(book);
    })
))
);
```

Look at the call to `grid.select(book)`. This is how you can select a row programmatically. But why is it needed here? Any time you click a row, the row is selected or deselected. When the row is selected, the details area is shown. When the row is clicked again, the row is deselected, and the details area is hidden. When the details area is visible, the click in the button we added is propagated to the row unselecting it and causing the details area to hide. To avoid this, we simply "reselect" the same row (book) again. With this, the user can click the button several times if needed without selecting the row every time.

Also, see how we changed the button's icon and added text to it in order to make it clear for the user what this button is all about. When the button was next to the *Quantity* column, it was easy to understand that the button increased the quantity, but this is not the case anymore if we move it to the details area. Figure 6-9 shows the result.

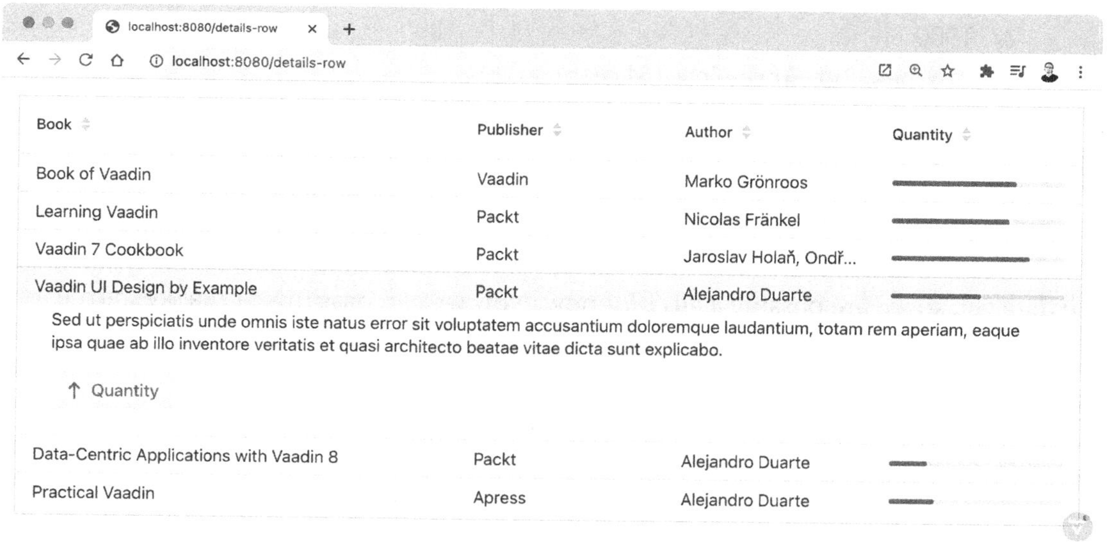

Figure 6-9. *Components in a details row*

Tip Be careful to not add complex layouts to details rows. This can make the UI messy and negatively impact the UX, especially when you use the application on small viewports such as those on mobile devices.

Exporting to CSV

To close this chapter, let's explore a common use case in business applications—export a Grid's content to a comma-separated values file (CSV). It's possible to export to many other formats as well, but CSV seems to be a popular requirement in the software industry. We'll use an Anchor component and *Opencsv*, a free library for reading, writing, and processing CSV files.

Let's start by coding the Anchor. An Anchor component can point to a defined URL that you specify as a string (href) or to a StreamResource which is a class that allows you to transfer dynamic data from the server to the client. Implementing a StreamResources is easy:

```
var streamResource = new StreamResource("books.csv",
    () -> {
      // TODO
      return new ByteArrayInputStream(null);
    }
);
```

When the link in the browser is clicked, the lambda expression is run, and you get the chance to return an InputStream that Vaadin uses to transfer the data. We don't have the data yet, so we are passing a null for now. Now we can pass this StreamResource to a new Anchor component that we can add to the UI:

```
var download = new Anchor(streamResource, "Download");

return new VerticalLayout(download, grid);
```

Time to generate the data. Before coding, we need to add the Opencsv library to the *pom.xml* file (check the latest version at `http://opencsv.sourceforge.net`):

```
<dependency>
    <groupId>com.opencsv</groupId>
    <artifactId>opencsv</artifactId>
    <version>5.4</version>
</dependency>
```

Now let's tackle the TODO part. We need the Book instances in the Grid. We can get them as follows:

```
var books = grid.getGenericDataView().getItems();
```

This returns an object (books) of type Stream<Book>. Data is ready. We need to transform it. To do this, we can use a StatefulBeanToCsvBuilder (from the Opencsv library). Here's how to use it:

```
StringWriter output = new StringWriter();
var beanToCsv =
    new StatefulBeanToCsvBuilder<Book>(output).build();
beanToCsv.write(books);
```

After the call to write(Stream), the output object will hold a String with the data in CSV format. We can pass the bytes forming this String to the InputStream (replacing the null that we used in a previous snippet of code):

```
return new ByteArrayInputStream(output.toString().getBytes());
```

Just so that you get the full picture, here's the complete StreamResource implementation:

```
var streamResource = new StreamResource("books.csv",
    () -> {
      try {
        var books = grid.getGenericDataView().getItems();
        StringWriter output = new StringWriter();
        var beanToCsv =
            new StatefulBeanToCsvBuilder<Book>(output).build();
```

```
        beanToCsv.write(books);
        return new ByteArrayInputStream(
            output.toString().getBytes());

    } catch (CsvDataTypeMismatchException |
        CsvRequiredFieldEmptyException e) {
        e.printStackTrace();
        return null;
    }
  }
);
```

If you run the application and download the file, you'll see that all the properties in the Book class are included in the file, while the Grid only shows some of them. This is expected as we transformed the Book objects that the grid contained. We can exclude properties as follows:

```
var beanToCsv = new StatefulBeanToCsvBuilder<Book>(output)
    .withIgnoreField(Book.class,
        Book.class.getDeclaredField("id"))
    .withIgnoreField(Book.class,
        Book.class.getDeclaredField("nextId"))
    .build();
```

Another issue is that the Publisher column shows the result of the default toString() method from the Object class instead of the publisher's name. The easiest way to solve this is by overriding the toString() method in the Book class to return the name of the publisher:

```
public class Publisher {

  private String name;

  @Override
  public String toString() {
    return name;
  }

  ...

}
```

160

> **Note**   Opencsv is a flexible library with much more functionality than described here. To learn more about it, see *http://opencsv.sourceforge.net*.

Summary

In this chapter, you learned how to use the most important functionality in one of the more complex UI components of Vaadin: the Grid component. You learned how to add columns automatically and manually and how to add rows holding data in memory or providing it to the Grid component using lazy loading to save memory. You saw how to enable sorting and how to react to selection changes in the rows of the Grid. You learned how to add UI components in a Grid's cell and how to show a "details view" when the user clicks a row in order to show more information about an item. You also learned a common use case in web applications—exporting data from a Grid to a CSV file. All this while exploring ways in which you can compose views by combining and connecting UI components using event listeners. The Grid class offers more functionality than we covered here. For example, you can freeze headers or add drag and drop functionality. See the official Vaadin documentation to learn more (https://vaadin.com/docs).

The next chapter covers a central topic in Vaadin: navigation and routing. Most applications require multiple views, so don't miss out on this topic!

PART III

Advanced Features

CHAPTER 7

Multiview Navigation and Routing

Although Vaadin abstracts away many of the Web platform and Java Servlet technology details, applications developed with the framework are still web applications. That sounds obvious, but it's worth reiterating. When you start implementing applications with Vaadin, you might get absorbed by the code and forget that you are developing a web application. I've been there.

A central part of web applications is the request-response model. Vaadin hides the complexities related to this model while letting you use its advantages. You already know you can have multiple views in the same application, each accessed through a different URL. You can also navigate from one view to another programmatically, run custom logic before or after the user enters a view, configure error views, have parameters in the URL, and more.

Routes

A route connects a Java class with a URL. This Java class is often a view and must implement Component. We have been defining routes with the @Route annotation:

```
@Route("hello")
public class Hello extends VerticalLayout {
  public Hello() {
    this.add(new Text("Hello!"));
  }
}
```

© Alejandro Duarte 2021
A. Duarte, *Practical Vaadin*, https://doi.org/10.1007/978-1-4842-7179-7_7

When the application starts (on Servlet initialization), Vaadin scans the classes to identify those annotated with @Route. For each class, it creates a registry with the configuration of each route. This configuration is later used when the user requests a URL managed by the VaadinServlet, for example, *http://localhost:8080/hello* on your development machine or *https://example.com/businessapp/hello* on production.

Tip   You can define multiple routes for a single view using the @RouteAlias annotation. If you decide to use this annotation, I recommend you follow the issue at *https://github.com/vaadin/flow/issues/7862*. Read this thread if you want to look at the kind of discussions that occurs during the development of an open source product like Vaadin.

Defining Routes at Runtime

Besides letting Vaadin automatically detect the routes from your classes, you can also define them programmatically at runtime. Let's develop a basic application with a login form. Depending on the credentials introduced in the login form, we grant access to one of two views. We'll make this simple, but you'll get the idea of how to adapt it to your applications. Let's say we have only two users:

- Username: user, password: user. Can access the UserView component only.

- Username: admin, password: admin. Can access the AdminView component only.

The views are simple Vaadin components that show a message. We won't annotate the implementation with @Route for now:

```
public class UserView extends Composite<Component> {

  @Override
  protected Component initContent() {
    return new Text("Welcome, user.");
  }

}
```

```
public class AdminView extends Composite<Component> {

  @Override
  protected Component initContent() {
    return new Text("Hello, admin.");
  }

}
```

If we annotated these classes with @Route, we would allow access to anybody. Instead, we want to tell Vaadin which routes are available depending on the logic run after a login form is shown. The easiest way to show a login form in a Vaadin application is by using the LoginOverlay (or alternatively, LoginForm) component:

```
@Route("login")
public class AppLoginForm extends Composite<Component> {

  @Override
  protected Component initContent() {
    LoginI18n i18n = LoginI18n.createDefault();

    LoginOverlay loginOverlay = new LoginOverlay(i18n);
    loginOverlay.setTitle("Chapter 7");
    loginOverlay.setDescription("Navigation and Routing");
    loginOverlay.setOpened(true);

    loginOverlay.addForgotPasswordListener(event ->
        Notification.show("Use admin/admin or user/user"));

    loginOverlay.addLoginListener(event -> {
      ... login logic here ...
    });

    return new VerticalLayout(loginOverlay);
  }

}
```

This class is annotated with @Route since we want everybody to be able to use it.

The LoginI18n is a class provided by Vaadin for customizing the texts in the LoginOverlay component. The LoginOverlay component shows a login form centered on the page, as shown in Figure 7-1. The component is fully responsive, meaning that it adapts according to the size of the screen in which it is displayed. Try implementing this example or run the project from the source code for this book (available on GitHub at *www.apress.com/ISBN*), and experiment with different window sizes.

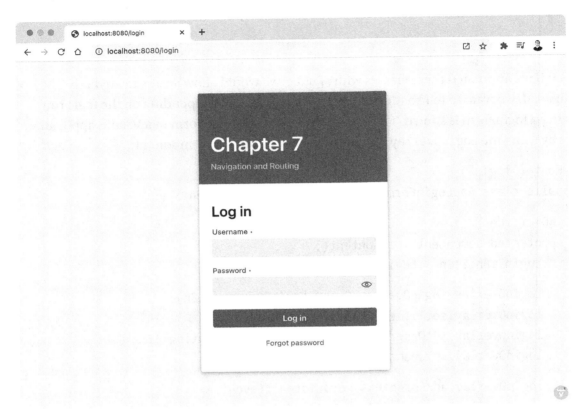

Figure 7-1. *The LoginOverlay component*

When you create a LoginOverlay, you can pass a LoginI18n object that allows you to customize things such as the error message, header, and the form to use. We'll leave that out for now. Explore the available methods in your IDE or the API documentation at *https://vaadin.com/api*.

See how we open the component, meaning we make it visible on the page. You can use the LoginOverlay component as an overlay on top of any view. Here, we don't have anything else but the login form itself. On other applications, you could, for example, add a button to show the login form.

Also, notice the listeners that we added. The first one handles the *Forgot password* option shown in the form, and it only shows a notification showing you the available users and passwords. I wouldn't recommend doing this in your applications. The second one reacts to the click event on the *Log in* button. Let's implement the logic for this button.

We needed to define or register the available views according to the credentials that the user introduced. To do this, we can use the `RouteConfiguration` class. For example, to make the `AdminView` component available as a route through the `admin` path, we can run

```
RouteConfiguration.forSessionScope().setRoute(
    "admin", AdminView.class
);
```

This tells Vaadin that for the current session, and only for the current session, the user can see the `AdminView` component as if the class had been annotated with `@Route("admin")`. We can use this to set the corresponding route according to the credentials in the login form as follows:

```
loginOverlay.addLoginListener(event -> {
  if ("user".equals(event.getUsername())
      && "user".equals(event.getPassword())) {
    RouteConfiguration.forSessionScope().setRoute(
        "user", UserView.class
    );
    UI.getCurrent().navigate(UserView.class);

  } else if ("admin".equals(event.getUsername())
      && "admin".equals(event.getPassword())) {
    RouteConfiguration.forSessionScope().setRoute(
        "admin", AdminView.class
    );
    UI.getCurrent().navigate(AdminView.class);

  } else {
    loginOverlay.setError(true);
  }
});
```

Caution   Using hardcoded strings to define users and passwords is far from being a good practice. This information should be securely stored in an external data source (like a SQL database) with appropriate encryption of passwords.

We are checking the username and password values from the event object in the login listener and setting the route accordingly. We also navigate to the appropriate view using the `navigate(Class)` method from the UI class. This code should be refactored to call a method to set the routes up instead of the copy-paste-based version I coded in this example. Alternatively, we could have used a `String` to specify the path to which we want to navigate. For example, to navigate to the admin view, we can use

```
UI.getCurrent().navigate("admin");
```

In both cases (user and admin), we have to close the `LoginOverlay` component; otherwise, it would continue to be visible, and we wouldn't see the view to which we navigated.

To check that the implementation works, see Figure 7-2. In the screenshot, note that only the login view is available. Vaadin only knows about the login view at this point.

Could not navigate to ''

Available routes:

* login

This detailed message is only shown when running in development mode.

Figure 7-2. *Only the login view is set before introducing valid credentials*

Once we go to the login view, enter valid credentials (e.g., *user/user*), and manually request the *empty* view in the browser (*http://localhost:8080/*), we see that a new view (user) is available (see Figure 7-3). Vaadin now knows about this view. It doesn't know about the admin view, which is precisely what we want—we want to restrict access to that view. If you try and request the admin view, Vaadin won't be able to show it since it hasn't been set.

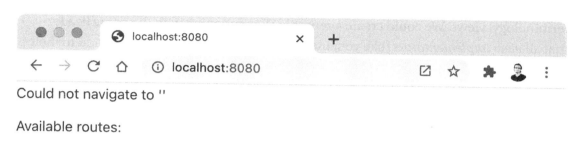

Could not navigate to ''

Available routes:

- login
- user

This detailed message is only shown when running in development mode.

Figure 7-3. *A view (user) added at runtime*

The example has a bug. If you log in with, say, user and then log in again with admin, you'll gain access to both views. How to solve this? I'll let that as an exercise to you. Maybe removing previous views? How about making the login view only available to unauthenticated users? How about implementing a logout option? Explore the APIs of the RouteConfiguration and UI classes and try to implement a solution.

Tip   In more complex applications, you can leverage the flexibility to create routes at runtime by, for example, reading the available views and its paths from an external system. For example, a SQL database can store the fully qualified name of the Java classes that implement the views alongside their paths. The application then takes this information to register the routes at runtime. Even the rules on which users have access to which routes can be stored in the database. Moreover, new views could potentially be implemented by third parties and added to the system at deployment time rather than compile time.

Router Layouts

Router layouts allow you to *decorate* views. Let's study an example. A common UI pattern in web applications is to have the same header in all the "pages" or, using Vaadin terminology, views. We could create a reusable UI component with the name Header that all *view implementators* (like you, me, or our colleagues) can manually add to their views:

```
@Route("my-fancy-view")
public class MyFancyView extends VerticalLayout {
  public MyFancyView() {
    ...
    var header = new Header();
    add(header, ... and other components ...);
  }
}
```

This works fine if we are sure that we'll never need to add something else like a footer or a menu that is also shared between all the views. For those cases in which we are not 100% sure about it, we can use router layouts.

A router layout is a class that implements RouterLayout and that sets up all the components that are shared by a set of views. Each view can use the @Route annotation to specify the router layout to use. Here's a simple router layout implementation that shows a header:

```
public class MainLayout extends Composite<Component>
    implements RouterLayout {

  @Override
  protected Component initContent() {
    var header = new Div(new Text("Chapter 7"));
    header.setWidthFull();
    header.getStyle().set("font-size", "2em");
    header.getStyle().set("font-weight", "bold");
    header.getStyle().set("color", "white");
    header.getStyle().set("background-color", "#002211");
```

```
    return new VerticalLayout(header);
  }

}
```

Please don't be distracted by the getStyle() method for now. Those lines just set CSS properties to make the header look more interesting for the screenshots you'll see later. We'll cover styling in Chapter 10. The important bit is that this class looks like any other custom UI component except it implements RouterLayout. The component itself consists of a Div with a Text inside that says *Chapter 7*. Here's how we can instruct Vaadin to use this router layout when it has to show the admin view in the browser (see Figure 7-4):

```
@Route(layout = MainLayout.class)
public class AdminView extends Composite<Component> {
  @Override
  protected Component initContent() {
    return new Text("Hello, admin.");
  }
}
```

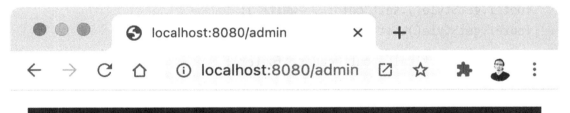

Hello, admin.

Figure 7-4. *A header implemented in a router layout*

Since in this example application we are defining the routes programmatically, we cannot use the @Route annotation. Instead, we have to specify the router layout when we define the route as follows:

```
RouteConfiguration.forSessionScope().setRoute(
  "admin", AdminView.class, MainLayout.class
);
```

The RouterLayout interface contains a default method that takes care of adding the view to the end of the layout. We can override the implementation to handle more complex layouts. To illustrate the point, let's try to add a footer to the router layout:

```
public class MainLayout extends Composite<Component>
    implements RouterLayout {

  @Override
  protected Component initContent() {
    ...

    var footer = new Div(
        new Text("Building UIs in Java is awesome!"));
    footer.setWidthFull();
    footer.getStyle().set("color", "white");
    footer.getStyle().set("background-color", "#002211");

    return new VerticalLayout(header, footer);
  }
}
```

Since the default is to append the view at the end of the layout, we'll end up with the header, then the container, and then the view, in that order inside a VerticalLayout (see Figure 7-5).

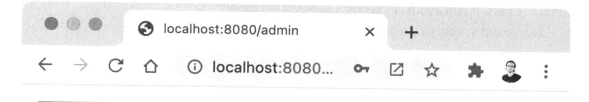

Figure 7-5. *The default behavior of a router layout*

What we want is to show the footer at the bottom of the page, not right after the header. To solve this, we can override the showRouterLayoutContent(HasElement) method of the RouterLayout interface. But first, we need to create a component that serves as a placeholder for the views. Let's call it container:

```
public class MainLayout extends Composite<Component>
    implements RouterLayout {

  private VerticalLayout container = new VerticalLayout();

  @Override
  protected Component initContent() {

    ...

    return new VerticalLayout(header, container, footer);
  }

}
```

Note how we are adding the header, container, and footer instances into the VerticalLayout in that order. Every time a view is going to be shown in the router layout, we need to empty the container and add the view to it:

```java
public class MainLayout extends Composite<Component>
    implements RouterLayout {

  private VerticalLayout container = new VerticalLayout();

  ...

  @Override
  public void showRouterLayoutContent(HasElement content) {
    container.removeAll();
    container.getElement().appendChild(content.getElement());
  }
}
```

Here again we are using something we haven't covered yet—the Element API. This API allows you to add and remove HTML elements. For some reason, in router layouts, Vaadin uses this API instead of the Component API that we are familiar with. In short, every component has an Element (a Java representation of the HTML element in the browser). We are using this more low-level API to add the view to the layout. You'll learn more about the Element API in Chapter 9. In practical terms, the effect of the code is the same as if we had used the add method of VerticalLayout. See the result in Figure 7-6.

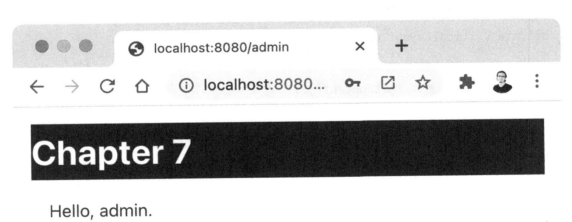

Figure 7-6. *A customized router layout*

Navigation Lifecycle

When you request a view, Vaadin looks for a matching class that either has been annotated with @Route or has been manually registered with the `RouterConfiguration` class. If a matching class is found, Vaadin renders it in the browser, and you can start using the view. Later, you might want to navigate to another view. You request the view through a URL or through a link in the application itself, and the process is repeated. We call this process the *navigation lifecycle*, and you can hook up custom logic primarily at two points:

- Before the user enters the view

- Before the user leaves the view

Note   There's a third point to run logic after the user has entered the view (or after the navigation event happens) that we won't cover here. If you want to learn more about it, see the Javadoc for the `AfterNavigationEvent` class at *https://vaadin.com/api*.

Before Enter Observer

A typical use case of the "before the user enters the view" scenario is when you want to redirect the user to a different view if there's no data to visualize. Let's see how to implement this.

Suppose we have this view, which is the "home" page of our application:

```
@Route("")
public class HomeView extends Composite<Component> {

  @Override
  protected Component initContent() {
    return new VerticalLayout(
        new H1("Welcome!"),
        new RouterLink("Go to my data", DataView.class)
    );
  }

}
```

This view is mapped to the empty route ("") and includes two components. The first is a title (H1), and the second is a link to another view (we'll implement this view next). The RouterLink component is useful to create menu options or links to views in your application. When you click *Go to my data*, Vaadin renders the DataView class. Figure 7-7 shows the HomeView component in the browser.

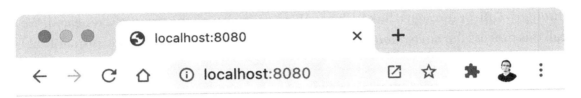

Figure 7-7. *The RouterLink component*

To implement the DataView class, let's say that the data is a simple String stored in the VaadinSession and that this data is shown in a TextArea component to allow changing it. Something like this:

```
@Route("data")
public class DataView extends Composite<Component> {

  private TextArea textArea;

  @Override
  protected Component initContent() {
    textArea = new TextArea("Data", getData().orElse(""),
        "type your data here");
```

```
    return new VerticalLayout(
        new H1("Data view"),
        new RouterLink("Home", HomeView.class),
        textArea,
        new Button("Save", event -> {
          setData(textArea.getValue());
          Notification.show("Thanks for your data");
        })
    );
  }

  private Optional<String> getData() {
    String data = (String) VaadinSession.getCurrent()
        .getAttribute("data");
    return Optional.ofNullable(data);
  }

  private void setData(String data) {
    VaadinSession.getCurrent().setAttribute("data", data);
  }
}
```

Figure 7-8 will help you to understand the code.

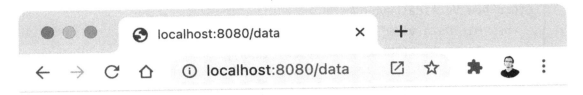

Data view

Home

Data

type your data here

Save

Figure 7-8. *A view that shows data stored in the* VaadinSession

The VaadinSession is a map where you can store key-value pairs. Each user of your application has its own VaadinSession object. The getData() method reads a value with the key data from the session. The setData(String) method sets a value with the key data in the session. These methods are used by the textArea object and the Button component to visualize and store the value, respectively.

We want to redirect the user to a different view if there's no data. We'll call this new view NoDataView, and we'll implement it later. First, we need to hook up the logic to check whether there's data or not and redirect if needed. This is the HomeView class responsibility. Vaadin uses the Observer Pattern to allow this. All we need to do is implement the BeforeEnterObserver interface in the HomeView class:

```
@Route("data")
public class DataView extends Composite<Component>
    implements BeforeEnterObserver {

  ...

  @Override
  public void beforeEnter(BeforeEnterEvent event) {
    if (getData().isEmpty() || getData().get().isEmpty()) {
      event.rerouteTo(NoDataView.class);
    }
  }

  ...
}
```

We have to implement the beforeEnter(BeforeEnterEvent) method with the logic that we need. We check if there's no data, and if so, we use the rerouteTo(Class) method to redirect the user to the NoDataView component. Here's the implementation of that component:

```
@Route("no-data")
public class NoDataView extends Composite<Component> {

  @Override
  protected Component initContent() {
    return new VerticalLayout(
        new H1("Oops! There's no data \uD83D\uDE31"),
        new Button("Create data \uD83E\uDDEF", event -> {
          VaadinSession.getCurrent()
              .setAttribute("data", "This is the default data");
          UI.getCurrent().navigate(DataView.class);
          Notification.show("Default data created");
        })
    );
  }
}
```

We added some interesting emojis using Unicode codes. But let's not get distracted by those! Let's understand what we implemented. If you go to *http://localhost:8080*, Vaadin creates an instance of the HomeView class and renders it in the browser (Figure 7-7). This class includes a RouterLink to the DataView component. You click this link and Vaadin creates an instance of DataView. However, before rendering the component in the browser, it calls the beforeEnter(BeforeEnterEvent) method that we implemented. This method realizes that there's no data in the session and redirects (or reroutes) to the NoDataView component which is what gets rendered instead of the DataView component (Figure 7-9).

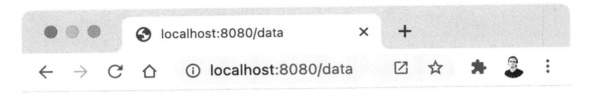

Oops! There's no data 😱

Create data 🗑

Figure 7-9. *Reroute caused by a "before enter" handler*

Once you click the Create data button, a default value with the key data is stored in the session, and the code directs the user to the DataView component again. This time, the beforeEnter(BeforeEnterEvent) method doesn't redirect because now it can see data. The view is finally rendered with the default data in the TextArea component (Figure 7-10).

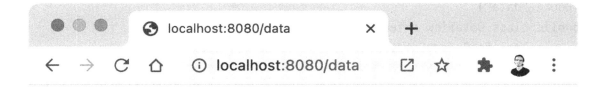

Data view

Home

Data

This is the default data

Save

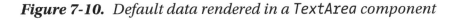

Figure 7-10. *Default data rendered in a* TextArea *component*

Before Leave Observer

Another common use case in business applications is to warn the user about changes that could be lost if they leave a view. We can implement this in the event that occurs just before the user is about to leave a view. This is done by implementing the BeforeLeaveObserver. Let's say we want to ask the user if they really want to leave the view when they have changed the value in the TextArea. Here's how:

```java
@Route("data")
public class DataView extends Composite<Component>
    implements BeforeEnterObserver, BeforeLeaveObserver {

  ...

  @Override
  public void beforeLeave(BeforeLeaveEvent event) {
    if (!getData().get().equals(textArea.getValue())) {
      ContinueNavigationAction action = event.postpone();
      Dialog dialog = new Dialog();
      dialog.add(
          new Text("Are you sure?"),
          new Button("Yeah", clickEvent -> {
            dialog.close();
            action.proceed();
          })
      );
      dialog.open();
    }
  }

  ...
}
```

The beforeLeave(BeforeLeaveEvent) method checks if the value in the textArea component is not the same as the one stored in the VaadinSession, and if that's true, it pauses the navigation action by calling the postpone() method and shows a Dialog to allow the user to confirm. If the user confirms, the dialog is closed, and the navigation action is continued by calling the proceed() method. You can test this by navigating to the DataView route, editing the data, and clicking the *Home* link. Figure 7-11 shows the result.

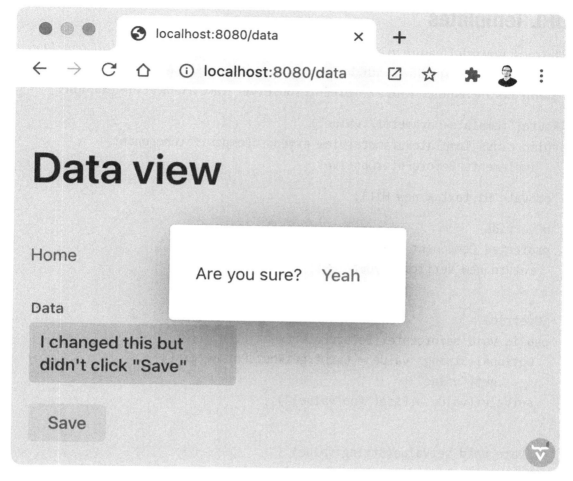

Figure 7-11. *A navigation action postponed by a BeforeLeaveObserver*

URL Parameters

A URL parameter is a value that is passed to a view through the URL that requested
the view. For example, a view implementation annotated with @Route("users") is
accessed through *http://localhost:8080/users*. A URL like *http://localhost:8080/
users?selectedId=3* contains a URL parameter (*selectedId*) with the value 3. The
URL parameter can be passed as part of the path in the URL. For example, in *http://
localhost:8080/users/3*, the number 3 can be a URL parameter that the view can use
to, say, select the user with ID 3.

URL Templates

The most powerful feature to handle URL parameters in Vaadin is called *URL templates*.
URL templates are specified with the @Route annotation, and the matching URL
parameters are handled with a BeforeEnterObserver. Take a look at this example:

```
@Route("template-parameter/:value")
public class TemplateParameterView extends Composite<Component>
    implements BeforeEnterObserver {

  private H1 text = new H1();

  @Override
  protected Component initContent() {
    return new VerticalLayout(text);
  }

  @Override
  public void beforeEnter(BeforeEnterEvent event) {
    Optional<String> value = event.getRouteParameters()
        .get("value");
    setValue(value.orElse("(no value)"));
  }

  private void setValue(String value) {
    text.setText(value);
  }

}
```

Pay close attention to the syntax in @Route("template-parameter/:value"). The
:value part indicates that the view expects a String at that position in the URL. That
string is later retrieved in the beforeEnter(BeforeEnterEvent) method and set as
the text content of the H1 component (text). Figure 7-12 shows an example. Pay close
attention to the URL in the browser.

42

Figure 7-12. URL parameter processed using a URL template

If you request the URL without the parameter (*http://localhost:8080/template-parameter*), you'll get an error despite the fact that the view checks this with an Optional. If you want to have URL parameters that can be absent (or null), you have to use the ? character in the URL template:

```
@Route("template-parameter/:value?")
```

You can declare multiple URL parameters and place them anywhere in the URL template. For example:

```
@Route("companies/:companyId/:employeeId/edit")
```

A URL like *http://localhost:8080/companies/6/7/edit* will match this route.

You can also use the wildcard character (*) to match the last segment of a URL. For example:

```
@Route("api/:path*")
```

You can get the value from a BeforeEnterEvent object as follows:

```
var path = event.getRouteParameters().get("path").orElse("");
```

If the URL *http://localhost:8080/api/com/company/list* is requested, the path variable would contain the string com/company/list.

It's also possible to use regular expressions. For example:

```
@Route("companies/:companyId?([0-9]/edit")
```

This will match only URLs that contain a single digit before */edit*.

> **Tip** You can get Integer and Long values using the getInteger(String) and getLong(String) methods of the RouteParameters object returned by getRouteParameters().

Typed Parameters

The HasUrlParameter interface is an alternative to URL templates that allows you to get a URL parameter of a specific type. The following example shows how to get an Integer value from the URL:

```java
@Route("typed-parameter")
public class TypedParameterView extends Composite<Component>
    implements HasUrlParameter<Integer> {

  private H1 text = new H1();

  @Override
  protected Component initContent() {
    return new VerticalLayout(text);
  }

  @Override
  public void setParameter(BeforeEvent beforeEvent,
      Integer number) {
    text.setText("" + number);
  }

}
```

See Figure 7-13 paying attention to the URL and the value rendered in the UI.

9

Figure 7-13. *A typed parameter handled by* `HasUrlParameter`

Tip   You can use the `@OptionalParameter` annotation in the parameter of the `setParameter(BeforeEvent, T)` method to make the parameter optional. Remember to check for null values if you use this annotation.

Query Parameters

A query parameter (or query string) is a set of key-value pairs that are included after the question mark character (?) in the URL. For example, we can pass a value like 13 in the `userId` parameter using URL `http://localhost:8080/query-parameter?userId=13`. The following example shows how to use this query parameter:

```
@Route("query-parameter")
public class QueryParameterView extends Composite<Component>
    implements BeforeEnterObserver {

  private H1 text = new H1("(no user ID)");

  @Override
  protected Component initContent() {
    return new VerticalLayout(text);
  }
```

```java
@Override
public void beforeEnter(BeforeEnterEvent event) {
  Location location = event.getLocation();
  Map<String, List<String>> list = location
      .getQueryParameters().getParameters();
  List<String> userIds = list.get("userId");
  if (!list.isEmpty()) {
    text.setText(userIds.get(0));
  }
}
```

Notice how we get a list of values for the `userId` parameter. This is because it's possible that the URL contains the parameter multiple times and hence gets multiple values under the same key. In the previous example, we are using only the first value in the list.

Updating the Page Title

To close this chapter, let's see how to set the title that the browser shows when you request a view. You might have noticed that up until now, the title shown in the browser tab shows the URL. You can easily set a title using the `@PageTitle` annotation (see Figure 7-14):

```java
@PageTitle("This is the title")
@Route("page-title")
public class PageTitleView extends Composite<Component> {

  @Override
  protected Component initContent() {
    return new H1("Hello!");
  }

}
```

Hello!

Figure 7-14. *A browser tab with a page title configured*

To set the title at runtime, you can use the HasDynamicTitle interface (see Figure 7-15):

```
@Route("dynamic-page-title")
public class DynamicPageTitleView extends Composite<Component>
implements HasDynamicTitle {

  @Override
  protected Component initContent() {
    return new H1("Hello again, and bye for now!");
  }

  @Override
  public String getPageTitle() {
    return "Title at " + LocalDateTime.now();
  }

}
```

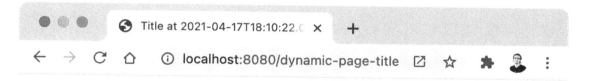

Hello again, and bye for now!

Figure 7-15. *A dynamic page title*

> **Caution**   Don't use @PageTitle and HasDynamicTitle at the same time. An exception is thrown when you do so.

Summary

There it is! In this chapter, you learned everything you need to connect URLs with views in Vaadin. You saw how to define routes using the @Route annotation or dynamically at runtime with the RouteConfiguration class. You learned how to decorate views using router layouts that allow you to implement UI structures that include headers, menus, footers, and any other areas in a web page. You also understood the navigation lifecycle and how to hook your logic up before the user enters a view and before it leaves it. You saw how to use URL parameters to configure the UI using URL templates, typed parameters, and query parameters.

The next chapter will cover an exciting feature in modern web applications: Server Push.

CHAPTER 8

Server Push

Server Push is a feature in Vaadin that allows you to update the UI without the need of user interaction. For example, you might want to show the progress of a task that's running in the server or notify the user about a new working item being available.

Activating and using Server Push in Vaadin is pretty straightforward and requires only an annotation and a call to the `UI:access(Command)` method. In this chapter, you'll learn what Server Push is, when to use it, how to use it, and the configuration options that are available to you.

When Is Server Push Used?

Server Push is used when you want to make changes in the UI from a thread different to the one that the server creates to handle a request from the client. For example, if you have a button that executes a long-running task in the server, you might want to create a new `Thread` to run the task logic and immediately return the control to the browser, so that the user can continue to use other functionality in the application. Once the task is completed, you can show the result in the UI. You cannot simply update the UI from the new thread, but fortunately that's the problem Server Push solves.

Let's see an example to understand why and when you have to use Server Push. Take a look at this view implementation:

```
@Route("no-push")
public class NoPushView extends Composite<Component> {

  private VerticalLayout layout;

  @Override
  protected Component initContent() {
    layout = new VerticalLayout(
        new Button("Run long task", event -> runLongTaks()),
```

```
        new Button("Does this work?", event -> addText()));
    return layout;
  }

  private void runLongTaks() {
    try {
      Thread.sleep(5000);
      Notification.show("Task completed.");
    } catch (InterruptedException ignored) {
    }
  }

  private void addText() {
    layout.add(new Paragraph("It works!"));
  }

}
```

This view contains a button with a click listener that simulates a long-running task that takes 5 seconds to complete. After 5 seconds, the code attempts to show a notification in the UI. There's also a button that simply adds text to the layout. If you run this application, you'll see that the UI is locked for 5 seconds. The client-side engine of Vaadin detects that the request is taking too long and shows a progress bar (see Figure 8-1).

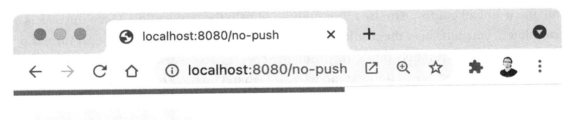

Figure 8-1. *A long-running task causes a progress bar displayed in the browser*

You'll also notice that the *Does this work?* button doesn't seem to work while the progress bar is displayed. However, after 5 seconds, the notification is shown in the browser, and the result of other interactions with the UI happens as well (see the text added to the layout in Figure 8-2). This shows that the long-running task blocks changes to the UI even when the client can send additional requests that are successfully processed by the server.

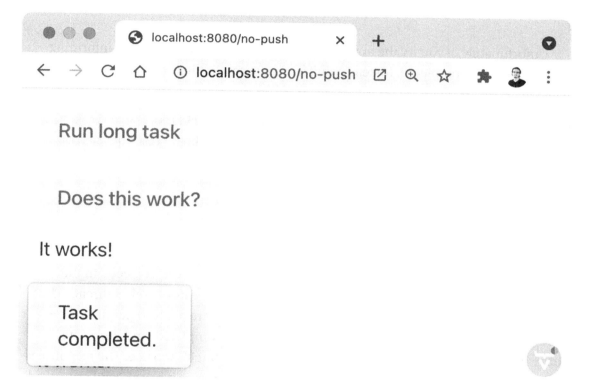

Figure 8-2. *UI changes happen at once after a long-running task in the server*

Let's make one step toward improving the application. Since the task takes too long to complete, we can move the logic to a separate thread. This allows the initial thread (started by the server) to finish and let Vaadin process the request and return a response immediately. We can also inform the user that the task is running before starting the new thread:

```
private void runLongTaks() {
  Notification.show("Running the task...");
```

```
new Thread(() -> {
  try {
    Thread.sleep(5000);
    Notification.show("Task completed.");
  } catch (InterruptedException ignored) {
  }
}).start();
}
```

Unfortunately, if you try the application, you'll never see a notification informing that the task was completed. Instead, you'll see an exception in the server's log:

`java.lang.IllegalStateException`: UI instance is not available. It means that you are calling this method out of a normal workflow where it's always implicitly set. That may happen if you call the method from the custom thread without 'UI::access' or from tests without proper initialization.

How Server Push Works

Let's study the example of the previous section in more detail. When you click the button, a new thread is created to handle the request in the server. The code in the click listener is executed in this thread. This code, in turn, creates another thread. The original thread ends, and both the browser and the server are ready to handle future UI interactions from the user. Later, the 5-second task is completed, and the call to `Notification.show("Task completed.")` is processed. But it's too late. The response is already closed. The browser is not expecting any changes since it has already processed the response 5 seconds ago. The new changes to the UI are lost.

Updates to the UI happen only when they are made in the thread of the original request. Take a look at Figure 8-3. An event in the browser (like a click on a button or a change in the value of a text field) generates a request to the server. Typically, this results in a change in the UI (e.g., showing a notification). This is the way we have been using the framework so far.

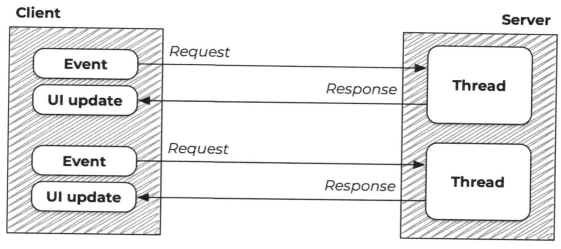

Figure 8-3. *Requests and responses changing the UI*

Server Push is a feature that you activate using an annotation in Vaadin (as you'll learn shortly) and that allows separate threads to update the UI in the browser. Figure 8-4 illustrates the concept. A UI event sends a request to the server which produces a response with a UI update. However, with Server Push, if a new separate thread was started, this new thread can send *push updates* that result in visible changes in the UI.

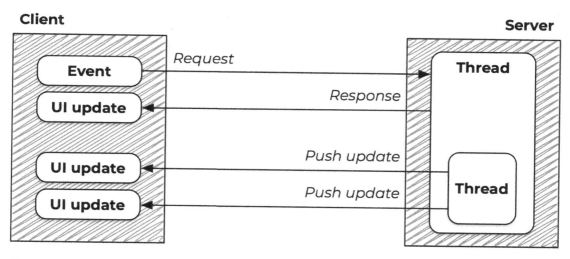

Figure 8-4. *Push updates from a separate thread in the server*

Performing Asynchronous UI Updates

To be able to update the UI using Server Push, you must enable it using the @Push annotation. This annotation needs to be placed in a class that implements the AppShellConfigurator interface:

```
@Push
public class AppConfiguration implements AppShellConfigurator {
}
```

Note   AppShellConfigurator instances are detected and used by Vaadin to configure the client-side engine when the user requests the application in the browser.

With Server Push enabled, you can now send updates to the client. These updates are asynchronous UI updates and can be sent to the client manually or automatically depending on the configuration you use.

Automatic Server Push Updates

By default, if you enclose the code that changes the UI in a Command object and call the access(Command) method of the UI class, Server Push changes are sent automatically to the client. For example, this is what we need to do to make the example of the previous section work:

```
private void runLongTaks() {
  Notification.show("Running the task...");
  var ui = UI.getCurrent();
  new Thread(() -> {
    try {
      Thread.sleep(5000);
      ui.access(() -> {
        Notification.show("Task completed.");
      });
    } catch (InterruptedException ignored) {
```

```
    }
  }).start();
}
```

This code gets a reference to the current UI and we initialize this reference before we start the thread. It's important to get this reference in the scope of the original thread (the request thread) since Vaadin uses Java's `ThreadLocal` to store these references.

Tip   Always enclose any code that is run in a separate thread in a `UI:access(Command)` call and make sure that you get the `UI` instance from outside this thread.

If you run the application, you see not only that you can add text to the layout while the long-running task is working but also that the notification is shown after 5 seconds when the task is completed (see Figure 8-5).

Run long task

Does this work?

It works!

Task
completed.

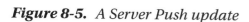

Figure 8-5. *A Server Push update*

Manual Server Push Updates

It's possible to control when exactly Server Push updates are sent to the client. To do so, you have to configure the Server Push mode using the @Push annotation:

```
@Push(value = PushMode.MANUAL)
public class AppConfiguration implements AppShellConfigurator {
}
```

You still have to use the access(Command) method when you perform changes to the UI from a separate thread, but you can now call the push() method of the UI class any time you want to send UI changes to the client:

```
doBusinessStuff();
ui.access(() -> {
  updateUI();
  ui.push();
}
doSomeMoreBusinessStuff();
ui.access(() -> {
  updateUI();
  ui.push();
}
```

Here's a version of the long-running task example that updates a ProgressBar component as the task progresses:

```
@Route("manual-push")
public class ManualPushView extends Composite<Component> {

  private VerticalLayout layout;
  private ProgressBar progressBar = new ProgressBar(0, 10);
  private Button button;

  @Override
  protected Component initContent() {
    button = new Button("Run long task", event -> runLongTaks());
    button.setDisableOnClick(true);
    layout = new VerticalLayout(button,
```

```
        new Button("Does this work?", event -> addText()),
        progressBar);
    return layout;
  }

  private void runLongTaks() {
    Notification.show("Running the task...");
    progressBar.setValue(0);
    var ui = UI.getCurrent();
    new Thread(() -> {
      try {
        for (int i = 0; i <= 10; i++) {
          Thread.sleep(1000);
          double progress = i;
          ui.access(() -> {
            progressBar.setValue(progress);
            ui.push();
          });
        }

        ui.access(() -> {
          Notification.show("Task completed.");
          button.setEnabled(true);
          ui.push();
        });
      } catch (InterruptedException ignored) {
      }
    }).start();
  }

  private void addText() {
    layout.add(new Paragraph("It works!"));
  }

}
```

We have added a `ProgressBar` with values between 0 and 10. A loop in the `runLongTask()` method updates the progress bar every second and sends the changes to the client using the `push()` method. When the loop ends, another Server Push update is sent to the client to inform about the completion of the task.

See how we called the `setDisableOnClick(boolean)` method on the button that invokes the long-running task. This is handy when you run this kind of task to prevent the user from starting the job more than once. Figure 8-6 shows a screenshot of the application as it runs the task.

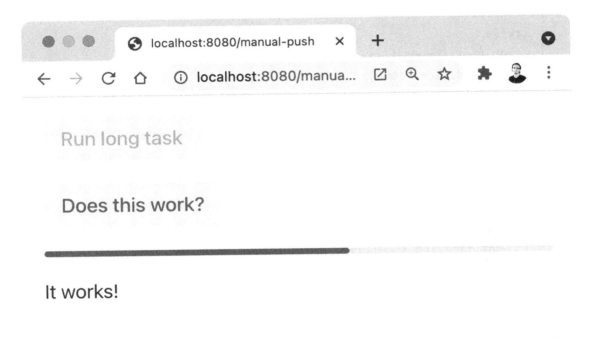

Figure 8-6. *A UI updated manually from a server-side thread*

The example also shows how the call to the `access(Command)` method is used only when we need to update the UI. A typical mistake is to call business logic in the `Command` when there's no need for this. For example:

```
ui.access(() -> {
  doBusinessStuff();
  updateUI();
  ui.push();
}
```

The negative impact of this is more evident when the business logic takes a considerable amount of time to run. Instead, move business logic calls to outside the Command implementation.

Caution   The access(Command) method locks the user session. This means that other threads are not able to make changes to the UI while the code in the Command implementation runs.

Using Thread Pools

In the previous examples, we have been using threads by directly creating new instances of Thread. Java threads are expensive and consume memory. To highlight this point, let's do an experiment (adapted from a talk by Petter Holmström):

```
public class MaxThreadsExperiment extends Thread {

  public static void main(String... args) {
    new MaxThreadsExperiment().start();
  }

  public static final AtomicInteger count = new AtomicInteger();

  @Override
  public void run() {
    try {
      System.out.println(count.incrementAndGet());
      new MaxThreadsExperiment().start();
      sleep(Long.MAX_VALUE);
```

```
  } catch (InterruptedException e) {
    e.printStackTrace();
  }
 }

}
```

This Java program recursively creates threads until you get an OutOfMemoryError. In the virtual machine I used to run this experiment, I got the error rather quickly:

```
...
1994
1995
1996
1997
1998
1999
2000
Exception in thread "Thread-1999" java.lang.OutOfMemoryError: unable to
create new native thread
        at java.lang.Thread.start0(Native Method)
        at java.lang.Thread.start(Thread.java:717)
        at MaxThreadsExperiment.run(MaxThreadsExperiment.java:15)
```

2000 threads was the limit. Depending on the server to which you deploy your application, this number could be smaller or larger. The key point is that 2000 (or approximately 4000 when I run it in my development machine) is probably too little for a web application, considering the Servlet Container creates threads to handle requests. Threads are a limited resource and should be treated like so.

In software design, a *pool* is a place where resources are created and initialized before they are used. Clients of a pool can request a resource, use it, and then return it to the pool. A resource can be a database connection, a service, a file, a thread, or any other resource. A thread pool is a software entity that creates a preconfigured number of threads that can execute tasks sent by a submitter.

Java includes the ExecutorService interface alongside ready-to-use thread pool implementations. A task submitter (your code) can submit (execute) tasks (Runnable objects) that run in threads queued and executed in a thread when one becomes available in the pool. Figure 8-7 depicts the process.

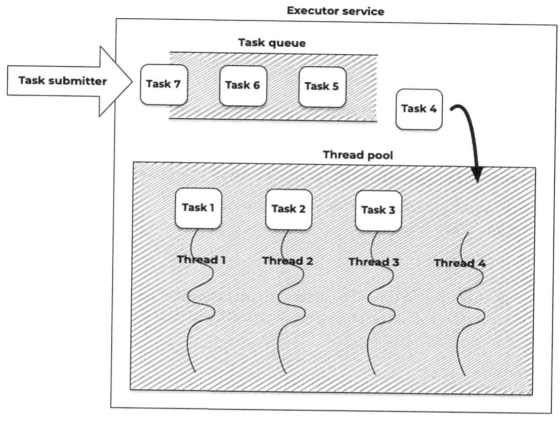

Figure 8-7. *The executor service with a pool of four threads*

Since a thread pool should be ready before the application starts to produce tasks, a good place to initialize it is a ServletContextListener. The ServletContextListener interface allows you to run logic when the ServletContext is initialized and destroyed.

Note   A ServletContext object is created when the application is started. There's only one ServletContext instance per instance of the web application.

Continuing with the example of the previous sections, we could create a new class that extends ServletContextListener or use an existing class if available. In fact, we have a good candidate, so instead of creating a new class (which you can do if you want), we'll use the AppConfiguration class that we previously created to enable Server Push. All we need to do is add the class to the extends list, implement the methods, and mark the class with @WebListener to allow the Servlet Container to detect the class:

```
@Push
@WebListener
public class AppConfiguration
    implements AppShellConfigurator, ServletContextListener {

  private static ScheduledExecutorService executorService;

  public static ExecutorService getExecutorService() {
    return executorService;
  }

  @Override
  public void contextInitialized(ServletContextEvent event) {
    executorService = Executors.newScheduledThreadPool(3);
  }

  @Override
  public void contextDestroyed(ServletContextEvent event) {
    executorService.shutdown();
  }

}
```

Here, we are using a static instance of type ScheduledExecutorService (which implements ExecutorService). A public getter allows other parts of the application to get a reference to the service and use it. We create a new instance using the Executors class and configure a thread pool with three threads. This number is used in this demo application for demonstration purposes so that you can play with it and see how the threads behave, but you should probably use a much bigger number in production or even make it configurable at runtime. Additionally, it's important to shut the executor service down when the application is stopped in order to prevent threads living in the JVM "forever."

The next step is to modify the view to use the thread pool (or executor service) instead of manually creating and starting threads there. Here's the result of the refactoring:

```
private void runLongTaks() {
  Notification.show("Running the task...");
  var ui = UI.getCurrent();

  AppConfiguration.getExecutorService().execute(() -> {
    try {
      Thread.sleep(5000);
      ui.access(() -> {
        Notification.show("Task completed.");
      });
    } catch (InterruptedException ignored) {
    }
  });
}
```

We get the reference to the ExecutorService and call the execute(Runnable) method to submit a new task. This task will be assigned to a free thread in the pool, if there is one, or queued until one becomes available. Try the application and click the *Run long task* button, say, ten times. See how the tasks are submitted but completed in batches of three. Figure 8-8 shows an example.

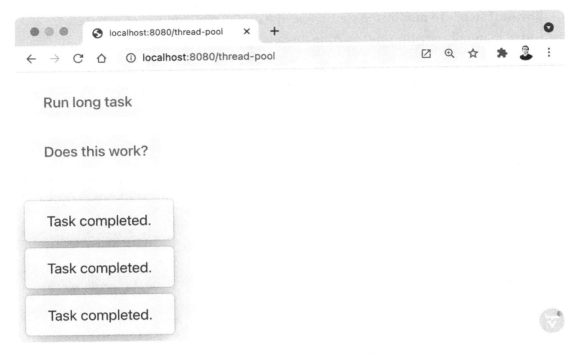

Figure 8-8. *Tasks completed in a pool of three threads*

Note   The result in Figure 8-8 doesn't imply that the tasks are executed simultaneously in batches of three. The result is a consequence of how the application was used. Several tasks were sent (by clicking the button) in a quick sequence. Since the threads sleep for 5 seconds in the server, all the three threads in the pool become busy. Since the tasks were sent quickly one after another, all the threads complete their tasks almost simultaneously.

WebSocket vs. Long Polling

By default, Vaadin uses the WebSocket protocol to send changes to the client when you enable Server Push. WebSocket is a communication protocol just like HTTP is. With WebSocket, the client establishes a permanent connection to the server that enables a full-duplex communication between the participants.

As an alternative to WebSocket, you can use HTTP for Server Push by setting the LONG_POLLING transport in the @Push annotation:

```
@Push(transport = Transport.LONG_POLLING)
public class AppConfiguration implements AppShellConfigurator {
}
```

Polling is a technique by which the client continuously sends requests to the server asking for UI changes. If the client-server was a conversation, regular polling would look like this:

> **Client:** Are there any changes for me?
>
> **Server:** No.
>
> **Client:** Are there any changes for me?
>
> **Server:** No.
>
> **Client:** Are there any changes for me?
>
> **Server:** Yes. Add a notification with the text "Hello".
>
> **Client:** Thanks. Are there any changes for me?
>
> **Server:** No
>
> ...

The client asking the server for changes represents HTTP requests. These requests are done periodically, for example, every certain number of seconds. If they are done, say, every 30 seconds, the UI is updated slowly. If you decrease the frequency to, say, 2 seconds, the UI is updated faster. Faster is better for the user but worst for the traffic in the network (especially if you are using a cloud provider that charges for usage).

Long polling is a technique by which the client polls the server in a smart way to reduce the number of requests while maintaining quick UI updates. With long polling, the client makes a request to the server, which the server holds until there are changes to be returned. Only at that point the response is sent to the client, which has been waiting quietly without making new requests. The conversation would look like this:

> **Client:** Are there any changes for me?
>
> (2 minutes later...)

Server: Yes. Add a notification with the text "Hello".

Client: Thanks. Are there any changes for me?

...

Selecting between WebSocket and long polling depends on the exact requirements of your application, the infrastructure in which you deploy it, and its usage. In general, WebSocket is more efficient, so, as a rule of thumb, use long polling only when the WebSocket protocol is not available, for example, when a web proxy blocks it.

Summary

In this chapter, you learned a lot about threads, asynchronous UI updates, and conversations between clients and servers. You learned when you need to enable Server Push with the @Push annotation. You saw how to automatically send Server Push updates to the client and how to send them manually. You also learned about thread pools and how they help you to avoid the infamous OutOfMemoryError. Finally, you got a general idea of how WebSocket and long polling work.

In the next chapter, you'll take control of the Document Object Model in the browser from the server by using Vaadin's Element API.

CHAPTER 9

The Element API

In Chapter 1, we learned about the Web platform and its core technologies. These are the technologies that power the Web in the browser. Vaadin abstracts away many of the concepts in the Web platform, but it doesn't get in your way when you need to go one level lower.

The Element API was introduced in Vaadin 10 to allow direct server-side manipulation of the DOM in the browser. In practice, the Element API is a set of Java classes with methods to read, create, and modify HTML elements in the web page.

Vaadin also includes functionality to execute JavaScript in the browser invoked from the server. It gives you access to the HTML History API and gets details of the browser configuration (vendor, version, underlying operating system) and more functionality.

Creating DOM Elements

Let's dive right into code. Here's how you can create a `<div>` element without typing any HTML code but only server-side Java:

```
@Route("creating-dom-elements")
public class CreatingDomElementsView extends Div {
}
```

Vaadin includes classes such as `Div`, `Span`, `H1`, `H2`, `H3`, and many others that you can use as a starting point for a UI component. If you inspect the DOM in the browser, you'll see that it contains the following:

```
...
<div id="outlet">
  <flow-container-root-2521314 id="ROOT-2521314" style="">
    <div></div>
  </flow-container-root-2521314>
</div>
...
```

© Alejandro Duarte 2021
A. Duarte, *Practical Vaadin*, https://doi.org/10.1007/978-1-4842-7179-7_9

The innermost empty <div> is ours. We created it with our own hands (through code, obviously). To prove it, let's define its id attribute:

```
@Route("creating-dom-elements")
public class CreatingDomElementsView extends Div {

  public CreatingDomElementsView () {
    Element div = getElement();
    div.setAttribute("id", "our-div");
  }

}
```

See how we got a reference (div) to the element using the getElement() method. An Element is a Java representation of an HTML element in the browser (in this case, a <div> element). With the Java reference ready, we call setAttribute(String, String) to set the id attribute as our-div. Here's what we get in the browser:

```
...
<div id="outlet">
  <flow-container-root-2521314 id="ROOT-2521314" style="">
    <div id="our-div"></div>
  </flow-container-root-2521314>
</div>
...
```

Note   The <flow-container-root-X> element is created by Vaadin alongside more elements and code in the page. These are implementation details required by the client-side engine of Vaadin, and you don't need to worry about when you implement views with the framework.

You don't need to create a whole class and extend one of the HTML UI components that Vaadin provides to add more elements to a page. You can create new instances of the Element class and append them to other instances. For example, we can append a new <span> element to our <div> as follows:

```
public CreatingDomElementsView () {
  Element div = getElement();
  div.setAttribute("id", "our-div");

  Element span = new Element("span");
  span.setText("Greetings from the low-level API!");
  div.appendChild(span);
}
```

The Element(String) constructor receives the name of the tag to create. We set the inner text of the <span> element using the setText(String) method. The HTML in the browser now looks like this:

```
...
<flow-container-root-2521314 id="ROOT-2521314" style="">
  <div id="our-div">
    <span>Greetings from the low-level API!</span>
  </div>
</flow-container-root-2521314>
...
```

Can we add a title? Yes! Let's do it (see the result in Figure 9-1):

```
Element div = getElement();
div.setAttribute("id", "our-div");

Element h1 = new Element("h1");
h1.setText("Element API example");
div.appendChild(h1);

Element span = new Element("span");
span.setText("Greetings from the low-level API!");
div.appendChild(span);
```

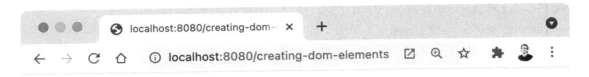

Element API example

Greetings from the low-level API!

Figure 9-1. *A UI implemented with the Element API of Vaadin*

We could have implemented this UI with the high-level API we have been using in previous chapters (the Component API). In fact, the code is much shorter:

```
@Route("with-components")
public class WithComponentsView extends Div {

  public WithComponentsView() {
    setId("our-div");
    add(
        new H1("Component API example"),
        new Span("Greetings from the high-level API!")
    );
  }

}
```

This highlights the advantage of using the Component API. The Element API is there in situations in which you might need it. Maybe you need to set an attribute in an HTML element that the Component API doesn't provide. Or you are creating a new component or integrating an existing one. You can always get an Element reference that represents the HTML element (the tag) in the browser from any Component in Vaadin, including your custom components.

> **Tip**   Vaadin includes the `ElementFactory` class with useful static methods to create many standard HTML elements. For example, instead of creating a `<span>` element by directly creating an instance of `Element` using new `Element("span")`, you can call `ElementFactory.createSpan()`.

Creating Custom Components

The Element API is a useful tool if you want to implement new client-side UI components that seamlessly connect to the server side. Let's develop an example.

In the previous sections, we use extension to create new views. The same approach can be used to create UI components. You can extend Div, Span, H1, H2, H3, Input, or other server-side components that render the respective HTML element in the browser. Another option is to use the @Tag annotation. For example, if we want to create a custom server-side component that renders an `<img>` element in the browser, we can use the following:

```
@Tag("img")
public class PictureButton extends Component {
}
```

The @Tag annotation tells Vaadin which tag to add to the DOM in the browser when you add an instance of the component into, say, a layout:

```
var button = new PictureButton();
var layout = new VerticalLayout(button);
```

In fact, Vaadin server-side components use this tag. For example, if you inspect its class hierarchy, you'll find that the Button class extends GeneratedVaadinButton, which in turn is annotated with

```
@Tag("vaadin-button")
...
public abstract class GeneratedVaadinButton ...
```

215

Note   The vaadin-button tag is a custom HTML element or Web Component. All server-side Vaadin components are implemented as Web Components. We won't dig into Web Components in this book. For now, it's enough to know that Web Components are a set of web standards that allow developers to define new HTML elements such as vaadin-button. It's possible to use these Web Components in non-Java applications. For more details on this, see the HTML examples for each component at *https://vaadin.com/components*.

Let's get back to the custom PictureButton component we are developing. We already know how to set attributes of an HTML element, so let's use that knowledge to set the src attribute of the <img> element:

```
@Tag("img")
public class PictureButton extends Component {

  public PictureButton(String imageUrl) {
    getElement().setAttribute("src", imageUrl);
  }

}
```

We can create a view that uses this component (see Figure 9-2):

```
@Route("custom-component")
public class CustomComponentView extends Composite<Component> {

  @Override
  protected Component initContent() {
    var button = new PictureButton(
    "https://live.staticflickr.com/65535/51154022090_22fd569976_k.jpg");

    var layout = new VerticalLayout(button);
    layout.setAlignItems(Alignment.CENTER);
    return layout;
  }

}
```

Figure 9-2. A custom component implemented with the Element API

It seems the image is too big. The creature in the picture is a mystery...

Styling

The Element API includes the Style class to allow you to set and unset CSS properties. You can get a reference to the Style class using the getStyle() method:

```
Style style = getElement().getStyle();
```

Let's use this object to set some CSS styles on the PictureButton component that we are developing:

```
public PictureButton(String imageUrl) {
  getElement().setAttribute("src", imageUrl);

  Style style = getElement().getStyle();
  style.set("border", "1em solid #333");
  style.set("box-sizing", "border-box");
  style.set("box-shadow", "1em 1em 1em #777");
}
```

217

Figure 9-3 shows the result in the browser, where I have scrolled all the way down to the bottom-right corner. The mystery remains.

Figure 9-3. *Setting CSS styles with the* `Style` *class*

Tip   The `boxing-sizing` CSS property is set to `border-box` to allow the border around the image to be included in the total width and height of the element. Without it, you might get an undesirable horizontal scroll bar in the browser.

Mixin Interfaces

We could solve the mystery right away by using the `Style` class to set a width:

```
style.set("width", "100%");
```

Or I could have just resized the browser window before taking the screenshot. But that's boring! Setting the width with the previous snippet of code would work in solving the mystery, but it won't add flexibility to the `PictureButton` class. What if a view requires a different width or size? We could refactor the code to add a public method to set the width:

```
public void setWidth(String width) {
  getElement().getStyle().set("width", width);
}
```

We would have to do something similar for getting the width, getting and setting the height, getting and setting the max width and height, shortcuts for setting a full size, full width, and undefined size... Sounds like a lot of work. Since adding this kind of API for managing the size of a component is pretty common, Vaadin includes an interface with default methods that implement exactly what we need. This interface is part of a set of interfaces collectively called *mixin interfaces*. Here's how we can easily add methods for sizing to the PictureButton class:

```
@Tag("img")
public class PictureButton extends Component implements HasSize {
  ...
}
```

There are many other mixin interfaces available, and you can use them in any custom component regardless of whether you use the @Tag annotation or not. These are some of them:

- HasSize: Component sizing

- HasStyle: Component styling

- ClickNotifier: Mouse click events

- HasEnabled: Enable or disable elements

- HasElement: Get the underlying Element instance

- HasText: Get and set text content

Note   You can find more details and a longer list with mixin interfaces at *https://vaadin.com/vaadin-reference-card*.

When using mixin interfaces, we don't need to implement any methods. Adding the interfaces to the `implements` declaration is enough to enable the features. With `HasSize`, we can now call the sizing methods that we have used with components such as `VerticalLayout` or `HorizontalLayout`. For example, we can set a width of a `PictureButton` component as follows:

```
var button = new PictureButton(
"https://live.staticflickr.com/65535/51154022090_22fd569976_k.jpg");
button.setWidth("65%");
```

Thanks to the `HasSize` interface, we can reveal the mystery. See Figure 9-4.

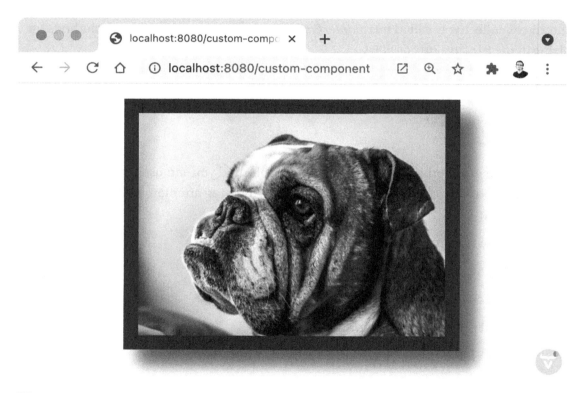

Figure 9-4. *A custom component that implements the* `HasSize` *mixin interface*

Note   If you are curious about the creature in Figure 9-4 (who also appears in Figure 4-26), his name is Draco—a funny, friendly, and sometimes hectic English Bulldog who likes to take the sun, look at people through his favorite window, and snore.

Handling Events

To handle interactions with the elements in the web browser, the Element API includes the addEventListener(String, DomEventListener) method. The first parameter specifies the name of the DOM event to handle. For example, we can add a click listener to an Element as follows:

```
getElement().addEventListener("click", event -> {
  ... server-side logic here ...
});
```

Note   There are many event types, and it'd be impossible to list them in this book. To explore the options, head to https://developer.mozilla.org/en-US/docs/Web/Events.

We can use this method to add a *button effect* to the PictureButton component. When the user presses the mouse button down over the image, we can remove the shadow and scale down the size of the component to give the effect of a button being pushed.

```
@Tag("img")
public class PictureButton extends Component implements HasSize {

  public PictureButton(String imageUrl) {
    getElement().setAttribute("src", imageUrl);

    Style style = getElement().getStyle();
    style.set("border", "1em solid #333");
    style.set("box-sizing", "border-box");
```

```
    String shadow = "1em 1em 1em #777";
    style.set("box-shadow", shadow);

    getElement().addEventListener("mousedown", event -> {
      style.set("transform", "scale(0.93)");
      style.remove("box-shadow");
    });
  }

}
```

We are using a CSS transformation to reduce the scale of the <img> element as well as removing its box-shadow attribute. This logic is run when the mousedown event happens on the element. This event is different from the click event. The mousedown event is fired when the mouse button is pressed but before it is released. The click event is fired after a complete click of the mouse button. Figure 9-5 shows the component when the mousedown event is fired.

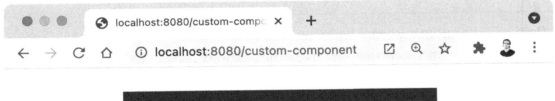

Figure 9-5. *Handling a mousedown event*

At this point, the `PictureButton` remains pressed (no shadow effect and scaled down in size), so no further clicks can be rendered. When the user releases the button, we need to reset the element's shadow and scale back to its original state. This can be done by adding a listener for the `mouseup` event:

```
getElement().addEventListener("mouseup", event -> {
  style.set("transform", "scale(1)");
  style.set("box-shadow", shadow);
});
```

There's still an edge case here. If the user presses the mouse button over the image, drags the pointer out of it, and then releases the mouse button, the button remains pressed. To fix this, we need to run the same logic we run on `mouseup`, but this time, when the mouse pointer leaves the image (`pointerleaves`). Since the logic is the same, we can assign the event listener to a variable and use it for both the `mouseup` and `pointerleaves` events:

```
DomEventListener listener = event -> {
  style.set("transform", "scale(1)");
  style.set("box-shadow", shadow);
};
getElement().addEventListener("mouseup", listener);
getElement().addEventListener("pointerleave", listener);
```

A button with no option for adding external click listeners is not a good button. We want to let clients of the `PictureButton` class add a listener so that they can react to click events. To do this, we can accept a listener in the form of a `SerializableConsumer` and invoke it (by calling its `accept(T)` method) when a click event is fired. For reference, here is the full implementation of the `PictureButton` class including the possibility to add an external click listener:

```
@Tag("img")
public class PictureButton extends Component implements HasSize {

  public PictureButton(String imageUrl,
      SerializableConsumer<DomEvent> clickListener) {

    getElement().setAttribute("src", imageUrl);
```

```
    Style style = getElement().getStyle();
    style.set("border", "1em solid #333");
    style.set("box-sizing", "border-box");

    String shadow = "1em 1em 1em #777";
    style.set("box-shadow", shadow);

    getElement().addEventListener("click", clickListener::accept)
        .addEventData("event.clientX")
        .addEventData("event.clientY");

    getElement().addEventListener("mousedown", event -> {
      style.set("transform", "scale(0.93)");
      style.remove("box-shadow");
    });

    DomEventListener listener = event -> {
      style.set("transform", "scale(1)");
      style.set("box-shadow", shadow);
    };
    getElement().addEventListener("mouseup", listener);
    getElement().addEventListener("pointerleave", listener);

  }

}
```

Look at how we add event data by using the addEventData(String) method right after adding the event listener. In this case, we are interested in getting the horizontal and vertical coordinates at which the click event happened. Here's the full implementation of a view that uses the component:

```
@Route("custom-component")
public class CustomComponentView extends Composite<Component> {

  @Override
  protected Component initContent() {
    var button = new PictureButton(
        "https://live.staticflickr.com/65535/51154022090_22fd569976_k.jpg",
```

```
    event -> {
      JsonObject data = event.getEventData();
      var x = data.getNumber("event.clientX");
      var y = data.getNumber("event.clientY");
      Notification.show("Clicked at " + x + ", " + y);
    });
  button.setWidth("65%");

  var layout = new VerticalLayout(button);
  layout.setAlignItems(Alignment.CENTER);
  return layout;
  }

}
```

We get the data from the event using the getEventData() method and specific values using the getNumber(String) method of the JsonObject class. Figure 9-6 shows the component after a click event is fired (the coordinates in the screenshot match the nose of the dog, in case you were wondering where I clicked).

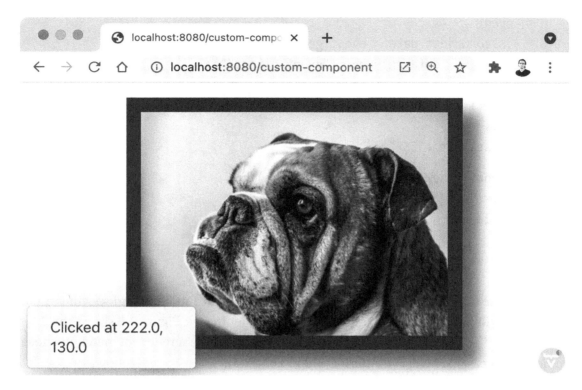

Figure 9-6. *A server-side click listener*

Caution   Make sure to use the correct getter in the `JsonObject` class when reading values. For example, the `clientX` property is a numeric value, so you have to use the `getNumber(String)` method. If the value is a `Boolean` or a `String`, use `getBoolean(String)` or `getString(String)`, respectively.

JavaScript Integration

Vaadin applications can integrate with JavaScript code in the browser. The integration allows you to call JavaScript functions from server-side Java and server-side Java methods from JavaScript in the browser. In short, there are two mechanisms that enable this:

- The executeJs(String, Serializable...) methods in the Page and Element classes for invoking JavaScript expressions that run in the browser

- The @ClientClickable annotation and the element.$server JavaScript object for invoking methods in the server from the browser

Adding JavaScript to a Vaadin Application

You can add your own JavaScript files to a Vaadin project in two locations depending on the packaging you use:

- For JAR packages, use *PROJECT_ROOT/frontend/*.

- For WAR packages, use *PROJECT_ROOT/src/main/resources/META-INF/resources/frontend/*.

You can create any subdirectory structure for your files.

Note   The files in the *frontend/* directory are processed by Vaadin (using a tool called Webpack) to produce a single *bundle* with all the client-side dependencies that your application needs.

For example, let's create a new JavaScript file, *PROJECT_ROOT/frontend/script.js*, with the following content:

```
alert("Hello there! It's me. The script!");
```

We can include this file in a Vaadin view as follows:

```
@Route("javascript-integration")
@JsModule("script.js")
public class JavascriptIntegrationView extends Div {
}
```

It's easy to think that the *script.js* JavaScript file is loaded only when the JavascriptIntegrationView is requested in the browser. However, as you can see in the screenshot of Figure 9-7, the file is loaded when you request any view of the application (the default *empty* view in the screenshot). This is easy to understand if you remember that the file is compiled into a single bundle.

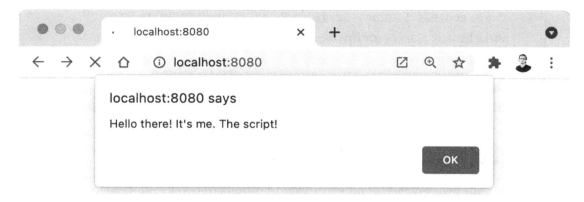

Figure 9-7. *A JavaScript file loaded in the browser*

Invoking JavaScript from Java

Let's develop a view that shows a button and an image. When the user clicks the button, the image visibility is toggled (visible/invisible). Let's start with the plumbing:

```java
@Route("javascript-integration")
@JsModule("script.js")
public class JavascriptIntegrationView extends Div {

    public JavascriptIntegrationView() {

        var image = new Image(
            "https://live.staticflickr.com/65535/51154022090_22fd569976_k.jpg",
            "dog");
        image.setMaxWidth("100%");

        Button button = new Button("Toggle visibility", event -> {
        });

        add(button, image);
        getElement().getStyle().set("display", "grid");
        getElement().getStyle().set("padding", "1em");
        getElement().getStyle().set("max-width", "700px");
    }

}
```

Nothing new here. The result is shown in Figure 9-8.

Figure 9-8. *A UI for toggling the visibility of an image*

We could develop all the functionality of the UI using the components we have covered in previous chapters of the book. In fact, that's exactly what I would suggest doing if you are implementing a view like this. However, we are here to learn about integration with the Web platform, so what we are going to implement will help you to understand how to integrate existing JavaScript components and libraries as well as implementing functionality that might not be provided out of the box by the core of Vaadin.

229

Back to the code. If you remember the earlier experiment, the script was executed immediately after the view was loaded. Instead of this, we want to run a JavaScript function when the button is clicked. Here's the **wrong** way of implementing the function in the *script.js* file:

```
function toggle() {
  ...
}
```

The reason this is incorrect is related to the scope in which this function is created and called later. We need to make sure that we know the scope. An easy way to achieve this is to create a *namespace* through a JavaScript object added to a well-known object in the DOM:

```
window.ns = {
  toggle: function() {
    ...
  }
}
```

This script adds an object with the name ns (you can use any name you want) to the window object that always exists in the browser. Inside this object, we can define the JavaScript function that we can invoke as follows:

```
ns.toggle();
```

And here's how to invoke it from a Vaadin view:

```
UI.getCurrent().getPage().executeJs("ns.toggle()");
```

We can accept parameters in the JavaScript function. For example, we might need the HTML element that we want to show/hide:

```
window.ns = {
  toggle: function(element) {
    ...
  }
}
```

Passing a parameter to the function from Java would look like this:

```
UI.getCurrent().getPage().executeJs("ns.toggle($0)",
    image);
```

As a reminder, the image object is a Vaadin component of type Image. The substring $0 is replaced with image when the invocation is made.

To implement the toggle functionality, we can use an existing library—jQuery. We can download the library file and place it into the project, but jQuery is also provided through a Content Delivery Network (CDN) which in practice means that we can get a link to the JavaScript file hosted in a public server. This is practical for our purposes here, so let's add it to the application:

```
@Route("javascript-integration")
@JsModule("script.js")
@JsModule("https://code.jquery.com/jquery-3.6.0.min.js")
public class JavascriptIntegrationView extends Div {
  ...
}
```

Now we can use jQuery in the script.js file:

```
window.ns = {
  toggle: function(element) {
    jQuery(element).fadeToggle();
    return `Toggled at ${new Date().toLocaleString()}`;
  }
}
```

The expression jQuery(element).fadeToggle() is one of the many functions available in the library. It hides or shows the selected element (element) using a fading animation. You'll have to run the example application if you want to see the fading effect.

We are returning the time in the browser at which the function was called just to learn how to use the returned value in the Java side. Here's the call to the function and how to use the returned value:

```
Button button = new Button("Toggle visibility", event -> {
  UI.getCurrent().getPage()
      .executeJs("return ns.toggle($0)", image)
      .then(value -> Notification.show(value.asString())));
});
```

Since the call to the JavaScript function is asynchronous, we have to use the then(SerializableConsumer) method to consume the returned value when it becomes available.

Invoking Java from JavaScript

We can also invoke a Java method in the server from a JavaScript function. For example, let's say we want to implement a click listener handled in the client side and call a server-side method from it. To set up things, we can add an init method to the script.js file:

```
window.ns = {
  init: function(element, view) {
  },

  toggle: function(element) {
    jQuery(element).fadeToggle();
    return `Toggled at ${new Date().toLocaleString()}`;
  }
}
```

We can call this method from Java as follows:

```
public JavascriptIntegrationView() {
  ...

  UI.getCurrent().getPage()
      .executeJs("return ns.init($0, $1)", image, this);

  ...
}
```

The init(element, view) function is called only once when the view is requested. We are passing the element (image) we want to initialize and the view itself. We can use the view object later to call Java methods from the script. But first, let's add the server-side method. This method should be annotated with @ClientCallable:

```
...
public class JavascriptIntegrationView extends Div {

  ...

  @ClientCallable
  public void showClickNotification(Integer x, Integer y) {
      var message = String.format("Clicked at %d, %d", x, y);
      Notification.show(message, 3000, Position.BOTTOM_END);
  }

}
```

Now, we can implement the function and see how to call the Java method from it:

```
window.ns = {
  init: function(element, view) {
    element.onclick = event =>
        view.$server.showClickNotification(event.clientX,
            event.clientY);
  },

  ...
}
```

The $server object is added by Vaadin. With this object, we can invoke the methods marked with @ClientCallable in the corresponding Java class. Figure 9-9 shows the result after clicking the toggle button and the image itself.

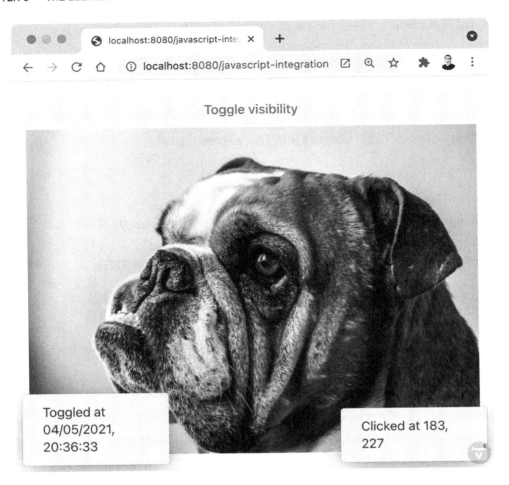

Figure 9-9. *A custom JavaScript component in action*

Summary

This chapter provided you with the tools you need to implement functionality that is not included in the core of Vaadin. You learned how to use the Element API to create and manipulate HTML elements in the browser. You saw how this API allows you to set CSS styles. You also learned how to include JavaScript files in your application and how to call JavaScript functions in the browser from server-side Java methods and server-side Java methods from JavaScript functions in the browser.

CHAPTER 10

Custom Styles and Responsiveness

In Chapter 1, you learned the fundamentals of Cascading Style Sheets (CSS) and how to write rules to change the appearance of an HTML document. Vaadin allows you to use CSS not only through the Element API (as you learned in Chapter 9) but in separate *.css* files that you can add to your project.

In addition to CSS, Vaadin includes components that ease the quick implementation of responsive UIs. A responsive UI adapts its structure according to the size of the screen in which it is rendered. This is something useful, when you want to support devices such as mobile phones that have narrow widths and long heights.

Built-In Themes

Vaadin manages the application styles in themes. A theme is a set of CSS files and associated resources, like fonts and images, that define the appearance of the application. Things such as the main background and foreground colors, fonts, spacing, and how the UI adapts to different view sizes are defined in the CSS rules that form the theme. There are two themes in Vaadin:

- **Lumo:** The default theme. We have been using this theme in the examples of the previous chapters.

- **Material:** A Vaadin theme based on Google's Material Design. Visit *https://material.io* for more information on Material Design.

Both themes come with two variants—light and dark.

© Alejandro Duarte 2021
A. Duarte, *Practical Vaadin*, https://doi.org/10.1007/978-1-4842-7179-7_10

An application can define a theme using the @Theme annotation in a class that implements the AppShellConfigurator interface. For example, the following snippet shows how to activate the Material theme (see Figure 10-1):

```
@Theme(themeClass = Material.class)
public class AppConfiguration implements AppShellConfigurator {
}
```

Figure 10-1. *The Material theme*

> **Tip**   You can deactivate the default Lumo theme using the @NoTheme annotation. This is useful when you want to take full control on the CSS files that are loaded and style your application from scratch. If Vaadin doesn't find a @Theme or @NoTheme annotation, the Lumo theme is used by default.

Using Theme Variants

Like a theme, a theme variant is a set of CSS files and associated resources. The difference lies in the fact that you can have only one theme per application while you can have multiple variants, one of which is active at a time. Both the Lumo and the Material themes include two variants. Here is how you can activate the dark variant of the Lumo theme (see Figure 10-2):

```
@Theme(themeClass = Lumo.class, variant = Lumo.DARK)
public class AppConfiguration implements AppShellConfigurator {
}
```

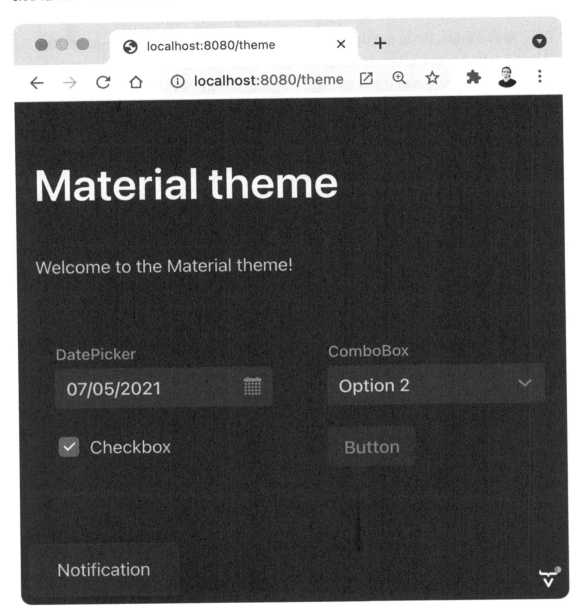

Figure 10-2. *The dark variant of the Lumo theme*

Note   If you have been trying the examples of this book or coding your own Vaadin applications, try changing their active theme. It's as simple as adding an annotation! Try the dark variant of the Material theme and see how it looks like. Keep in mind that it's not possible to have multiple themes. It is possible to have several theme variants (even custom ones) and change them at runtime (see *https://vaadin.com/learn/tutorials/toggle-dark-theme*).

Using Component Variants

Several Vaadin components include theme variants. A component theme variant affects only the component that includes the variant. For example, you can make a button look more prominent by adding the ButtonVariant.LUMO_PRIMARY variant:

```
Button button = new Button("Primary ");
button.addThemeVariants(ButtonVariant.LUMO_PRIMARY);
```

Figure 10-3 shows several buttons and text fields with different theme variants.

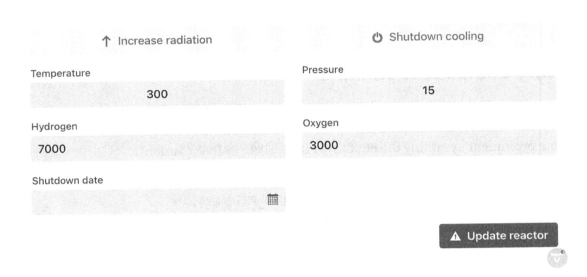

Figure 10-3. *Component theme variants*

Tip   Explore the variants that are available using the autocompletion feature of your IDE.

Styling with CSS

With what we have seen so far, we have four possible styles for Vaadin applications—two themes with two variants each. Now let's see how to expand the options by adding custom CSS rules that modify the available themes.

Importing CSS Files

We saw in Chapter 9 how to set custom CSS properties for a specific component or HTML element in the UI using the Element APIs. For example, we can add a border with a shadow to a Div component as follows:

```
Div div = new Div();
Style style = div.getStyle();
style.set("border", "1em solid #333");
style.set("box-shadow", "1em 1em 1em #777");
```

This is a quick and easy way to change the styles of UI components. However, when you want to change the overall look and feel of your application, it's better to have separate CSS files that can be used by multiple views.

Let's see how we can add custom CSS rules to a Vaadin application. Figure 10-4 shows a simple view with an H1, a TextField, a Button, and no custom CSS.

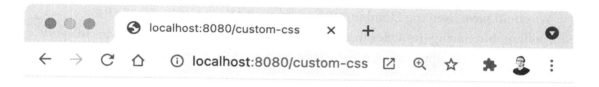

Figure 10-4. *A view with default theme and styles*

A frequent question developers ask me is how to decrease the space before and after an H1 component. This is understandable since often an H1 component is the topmost component in a view or section of a UI, and it might be necessary to optimize space usage. Fortunately, adjusting this is easy with CSS:

```
h1 {
  margin-top: 0.15em;
  margin-bottom: 0;
}
```

We can put this CSS in a file inside the *frontend/* directory, use any name we want for the file (e.g., *custom-styles.css*), and load it in a view using the @CssImport annotation:

```
@Route("custom-css")
@CssImport("./custom-styles.css")
public class CustomCss extends Composite<Component> {
}
```

We could have used the Element API and set the CSS properties for the H1 component, but having the styles in a separate file allows us to reuse the styles in every H1 component in the application more easily. Figure 10-5 shows the result.

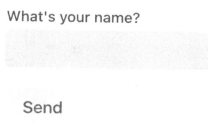

Figure 10-5. *Custom CSS files added to a view*

Caution   The files that you import using the @CssImport annotation are included in the application bundle. This means that a view will be affected by the contents of CSS files imported by other views.

Using Lumo Theme Properties

The Lumo theme includes a set of CSS properties (or variables) that allow quickly making general changes to the theme. These properties can be seen as parameters of the theme and adjust the styles of all the components when applicable.

Tip   CSS properties start with --.

You can set the value of the CSS properties used by the Lumo theme in a CSS file that you can import using the @CssImport annotation as shown in the previous section. The following example shows how to change the font and the roundness of the UI components (see the result in Figure 10-6):

```
html {
  --lumo-font-family: "Courier New", Courier, monospace;
  --lumo-border-radius: 0px;
}
```

Figure 10-6. *Customizing the Lumo theme with CSS properties*

There are many CSS properties defined in the Lumo theme. Listing 10-1 shows an example of some of the properties that are available.

Listing 10-1. A custom Vaadin theme based on Lumo properties

```
html {
  --lumo-font-family: "Courier New", Courier, monospace;
  --lumo-font-size: 1rem;
```

```
--lumo-font-size-xxxl: 3rem;
--lumo-font-size-xxl: 2.25rem;
--lumo-font-size-xl: 1.75rem;
--lumo-font-size-l: 1.375rem;
--lumo-font-size-m: 1.125rem;
--lumo-font-size-s: 1rem;
--lumo-font-size-xs: 0.875rem;
--lumo-font-size-xxs: 0.8125rem;
--lumo-line-height-m: 1.4;
--lumo-line-height-s: 1.2;
--lumo-line-height-xs: 1.1;
--lumo-border-radius: 0px;
--lumo-size-xl: 4rem;
--lumo-size-l: 3rem;
--lumo-size-m: 2.5rem;
--lumo-size-s: 2rem;
--lumo-size-xs: 1.75rem;
--lumo-space-xl: 1.75rem;
--lumo-space-l: 1.125rem;
--lumo-space-m: 0.5rem;
--lumo-space-s: 0.25rem;
--lumo-space-xs: 0.125rem;
--lumo-shade-5pct: rgba(26, 26, 26, 0.05);
--lumo-shade-10pct: rgba(26, 26, 26, 0.1);
--lumo-shade-20pct: rgba(26, 26, 26, 0.2);
--lumo-shade-30pct: rgba(26, 26, 26, 0.3);
--lumo-shade-40pct: rgba(26, 26, 26, 0.4);
--lumo-shade-50pct: rgba(26, 26, 26, 0.5);
--lumo-shade-60pct: rgba(26, 26, 26, 0.6);
--lumo-shade-70pct: rgba(26, 26, 26, 0.7);
--lumo-shade-80pct: rgba(26, 26, 26, 0.8);
--lumo-shade-90pct: rgba(26, 26, 26, 0.9);
--lumo-primary-text-color: rgb(235, 89, 5);
--lumo-primary-color-50pct: rgba(235, 89, 5, 0.5);
--lumo-primary-color-10pct: rgba(235, 89, 5, 0.1);
```

```
  --lumo-error-text-color: rgb(231, 24, 24);
  --lumo-error-color-50pct: rgba(231, 24, 24, 0.5);
  --lumo-error-color-10pct: rgba(231, 24, 24, 0.1);
  --lumo-success-text-color: rgb(62, 229, 170);
  --lumo-success-color-50pct: rgba(62, 229, 170, 0.5);
  --lumo-success-color-10pct: rgba(62, 229, 170, 0.1);
  --lumo-shade: hsl(0, 0%, 10%);
  --lumo-primary-color: hsl(22, 96%, 47%);
  --lumo-error-color: hsl(0, 81%, 50%);
  --lumo-success-color: hsl(159, 76%, 57%);
  --lumo-success-contrast-color: hsl(159, 29%, 10%);
}
```

Note   Explaining each property is out of the scope of this book. The properties are well documented in the official documentation at *https://vaadin.com/docs/ latest/ds/foundation*. At the time of writing, there's an online theme editor available at *https://demo.vaadin.com/lumo-editor*.

Adding CSS Classes to UI Components

You can add CSS classes to any component to style the component. For example:

```
Div div = new Div();
div.addClassName("styled-div");
```

And the corresponding CSS rule:

```
.styled-div {
  border: 1px solid red;
}
```

As your application grows, you'll need a consistent convention for the CSS classes that you define. A good way to improve maintainability is to use the name of the Java class (the view) in the CSS class name. Suppose we have the following view:

```
@Route("css-classes")
public class CssClassesView extends Composite<Component> {

  @Override
  protected Component initContent() {
    var header = new Div(VaadinIcon.VAADIN_H.create(),
        new H1("Title"),
        new Anchor("https://vaadin.com?utm_source=apressbook",
            "Log out"));

    Grid<String> grid = new Grid<>(String.class);
    grid.setItems("item1", "item2", "item3", "");

    var content = new Div(grid);

    var layout = new Div();
    layout.add(header, content);

    return layout;
  }

}
```

We are grouping the components in coherent parts (using the Div class), but other than that, we don't "care" how the view looks like when rendered in the browser. Figure 10-7 shows that this is indeed true!

Figure 10-7. *A view made of* Divs *without CSS styling*

However, if we add CSS class names to the important bits, we—or even better, a web designer who masters CSS—can completely change how the view looks like. We'll use the name of the Java class (CssClassesView) in the names of the CSS classes appending an appropriate string to differentiate between the components we want to style:

```
layout.addClassName(getClass().getSimpleName());
header.addClassName(getClass().getSimpleName() + "-header");
content.addClassName(getClass().getSimpleName() + "-content");
```

In the browser, these components are rendered as

```
<div class="CssClassView">
...
  <div class="CSSClassView-header">
...
<div class="CssClassView-content">
...
```

We can load a new CSS file as follows:

```
@Route("css-classes")
@CssImport("./custom-classes.css")
public class CssClassesView extends Composite<Component> {
    ...
}
```

Finally, we can style the view in the *custom-classes.css* file. Here's a backend Java developer's attempt (see Figure 10-8 for the result):

```
.CssClassesView {
    display: flex;
    flex-direction: column;
}

.CssClassesView-header {
    display: flex;
    flex-direction: row;
    justify-content: space-between;
    align-items: center;
    background: var(--lumo-primary-text-color);
    color: var(--lumo-primary-contrast-color);
    padding-left: 1em;
    padding-right: 1em;
}

.CssClassesView-header h1 {
    color: var(--lumo-primary-contrast-color);
}

.CssClassesView-header a {
    color: var(--lumo-primary-contrast-color);
}
```

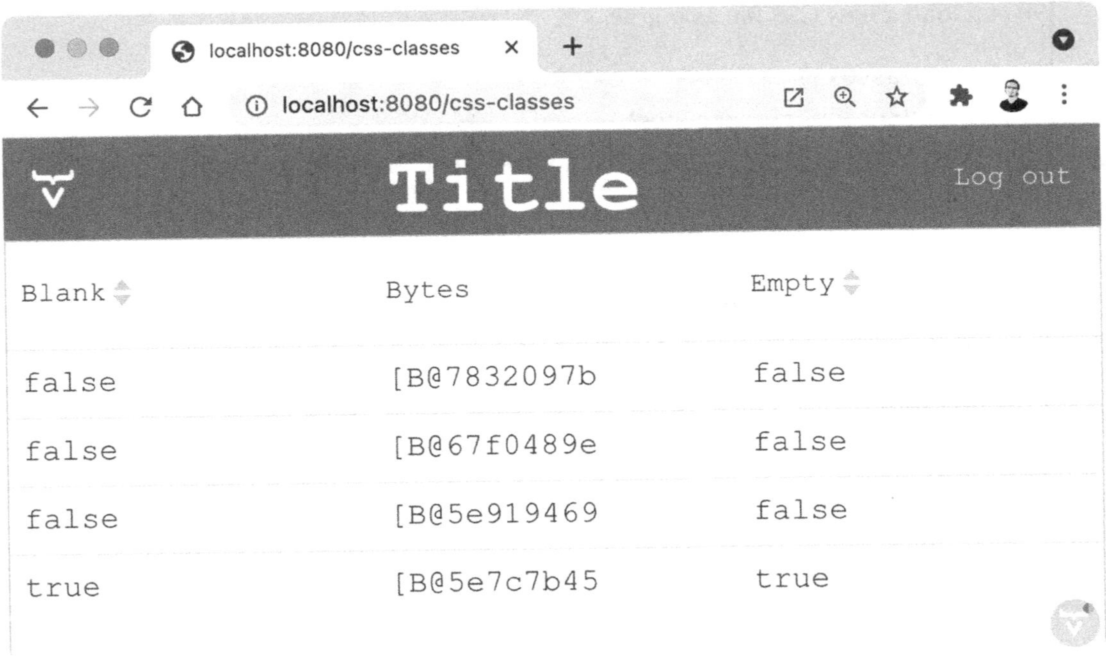
localhost:8080/css-classes
localhost:8080/css-classes
Title
Log out
Blank
Bytes
Empty
false
[B@7832097b
false
false
[B@67f0489e
false
false
[B@5e919469
false
true
[B@5e7c7b45
true

Figure 10-8. *Using CSS classes to style a view*

Styling Shadow DOM

Vaadin components are implemented as Web Components. A Web Component is a set of HTML resources that are encapsulated in a single reusable unit. For example, a `Button` is rendered in the browser as `<vaadin-button>`. Web Components include *shadow DOM* which is HTML that doesn't "contaminate" the HTML document in a page. This means that the styles in the Web Component won't be leaked to the rest of the page, and the styles in the page won't affect the Web Components. You can still style Web Components, but you need to do it in a special way.

Suppose we want to change the styles in the header of the `Grid` in the example of the previous section. If we inspect the DOM in the browser, we'll see that there's a `<th>` element inside the shadow DOM of a `<vaadin-grid>` Web Component. We can style this element using the following CSS selector:

```
:host th {
  background: var(--lumo-primary-color-10pct);
}
```

:host selects the shadow DOM. We are selecting <th> elements inside the shadow DOM of a Web Component. Which Web Component? We answer that in the @CssImport annotation. Suppose we put the previous CSS rule in a file with the name *vaadin-grid. css* (you can use any name). When we load this file, we can specify the Vaadin Web Component that we want to style (Figure 10-9 shows the result):

```
...
@CssImport(value = "./vaadin-grid.css", themeFor = "vaadin-grid")
public class CssClassesView extends Composite<Component> {
  ...
}
```

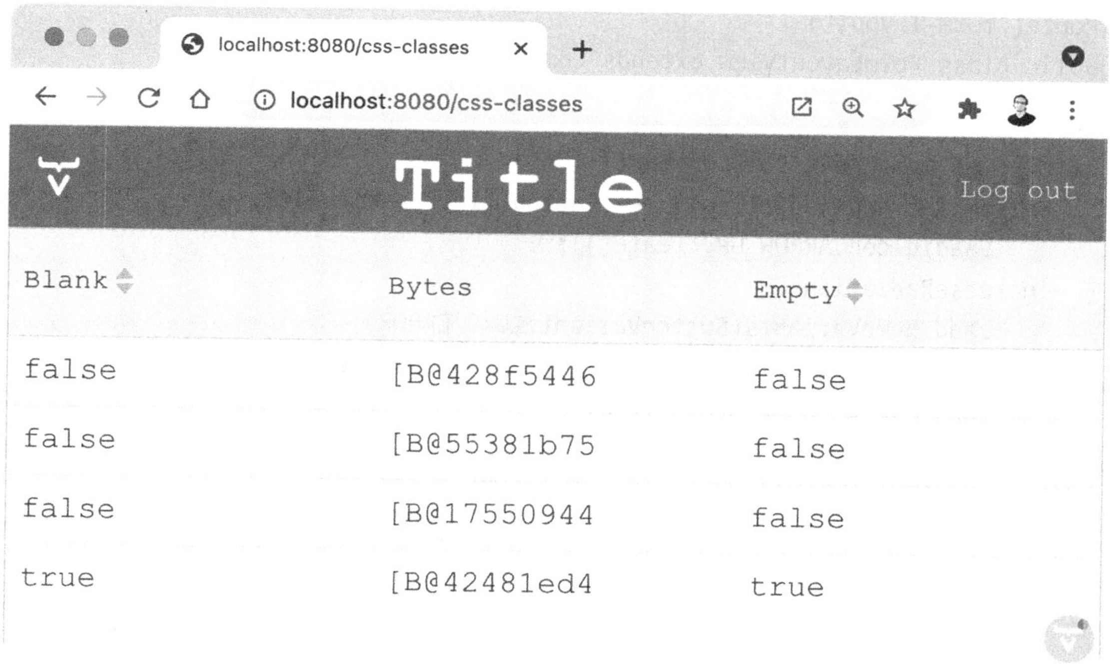

Figure 10-9. *Styling a Vaadin Web Component*

Responsive Web Design

Responsive web design is the use of techniques to make layouts and components adapt to different devices. Responsive web applications change their layout when used in different screen sizes.

Vaadin provides special components that ease the implementation of responsive UIs. When these components don't match your requirements, you can always use CSS to accomplish your goals.

FormLayout

The FormLayout component makes it easy to display other components in a number of columns that varies according to the width of the screen. It also places input components' labels on top of the components rather than to the side. In fact, we used FormLayout in Figure 10-3. Here's the implementation (focus your attention on the end of the constructor):

```
@Route("form-layout")
public class FormLayoutView extends Composite<Component> {

  @Override
  protected Component initContent() {
    Button increaseRadiation = new Button("Increase radiation",
        VaadinIcon.ARROW_UP.create());
    increaseRadiation
        .addThemeVariants(ButtonVariant.LUMO_ERROR);
    Button shutDownCooling = new Button("Shutdown cooling",
        VaadinIcon.POWER_OFF.create());
    shutDownCooling
        .addThemeVariants(ButtonVariant.LUMO_SUCCESS);
    NumberField temperature = new NumberField("Temperature");
    temperature
        .addThemeVariants(TextFieldVariant.LUMO_ALIGN_CENTER);
    NumberField pressure = new NumberField("Pressure");
    pressure
        .addThemeVariants(TextFieldVariant.LUMO_ALIGN_CENTER);
    NumberField hydrogen = new NumberField("Hydrogen");
    hydrogen
        .addThemeVariants(TextFieldVariant.LUMO_ALIGN_CENTER);
    NumberField oxygen = new NumberField("Oxygen");
    oxygen.addThemeVariants(TextFieldVariant.LUMO_ALIGN_CENTER);
```

```
DatePicker shutdownDate = new DatePicker("Shutdown date");
Button update = new Button("Update reactor",
    VaadinIcon.WARNING.create());
update.addThemeVariants(ButtonVariant.LUMO_PRIMARY);

FormLayout form = new FormLayout(increaseRadiation,
    shutDownCooling, temperature, pressure, hydrogen,
    oxygen, shutdownDate);

VerticalLayout layout = new VerticalLayout(
    new H1("Nuclear Reactor"), form, update);
layout.setAlignItems(Alignment.CENTER);
layout.setAlignSelf(Alignment.END, update);
return layout;
  }

}
```

Just by adding input components to a FormLayout, we get two columns in wide screens and one column in narrow ones. Figure 10-10 shows the view in a narrow window.

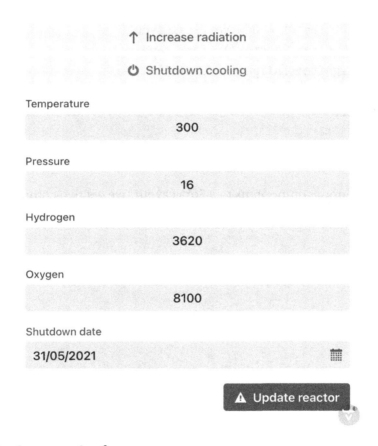

Figure 10-10. *A responsive form*

You can configure the number of columns to use for specific minimum widths. Here's an example:

```
form.setResponsiveSteps(
    new ResponsiveStep("1px", 1),
    new ResponsiveStep("600px", 2),
    new ResponsiveStep("800px", 3)
);
```

If a viewport (screen) is 800 pixels wide or more, the form will show three columns. If it's 600 pixels wide, two columns are used, and so forth. Figure 10-11 shows the form in a wide screen.

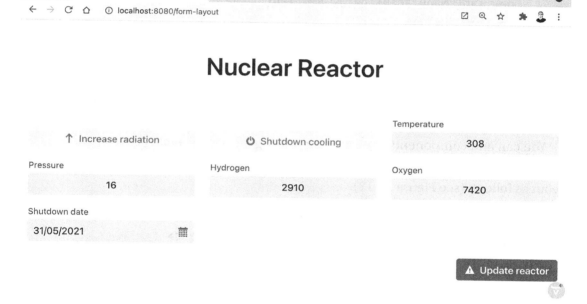

Figure 10-11. *Custom responsive steps*

AppLayout

The AppLayout component offers a popular style of layout for web applications. It includes a shared *navbar* (header), *drawer* (menu), and content area. This component implements RouterLayout so you can use the layout in multiple views. To use it as a router layout, you need to extend AppLayout. The following example shows how to add a logo to the navbar and a Tabs component to the drawer:

```java
public class BusinessAppLayout extends AppLayout {

  public BusinessAppLayout() {
    Image logo = new Image("https://i.imgur.com/GPpnszs.png",
        "Vaadin Logo");
    logo.setHeight("44px");
    addToNavbar(new DrawerToggle(), logo);

    Tabs tabs = new Tabs(new Tab("Home"), new Tab("CRM"),
        new Tab("Financial"), new Tab("Marketing"),
        new Tab("Sales"), new Tab("Inventory"),
        new Tab("Manufacturing"), new Tab("Supply chain"),
        new Tab("HR"));
    tabs.setOrientation(Tabs.Orientation.VERTICAL);
    addToDrawer(tabs);
  }

}
```

You can add components to each section using the addToNavbar(Component...) and addToDrawer(Component...) methods. The views in your application can use this layout as follows (see Figure 10-12):

```java
@Route(value = "app-layout", layout = BusinessAppLayout.class)
public class AppLayoutView extends Composite<Component> {

  @Override
  protected Component initContent() {
    return new VerticalLayout(new H1("Business Application"),
        new Button("Let's do business!",
            event -> Notification.show("Success!")));
  }

}
```

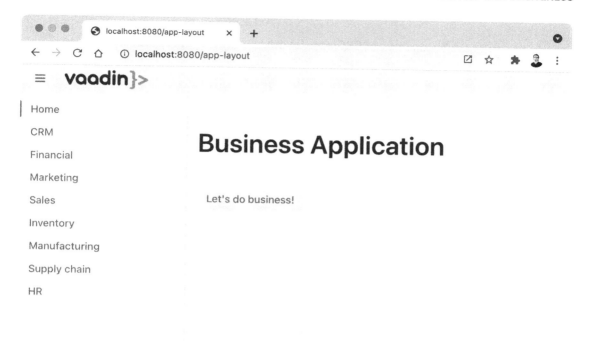

Figure 10-12. *A view using a router layout implemented with* AppLayout

The AppLayout component is responsive. If you resize the browser's window, you'll see that the drawer is shown or hidden accordingly. Users can toggle the visibility of the drawer by clicking the DrawerToggle in the upper-left corner of the view. Figure 10-13 shows the same view in a smaller window.

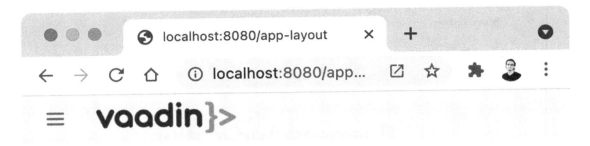

Business Application

Let's do business!

Figure 10-13. AppLayout *hiding the drawer in small viewports*

CSS Media Queries

CSS allows you to target different screen sizes to selectively apply styles. Let's see this in action as we develop a responsive view with a menu and a content area:

```
@Route("css")
@CssImport("./styles.css")
public class CssView extends Composite<Component> {

  @Override
  protected Component initContent() {
    Div menu = new Div(new RouterLink("Option 1", getClass()),
        new RouterLink("Option 2", getClass()),
        new RouterLink("Option 3", getClass()));
```

```
    menu.addClassName(getClass().getSimpleName() + "-menu");

    Div content = new Div(new H1("Hello!"), new Paragraph(
        "Try resizing the window to see the effect in the UI"));
    content
        .addClassName(getClass().getSimpleName() + "-content");

    Div layout = new Div(menu, content);
    layout.addClassName(getClass().getSimpleName());
    return layout;
  }

}
```

We added CSS class names to the important parts and imported the *styles.css* file. Let's use a mobile-first approach and style the application so that it looks good on small screens. For now, this is how the view is going to look like in all screen sizes. Here's the CSS (Figure 10-14 shows the result):

```
.CssView {
  display: flex;
  flex-direction: column;
  height: 100%;
}

.CssView-menu {
  display: flex;
  flex-direction: row;
  background-color: var(--lumo-primary-color-10pct);
}

.CssView-menu a {
  margin-left: 1em;
  white-space: nowrap;
}

.CssView-content {
  margin-left: 1em;
}
```

Since we are targeting mobile devices which most likely are used in portrait mode (height longer than width), it makes sense to show the components in a column. That's why we set a column direction in a flex display for the view. The menu is configured as a flex row so that all the options are shown in a horizontal fashion on the top of the screen. We also added a margin to the left of each option (`<a>` elements) and configured `nowrap` to avoid showing multiple lines of text in some browsers. For the content area, we added a small margin to separate it from the border of the view.

Figure 10-14. *A mobile-first design*

With the mobile version ready and set by default, we can target larger screens by adding CSS Media Queries. These queries allow you to apply styles according to the characteristics of the device in which the page is shown. For example, we can target screens with a minimum width of 800 pixels as follows:

```
@media screen and (min-width: 800px) {
  .CssView {
    display: flex;
    flex-direction: row;
  }

  .CssView-menu {
    display: flex;
    flex-direction: column;
     padding: 1em;
  }

  .CssView-menu a {
    margin-bottom: 1em;
    margin-left: 0em;
  }
}
```

These styles will override any styles that are set outside the media query (i.e., the mobile styles we already have in place). We are changing a few things here. First, the view is now a row instead of a column. We can show the menu on the left instead of on the top on larger screens. Second, the options in the menu are a column. And third, we adjust the margin of the options by adding space at the bottom of each option and removing the space on the left that we added for the mobile version (remember that we are overriding styles). Figure 10-15 shows the effect on the view on a bigger browser window.

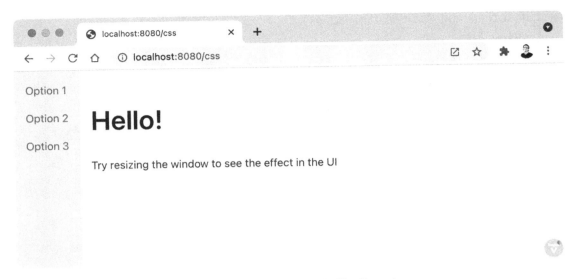

Figure 10-15. *Responsive design using CSS Media Queries*

Summary

This chapter really boosted your Vaadin skills! You learned about the built-in themes available in Vaadin and how to use both theme and component variants. You learned how to style your applications with CSS by importing custom CSS files and how to quickly adjust the look and feel using Lumo theme properties. You saw how you can add CSS classes to individual UI components and how to set styles in the shadow DOM of a Vaadin Web Component.

You also learned about responsive web design using the `FormLayout` and `AppLayout` components, as well as CSS Media Queries to target different screen sizes.

The next chapter continues the exploration of client-side technologies by introducing you to Vaadin Flow—a way to implement views in TypeScript.

CHAPTER 11

Client-Side Views with TypeScript

We have been writing Java code in the previous chapters of this book. Let's take a quick break and have some fun implementing views using a different programming language: TypeScript.

Vaadin Flow vs. Vaadin Fusion

The term *Vaadin* is widely used to refer to the server-side classes that allow you to code web UIs in Java. However, Vaadin also lets you implement UIs using the TypeScript programming language. Online, you'll find terms such as the Vaadin Platform, Vaadin Flow, Vaadin Fusion, and (plain) Vaadin. Let's clear up some definitions:

- **Vaadin:** A set of tools to develop Java web applications. This includes a free open source web framework, an online tool to generate new projects, documentation, and paid subscriptions with additional tools and services on top of the free offer. You can implement UI using Java, TypeScript, or both. Often, the term *Vaadin* is used to refer to *Vaadin Flow* or *Vaadin Fusion*.

- **Vaadin Platform:** A synonym of *Vaadin* that is declining in use.

- **Vaadin Flow:** The part of Vaadin that allows you to implement UIs in Java.

- **Vaadin Fusion:** The part of Vaadin that allows you to implement UIs in TypeScript and which this chapter serves as an introduction to.

© Alejandro Duarte 2021
A. Duarte, *Practical Vaadin*, https://doi.org/10.1007/978-1-4842-7179-7_11

> **Note**   Some refer to Vaadin Flow and Vaadin Fusion as the two *web frameworks* in Vaadin. Some use the word *library*. Others, the term *module*. I prefer to think of them as *features*. I think of Vaadin Flow as Java and Vaadin Fusion as TypeScript.

Quick Introduction to TypeScript

TypeScript is a superset of JavaScript. Every JavaScript program is also a TypeScript program. TypeScript adds static typing and compiles programs to JavaScript.

Installing the TypeScript Compiler

You don't have to install any additional tools if you want to use TypeScript in a Vaadin application. However, if you want to try the code in the next sections, you'll need *Node.js*. You can download an installer at `https://nodejs.org`. Node.js includes *npm*—a tool to manage JavaScript packages. You can check that the tool works by running the following command and confirming that you get a version reported as output:

```
> npm --version
```

Using *npm*, you can install the TypeScript package as follows:

```
> npm install --global typescript
```

This package includes a TypeScript compiler. You can check that the compiler is ready by running the following command and confirming that you get a version reported:

```
> tsc -version
Version 4.2.4
```

Implementing "Hello, World" in TypeScript

A "Hello, World" in TypeScript requires one line of code:

```
console.log("Hello, World!");
```

If we put this line in a file named *hello.ts*, we can compile it using the following command:

```
> tsc hello.ts
```

By default, the TypeScript compiler creates a new *hello.js* file in the same directory. To run the program, we can execute the following command:

```
> node hello.js
```

We should get the expected output in the terminal:

```
Hello, World!
```

Let's make a parallel with the Java world. The Java compiler, *javac*, takes a *.java* source file and produces a *.class* bytecode file. The *java* tool starts a JVM and runs the *.class* file. On the TypeScript side, the TypeScript compiler, *tsc*, takes a *.ts* source file and produces a *.js* JavaScript file. The *node* tool runs the *.js* file. Node.js is a runtime for JavaScript, just like a web browser also is.

Static Typing

Reading TypeScript code is easy if you have experience with Java. Take a look at this example:

```
class Bicycle {
  private color: string;
  private speed: number = 0;
  private gear: number = 1;

  public constructor(color: string) {
    this.color = color;
  }

  public speedUp(increase: number): void {
    this.speed += increase;
  }

  public applyBreak(decrease: number): number {
    return this.speed -= decrease;
  }
```

```typescript
  public changeGear(newGear: number): number {
    return this.gear = newGear;
}

public print(): void {
    console.log(
`${this.color} bicycle: ${this.speed} Km/h (${this.gear})`);
  }
}
```

I'm pretty sure that you understand every single bit of this class. I coded it in a way that would be as easy as possible to understand for a Java developer, but TypeScript includes features to make the code more concise.

Note   Teaching all the features of TypeScript is out of the scope of this book. You can find excellent learning resources online. For example, the official TypeScript website (*www.typescriptlang.org*) includes documentation and a handbook. I also recommend *Essential TypeScript* by Adam Freeman if you want to learn the language and its ecosystem in depth.

We can use the Bicycle class by adding some code at the end of the file (that I have named *bicycle.ts*):

```typescript
class Bicycle {
  ...
}

let redBicycle = new Bicycle("red");
redBicycle.print();
redBicycle.speedUp(10);
redBicycle.changeGear(2);
redBicycle.speedUp(10);
redBicycle.changeGear(3);
redBicycle.speedUp(8);
redBicycle.applyBreak(5);
redBicycle.print();
```

We can compile the file, run it, and see the output:

```
> tsc bicycle.ts
> node bicycle.js
red bicycle: 0 Km/h (1)
red bicycle: 23 Km/h (3)
```

One of the advantages of TypeScript code over plain JavaScript is that it is type-safe. If we use an incorrect type in a parameter when calling, say, the speedUp function wrongly passing a string instead of a number, we'll see a compilation error:

```
> tsc bicycle.ts
bicycle.ts:38:20 - error TS2345: Argument of type 'string' is not
assignable to parameter of type 'number'.

38 redBicycle.speedUp("10");
                      ~~~~

Found 1 error.
```

The type-safe syntax is optional in TypeScript. You can use plain JavaScript if and where you want. This makes it possible to include any other JavaScript library in your TypeScript programs.

Web Components with Lit

Like we saw in Chapter 1, a Web Component is a custom element with encapsulated logic, styles, and structure. On the client side, Vaadin components are implemented as Web Components. For example, a Button is rendered as a <vaadin-button> in the browser. *Lit* is a JavaScript library for implementing Web Components, and it's the base for creating client-side views in TypeScript using Vaadin Fusion.

Creating a New Lit Project

To help you play with Lit and experiment with your own Web Components, let's create a new project with the minimum configuration needed. The project is based on *npm* and will include a web server for quick experimentation. We can start by creating a new directory for the project in the hard drive with the name *lit-element/* (you can use any name you want). Inside this project, we need a *package.json* file with the following contents:

```
{
  "scripts": {
    "start": "tsc && wds"
  },
  "dependencies": {
    "lit": "*"
  },
  "devDependencies": {
    "@web/dev-server": "^0.1.17"
  }
}
```

The *package.json* file is similar to the *pom.xml* file which declares the dependencies of a Java project. You can add more dependencies to this file when you need them. In this case, we are defining a script with the name start that invokes the TypeScript compiler and starts the web server. We are adding Lit as a runtime dependency and a web server (dev-server) as a development dependency.

Next, we need to configure the TypeScript compiler. This can be done with a *tsconfig. json* file. This file is read by the *tsc* tool and allows us to configure things such as the source directory, target directory, and many other options. Here's what we need for now:

```
{
  "compilerOptions": {
    "target": "es2018",
    "module": "esnext",
    "moduleResolution": "node",
    "experimentalDecorators": true
  }
}
```

This sets the compiled JavaScript version we want to generate (ES2018), the module system to use (ESNext), how TypeScript looks up modules in files (Node), and enables experimental decorators.

In addition to this, we need to configure the web server by creating a *web-dev-server. config* file with the following content:

```
export default ({
  nodeResolve: true
});
```

To install the dependencies, run

```
> npm install
```

The *npm* tool autogenerates a *package-lock.json* file. This file could be seen as the equivalent of the *effective POM* in Maven, and it contains the exact dependency trees used to build the project. Additionally, the *npm* tool creates a *node_modules/* directory where the actual files that make up the libraries are. This is similar to the *WEB-INF/libs* in a Java WAR file.

Now we are ready to code!

Creating a "Hello, World" Web Component

We need a new TypeScript file to implement the Web Component. Let's call it *hello-web-component.ts*. In this file, the first thing we need is to include the objects and classes we want to use from the Lit library. Here's how:

```
import {LitElement, html} from 'lit';
import {customElement } from 'lit/decorators.js';
```

We are importing the LitElement class to create new custom elements, the html tagged template (a function that can process a template literal), and the customElement decorator (like an annotation in Java).

Let's code the simplest "Hello, World" as a Web Component now:

```
import { LitElement, html } from 'lit';
import { customElement } from 'lit/decorators.js';

@customElement('hello-web-component')
export class HelloWebComponent extends LitElement {
  render() {
    return html`
```

```
      <div>Hello, World!</div>
    `;
  }
}
```

To define a custom HTML element, we need a class that extends `LitElement` and that is decorated with `@customElement`. The name of the tag should always contain a dash (-). In the `render()` function, we can return the HTML that will form the structure of the Web Component in the browser using the `html` tagged template function.

To use the Web Component, we only need to create an HTML file that imports the JavaScript file produced by the TypeScript compiler and add the `<hello-web-component>` element somewhere in the document. For example, we can create the following *demo.html* file:

```
<html>
<head>
<meta charset="UTF-8">
<title>Web Component example</title>
</head>
<body>

<script type="module" src="hello-web-component.js"></script>
<hello-web-component></hello-web-component>

</body>
</html>
```

To start the web server, we can invoke the `start` script that we defined in the *package.json* file:

```
> npm run start
```

You can request the page using *http://localhost:8000/demo.html*. Figure 11-1 shows the result in the browser.

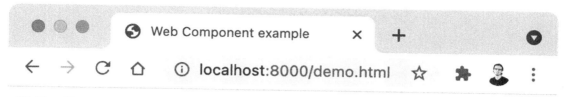

Hello, World!

Figure 11-1. *A Web Component implemented with Lit*

Client-Side Views with Vaadin Fusion

Now that we have a basic understanding of TypeScript and Lit, let's put everything together and implement a client-side view with Vaadin Fusion. Client-side views are a good option when you want to introduce horizontal scaling (adding more servers) or need client-side functionality not currently provided by Vaadin Flow (e.g., offline capabilities).

Enabling Client-Side Bootstrapping

Let's say you have a regular Vaadin application with one view:

```
@Route("flow")
public class FlowView extends Composite<Div> {

  public FlowView() {
    getContent().add(new Text("Hello from Vaadin Flow!"));
  }

}
```

When you have at least a view implemented with Vaadin Flow, the framework detects it and sets up a client-side bootstrap to handle all further communication between the server and the client. If you inspect the *target/* directory of a Vaadin application, you'll find two files that are autogenerated by Vaadin (see Figure 11-2).

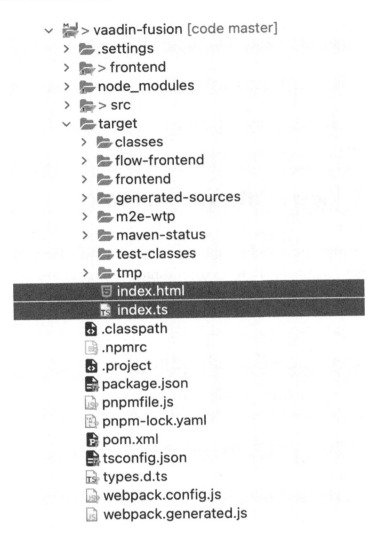

Figure 11-2. Generated index.html and index.ts files

The *index.html* and *index.ts* files are served when you request the application in the browser and are created when you compile the application. To be able to implement client-side views with Vaadin Fusion, we need to set up our own versions of these files. The easiest way to do this is to compile the project and simply copy the two files from the *target/* directory to the *frontend/* directory. You can do this using your IDE or the command line:

```
> mvn package
> cp target/index.* frontend/
```

In the *index.html* file, we need to add a custom style to make sure that the client-side views match the theme of the application. We just have to add the following inside the `<style>` section:

```
<custom-style>
  <style include="lumo-typography"></style>
</custom-style>
```

And in the *index.ts* file, import the Lumo theme:

```
import '@vaadin/vaadin-lumo-styles/all-imports';
```

That's it. The application is ready for client-side views with Vaadin Flow!

Adding a Client-Side View

To add a client-side view implemented with TypeScript and Lit, we need to create a new *.ts* file in the *frontend/* directory, import it, and define the route in the *index.ts* file. You can use any name you want for the file. As an optional convention, let's use the name of the custom HTML element (configured with the `@customElement` decorator) as the name of the file adding the *.ts* extension (*fusion-view.ts*):

```
import { LitElement, customElement, html } from 'lit-element';

@customElement('fusion-view')
export class FusionView extends LitElement {
  render() {
    return html`
      <div>Hello from Vaadin Fusion!</div>
    `;
  }
}
```

In the *index.ts* file, we can import this file as follows (no need to specify the file extension):

```
...
import './fusion-view';
...
```

Finally, we need to define the route for the view. A client-side route specifies a route (used in the URL) and an HTML element to show when the route is invoked. For this, we can modify the routes constant as follows:

```
const routes = [
  { path: 'fusion', component: 'fusion-view'},
  // for server-side, the next magic line sends all unmatched routes:
  ...serverSideRoutes // IMPORTANT: this must be the last entry in the
array
];
```

This sets the fusion as the route to render the fusion-view Web Component that we previously created. This means that the view can be invoked using *http://localhost:8080/fusion*. See Figure 11-3.

Hello from Vaadin Fusion!

Figure 11-3. *A client-side view implemented with Vaadin Fusion*

Adding Vaadin Components

The UI components that we have been using in Java throughout the book are implemented in the client side as Web Components. The Web can use this Web Components in client-side views as well without having a Java counterpart in the server. To use a Vaadin component, we have to import it first. For example, to use a Vaadin button, we can add the following import declaration in the TypeScript file that contains the view implementation:

```
import '@vaadin/vaadin-button/vaadin-button';
```

Then, we can use the `<vaadin-button>` component in the `render()` function:

```
@customElement('some-view')
export class SomeView extends LitElement {
  render() {
    return html`
      <vaadin-button>Click me!</vaadin-button>
    `;
  }
}
```

We can apply the same concept to all the components in the Vaadin collection. Here's an example that shows how to combine input components and layouts in a client-side view:

```
import { LitElement, customElement, html } from 'lit-element';
import '@vaadin/vaadin-ordered-layout/vaadin-vertical-layout';
import '@vaadin/vaadin-ordered-layout/vaadin-horizontal-layout';
import '@vaadin/vaadin-combo-box/vaadin-combo-box';
import '@vaadin/vaadin-button/vaadin-button';
import '@vaadin/vaadin-text-field/vaadin-text-field';
import '@vaadin/vaadin-icons';

@customElement('vaadin-components-view')
export class VaadinComponentsView extends LitElement {
  render() {
    return html`
      <vaadin-vertical-layout theme="padding">
        <h1>Vaadin Components</h1>
        <vaadin-horizontal-layout>
          <vaadin-combo-box
            placeholder='Select a language...'
            items='[
              "Java", "TypeScript", "JavaScript"
            ]'
          ></vaadin-combo-box>
```

```
      <vaadin-button>
        <iron-icon icon="vaadin:check"></iron-icon>
        Select
      </vaadin-button>
    </vaadin-horizontal-layout>
  </vaadin-vertical-layout>
  `;
  }
}
```

Always remember to import the file and define a route for the view in the *index.ts* file (see Figure 11-4):

```
import './vaadin-components-view';
...
const routes = [
  { path: 'fusion', component: 'fusion-view'},
  { path: 'vaadin-components', component: 'vaadin-components-view'},
  ...serverSideRoutes
];
```

Vaadin Components

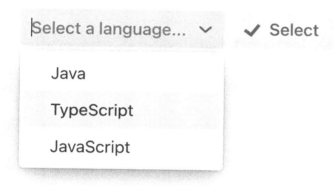

Figure 11-4. *Vaadin web components*

Event Listeners

To respond to user interaction, we can use listeners. For example, we can add a click listener to a button as follows:

```
<vaadin-button @click='${this.clickHandler}'>Click me!</vaadin-button>
```

The greet function is then defined at the class level:

```
clickHandler() {
  ... logic here ...
}
```

When we need to modify other HTML elements, we can use the query decorator. Here's a view that contains a <vaadin-text-field>, a <vaadin-button>, and a <vaadin-notification> that work together to show a personalized greeting to the user (see Figure 11-5):

```
import { LitElement, customElement, html, query } from 'lit-element';
import '@vaadin/vaadin-ordered-layout/vaadin-vertical-layout';
import '@vaadin/vaadin-text-field/vaadin-text-field';
import '@vaadin/vaadin-button/vaadin-button';
import '@vaadin/vaadin-notification/vaadin-notification';

@customElement('greeting-view')
export class GreetingView extends LitElement {

  @query('#greeting-notification')
  private notification: any;

  private name: string = '';

  render() {
    return html`
      <vaadin-vertical-layout theme="padding">
        <h1>Greeting</h1>
        <vaadin-text-field
          id='name'
          label="What's your name?"
          @value-changed=
             '${(event:any) => this.setName(event.detail.value)}'
        ></vaadin-text-field>
        <vaadin-button @click='${this.greet}'>
          Send
        </vaadin-button>
      </vaadin-vertical-layout>
      <vaadin-notification id='greeting-notification'>
      </vaadin-notification>
    `;
  }
```

```
  setName(newName: string) {
    this.name = newName;
    this.notification.close();
  }

  greet() {
    let message:string = 'Hello, ' + this.name;
    this.notification.renderer = (root:any) =>
        root.textContent = message;
    this.notification.open();
  }
}
```

The @query decorator makes the notification object to hold the <vaadin-notification> element. We can later use this object to set a custom renderer to show a customized message in the notification that is shown to the user. Notice also how we update the *model* when the value in the text field changes. In this example, the model is simply a string object in the class (name).

Reactive Views

Even when the example of the previous section is valid and works well, one of the most interesting features of Lit is the possibility to define the HTML content of a component as a function of the state encapsulated in the class that implements the Web Component. Let's see this in action by reimplementing the previous example in a reactive way.

We need a set of imports and a class:

```
import { LitElement, customElement, html, state } from 'lit-element';
import '@vaadin/vaadin-ordered-layout/vaadin-vertical-layout';
import '@vaadin/vaadin-text-field/vaadin-text-field';
import '@vaadin/vaadin-button/vaadin-button';
import '@vaadin/vaadin-notification/vaadin-notification';

@customElement('reactive-view')
export class ReactiveView extends LitElement {
  // TODO
}
```

Inside the class, we can define the state of the view. What constitutes the state of this view? We have a text field and a notification both with values we cannot predict. The state of the view is determined by the name in the text field and the visibility of the notification (visible/hidden). We can add these two values as properties of the ReactiveView class and decorate them with state():

```
@customElement('reactive-view')
export class ReactiveView extends LitElement {

  @state()
  private notificationOpen = false;

  @state()
  private name = '';

}
```

The state() decorator marks the property as reactive. We can use these reactive properties in the render() method. But before doing this, it's worth thinking about other operations that are needed. What changes do we need to make to the view? When the user types a name, we need to update the model (the name and notificationOpen properties). When the user clicks the button, we need to update the model (the notificationOpen property). Additionally, we also need to set the text in the notification, but we'll implement this later. Let's add the following method for now:

```
@customElement('reactive-view')
export class ReactiveView extends LitElement {

  ...

  setName(newName: string) {
    this.name = newName;
    this.notificationOpen = false;
  }
```

```
  greet() {
    this.notificationOpen = true;
  }
}
```

Now we can implement the render() method as a function of the state:

```
...

@customElement('reactive-view')
export class ReactiveView extends LitElement {

  ...

  render() {
    return html`
      <vaadin-vertical-layout theme="padding">
        <h1>Greeting</h1>
        <vaadin-text-field
          label="What's your name?"
          @value-changed='${(event:CustomEvent) => this.setName(event.
          detail.value)}'
        ></vaadin-text-field>
        <vaadin-button @click='${this.greet}'>Send</vaadin-button>
      </vaadin-vertical-layout>
      <vaadin-notification
        .opened="${this.notificationOpen}"
      ></vaadin-notification>
    `;
  }

  setName(newName: string) {
    this.name = newName;
    this.notificationOpen = false;
  }
```

```
greet() {
  this.notificationOpen = true;
}
}
```

The way the `<vaadin-notification>` element works requires us to define a renderer to show the text we want to show in the notification. To do this, we can modify the element as follows:

```
<vaadin-notification
  .opened="${this.notificationOpen}"
  .renderer=${this.greetingRenderer}
></vaadin-notification>
```

And `greetingRenderer` needs to be defined as a property in the class:

```
greetingRenderer = (root: HTMLElement) => {
  let message = 'Hello, ' + this.name;
  root.textContent = message;
}
```

That's it. We now have a reactive view! Figure 11-5 shows a screenshot.

Greeting

What's your name?

Reactive Jussi

Send

Hello, Reactive
Jussi

Figure 11-5. *A reactive client-side view*

A Word on Offline Capabilities

So far, we haven't directly "talked" to the server. All the views are 100% client side. Once loaded in the browser, a view continues to operate even if you deactivate the network connection. You cannot request the view again nor request other views, but the view already rendered in the browser should keep working. There's no communication going on between the client and the server. Figure 11-6 shows a screenshot of the previous section's example working without a network connection (in Chrome you can simulate this using the developer tools and selecting *Offline* in the *Network* tab).

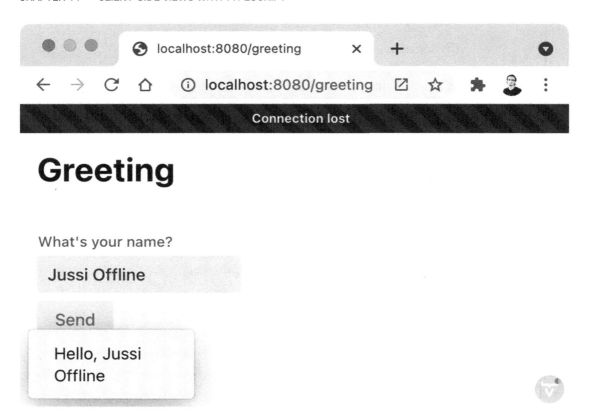

Figure 11-6. *A client-side view continues to work without a network connection*

Implementing offline capabilities is out of the scope of this book. If you want to learn more about this topic, the official Vaadin documentation has plenty of resources on this topic (see *https://vaadin.com/docs/latest/fusion/tutorials/in-depth-course/ installing-and-offline-pwa*).

Note   In case you are curious, Jussi is a friend of mine who predicted that I would write a new book this year (2021) well before Apress reached out to me with the idea.

Summary

In this chapter, you learned the basics of Vaadin Fusion. You learned how to compile TypeScript programs and how to use Lit to implement Web Components. You also learned how to implement client-side views as Web Components implemented with TypeScript and the Lit library.

My objective with this chapter was to offer you a first approach to Vaadin Fusion. There are many topics that we didn't cover here. I believe that explaining Vaadin Fusion in depth would require a complete book. However, it's important that you got the big picture so that you can take over more advanced tutorials and in-depth documentation. You can find good learning resources at `https://vaadin.com/docs`.

The next chapter gets back to Java and an exciting framework: Spring Boot.

PART IV

Integrations and Database Connectivity

CHAPTER 12

Spring Boot

Spring is a set of projects that increase the productivity of enterprise application developers. There are many projects and modules in Spring, but you don't have to master them all in order to take advantage of it. One of the key projects in Spring is the *Spring Framework*, a programming and configuration model for enterprise applications. We'll be using Spring Framework and *Spring Boot*, a project that simplifies, among many other things, the creation of standalone applications with automatically configured libraries (such as JPA for connecting to SQL databases).

This chapter shows how to use Vaadin in the context of a Spring Boot application and how to quickly implement a CRUD view that connects to a MySQL database.

Creating a New Spring Boot Project

The most common way to create Spring Boot projects is by using the *Spring Initializr* tool available at *https://start.spring.io*. This is an online tool where you can fill in your project details and add the dependencies that you want to use. Vaadin is one of the dependencies available there alongside many other Java libraries.

We'll create a Maven project with the name *spring* and use Java 11—the Long Term Support (LTS) version of Java at the time of writing. We'll use the following dependencies:

- **Vaadin:** This book's favorite web framework

- **Spring Data JPA:** To persist data in SQL databases using the Jakarta Persistence API (JPA; formerly Java Persistence API)

- **MySQL Driver:** The JDBC driver to connect to MySQL databases

© Alejandro Duarte 2021
A. Duarte, *Practical Vaadin*, https://doi.org/10.1007/978-1-4842-7179-7_12

Note   You need a MySQL server running in your machine to follow this chapter. You can download the free MySQL Community Server at *https://dev.mysql. com/downloads*. If you want to use a different database system, select the correct driver when creating the project. If you prefer not to install any additional software, add the *H2 database* dependency in the Spring Initializr instead. The H2 database can be configured as an embedded server that runs alongside your Java application.

Figure 12-1 shows a screenshot of the Spring Initializr configuration that I used to create the example project.

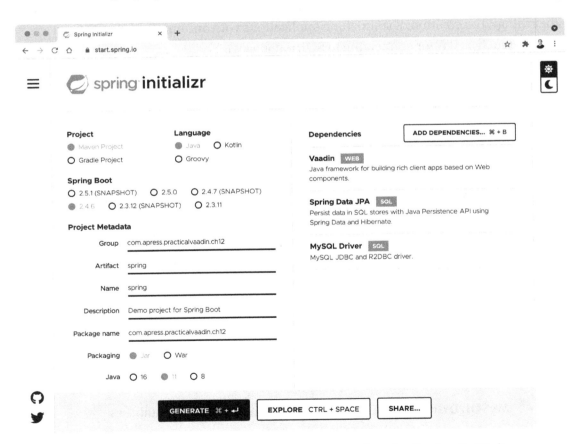

Figure 12-1. *Creating a new Spring Boot project using the Spring Initializr*

When you click the *GENERATE* button, you'll get a ZIP file that contains a Maven project. Extract this file and import the project in your IDE.

The main files in the generated project are

- **pom.xml:** The Project Object Model file that defines a Maven project. You'll see that there's no `<packaging>` declaration, meaning that the default is used (JAR). By default, Spring Boot applications are packaged as standalone Java applications that you can directly run with the *java* tool provided by the JDK binaries.

- **Application.java:** Defines the `public static void main(String...)` standard entry point of a Java application. This allows the application to be built as a JAR file using `mvn package` that you can then run with `java -jar spring.jar`. During development, you can simply run the entry point like you would do with any other standard Java application.

- **application.properties:** Application configuration properties such as server port and database connection strings. The file is empty by default. Spring Boot uses default configurations that can be overridden in this file.

Creating a New Database

Before establishing a connection, we need the database server running. Make sure you have MySQL installed and connect to the server with a username and a password. I'm going to use the default user (`root`):

```
mysql -u root -p
```

After introducing the password, create a new database for this chapter's example application:

```
CREATE DATABASE spring_example;
```

Caution   In a production environment, make sure you create a database user for your application and configure the required privileges to the database.

In this database, let's create a new table to store information about users:

```
USE spring_example;

CREATE TABLE users(
  id INT NOT NULL AUTO_INCREMENT,
  email VARCHAR(255),
  user_password VARCHAR(255),
  birth_date DATE,
  favorite_number INT,
  PRIMARY KEY (id)
);
```

Finally, we can insert some initial data in this table:

```
INSERT INTO users(email, user_password, birth_date,
    favorite_number)
VALUES ("marcus@test.com", "pass1", "1990-03-11", 888);
INSERT INTO users(email, user_password, birth_date,
    favorite_number)
VALUES ("sami@test.com", "pass2", "1991-05-13", 777);
INSERT INTO users(email, user_password, birth_date,
    favorite_number)
VALUES ("guillermo@test.com", "pass3", "1992-07-15", 666);
```

Check that you have some rows in the table:

```
SELECT * FROM users;
```

The database is ready!

Configuring the Database Connection

The Java technology that allows applications to connect to databases is called *Java Database Connectivity* (JDBC). JDBC is an API that database vendors can implement to offer Java programs connectivity to their database systems. The important concept here is the *JDBC driver*. This is a JAR file that encapsulates the logic to "speak" to a specific database. We already added the driver for MySQL in the previous section.

With JDBC, a database connection is specified through a connection string. We need to find the correct connection string for the database we are using and configure it in a specific property in the *resources/application.properties* file that Spring Boot uses. We also have to set the user and password to connect to the database. The following are the properties we need to add to connect to the `spring_example` MySQL database (make sure to use the correct user and password):

```
spring.datasource.url=jdbc:mysql://localhost:3306/spring_example
spring.datasource.username=root
spring.datasource.password=password
```

Here are examples of JDBC connection strings for some other popular databases:

- **PostgreSQL:** `jdbc:postgresql://localhost:5432/spring_example`

- **Oracle:** `jdbc:oracle:thin:@localhost:1521:spring_example`

- **SQL Server:** `jdbc:sqlserver://localhost;databaseName=spring_example`

- **H2 (file-based):** `jdbc:h2:~/some-directory/spring_example`

- **H2 (in-memory):** `jdbc:h2:mem:spring_example`

Spring will set up a connection pool to connect to the configured database. A connection pool is a set of connections to the database that are available by the application. Instead of creating connections as transactions happen, the connections in the pool are reused to avoid wasting computing resources. This happens automatically, and you don't need to worry about it for now.

Implementing an Entity

We are going to use the Jakarta Persistence API (JPA) to connect to and to read and write data. JPA is a specification, not an implementation. Spring Boot uses Hibernate (a JPA implementation). JPA builds on top of JDBC and allows you to *map* Java classes to SQL tables. For example, we can create a `User` class that matches the `users` SQL table that we previously created.

> **Note**   You can learn more about JPA at `https://eclipse-ee4j.github.io/jakartaee-tutorial/#persistence`.

Let's start by simply defining a Java class with matching properties for the users SQL table:

```
public class User {

  private Integer id;
  private String email;
  private String password;
  private LocalDate birthDate;
  private Integer favoriteNumber;

  ... getters and setters ...

}
```

Classes of which instances can be persisted in a database through JPA are called *Entities*. An Entity class must be annotated with @Entity and must contain a property marked with @Id (corresponding to the primary key of the table). By default, Hibernate uses the name of the class and its properties converting camelCase to snake_case to look for the matching SQL table and columns in the database. We can customize this by using the @Table and @Column annotations. Here's what we need to configure to match the users table:

```
@Entity
@Table(name = "users")
public class User {

  @Id
  @GeneratedValue(strategy = GenerationType.IDENTITY)
  private Integer id;

  private String email;

  @Column(name = "user_password")
  private String password;
```

```
  private LocalDate birthDate;

  private Integer favoriteNumber;

  ...
}
```

We are changing the defaults for the table's name and the password column. We also configured the id property to let JPA know that the value is generated by the database, so we don't have to set its value when we create instances of the User class.

It's also important to add proper implementations of the hashCode() and equals(User) methods based on the identity property (id). Most IDEs have tools to generate these methods. Here's an example:

```
@Override
public int hashCode() {
  return Objects.hash(id);
}

@Override
public boolean equals(Object obj) {
  if (this == obj)
    return true;
  if (obj == null)
    return false;
  if (getClass() != obj.getClass())
    return false;
  User other = (User) obj;
  return Objects.equals(id, other.id);
}
```

The class is persistence-ready now!

Adding a Repository

A *repository* is an object used to read and write data from a database. It contains methods to perform all or some of the CRUD operations. With Spring, creating repositories is straightforward as it can be done declaratively through a Java interface that you don't have to implement. To create a repository, we have to use the @Repository annotation and extend one of the repository interfaces that are available. Take a look at this repository interface:

```
@Repository
public interface UserRepository
    extends JpaRepository<User, Integer> {
}
```

The JpaRepository<T, ID> interface that we are extending takes as arguments the domain type or Entity that we want to use and the type of its id property. The interface declares useful methods for data manipulation. Here are some of them:

- List<T> findAll(): Returns all the instances or rows in the table that correspond to the Entity type (e.g., User)

- Optional<T> findById(ID id): Returns an Entity by its id

- S save(S entity): Saves the given Entity

- void delete(T entity): Deletes the given Entity

- long count(): Returns the number of Entities

There are many more methods available. Use the autocompletion feature of your IDE to get familiar with what is available to you. Remember, we won't implement this interface. Spring will provide the implementation at runtime.

Tip   You can add your own queries to repositories by adding methods that match the convention used by Spring. At runtime, the name of the method is used to create the appropriate query. See *https://docs.spring.io/spring-data/jpa/docs/current/reference/html*.

Inversion of Control and Dependency Injection

A central part of Spring is its *Inversion of Control* and *Dependency Injection* features. When the Spring application starts, you run Spring's code (the Application class in your project), that is, you yield control of your application execution to Spring. Spring then scans your project looking for classes annotated with, for example, @Repository and creating instances of these classes that you can use through the Dependency Injection mechanism. This is easy to understand with an example.

Let's implement a Vaadin view that uses the repository class to show the number of users in the database. Let's start with this:

```
@Route("user-count")
public class UserCountView extends Composite<Component> {

  @Override
  protected Component initContent() {
    long count = 999; // TODO!
    return new VerticalLayout(new H1("How many users?"),
        new Text(count + " users found."));
  }

}
```

For now, we are hardcoding the number of users (999). To fix this, we need an instance of type UserRepository, the repository interface that we coded in a previous section. We cannot use new UserRepository() since this is an interface. Instead, we can accept a reference of this type in the constructor and tell Spring to inject an instance. Since the UserRepository interface is marked with @Repository, Spring knows that it needs to create a new instance of this type if another class needs it in the constructor:

```
@Route("user-count")
public class UserCountView extends Composite<Component> {

  private final UserRepository userRepository;

  @Autowired
  public UserCountView(UserRepository userRepository) {
    this.userRepository = userRepository;
  }

  @Override
  protected Component initContent() {
    long count = userRepository.count();
```

```
    return new VerticalLayout(new H1("How many users?"),
        new Text(count + " users found."));
  }

}
```

As you can see, we are marking the constructor with @Autowired. In fact, this annotation is optional, but we'll keep it for clarity.

How can Spring pass an instance of UserRepository to the UserCountView class? The truth is that the UserCountView is also created by Spring! This happens thanks to a Vaadin-Spring integration that is included in the project (see the pom.xml file). Before creating an instance of UserCountView, Spring sees that it depends on a UserRepository and passes it to the constructor using Dependency Injection. Later in the initContent() method, we can use the instance to get the number of users in the database.

You can run the application by executing the main(String...) method in the Application class. Most IDEs include an option to do this when you right-click the file. Alternatively, you can run the spring-boot:run Maven goal. Figure 12-2 shows a screenshot of the view.

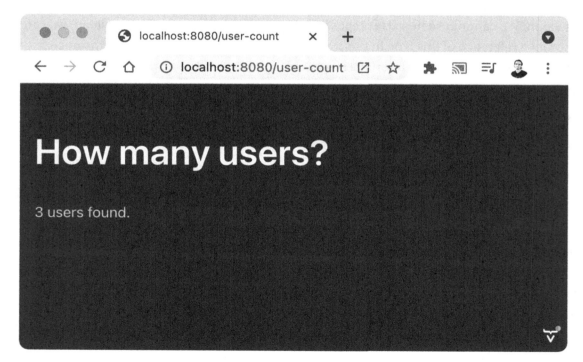

Figure 12-2. *A Vaadin view that consumes an SQL database*

Tip   In the previous example, we directly used the repository interface in the view. In more serious applications, a view should use a service class instead. This service class can use the repository interface to connect to the database, effectively decoupling the presentation layer (views) from persistence technologies (JPA).

Implementing a CRUD

By now, you should have a clear idea of how to combine the knowledge you have acquired throughout the book. You can use the `Binder` class and repository classes to connect the domain model to a database through a UI. In this section, I want to show you a quick way (one of the quickest I know) to implement a fully functional CRUD using an open source Vaadin add-on that I created and that is available for free at *https://vaadin.com/directory/component/crud-ui-add-on*.

Note   The *Vaadin Directory* contains numerous useful add-ons contributed by the Vaadin Community. You can also publish your own add-ons there!

To start, let's add the Crud-UI add-on to the `pom.xml` file:

```
<repositories>
    <repository>
        <id>vaadin-addons</id>
        <url>https://maven.vaadin.com/vaadin-addons</url>
    </repository>
</repositories>
<dependencies>
    ...
    <dependency>
        <groupId>org.vaadin.crudui</groupId>
        <artifactId>crudui</artifactId>
        <version>4.4.1</version>
    </dependency>
<dependencies>
```

This add-on includes the `GridCrud<T>` class that allows us to render a CRUD UI component by using a single line of code:

```
var crud = new GridCrud<>(User.class);
```

We can connect the CRUD operations using lambda expressions. For example, to use the repository to delete users, we can configure the following operation:

```
crud.setDeleteOperation(userRepository::delete);
```

We can configure the visibility of the columns and fields displayed by the component:

```
crud.getGrid().setColumns("email", "birthDate", "favoriteNumber");
crud.getCrudFormFactory().setVisibleProperties("email",
    "password", "birthDate", "favoriteNumber");
```

And finally, we can also configure the type of input component to use for a particular property. For example:

```
crud.getCrudFormFactory().setFieldType("password", PasswordField.class);
```

Putting it all together, we can implement a fully functional CRUD view connected to a Spring repository as follows:

```
@Route("user-crud")
public class UserCrudView extends Composite<Component> {

  private final UserRepository userRepository;

  public UserCrudView(UserRepository userRepository) {
    this.userRepository = userRepository;
  }

  @Override
  protected Component initContent() {
    var crud = new GridCrud<>(User.class);
    crud.getGrid().setColumns("email", "birthDate",
        "favoriteNumber");
    crud.getCrudFormFactory().setVisibleProperties("email",
        "password", "birthDate", "favoriteNumber");
```

```
crud.getCrudFormFactory().setFieldType("password",
    PasswordField.class);
crud.setFindAllOperation(userRepository::findAll);
crud.setAddOperation(userRepository::save);
crud.setUpdateOperation(userRepository::save);
crud.setDeleteOperation(userRepository::delete);

    return new VerticalLayout(crud);
  }

}
```

Figure 12-3 shows a screenshot of the view.

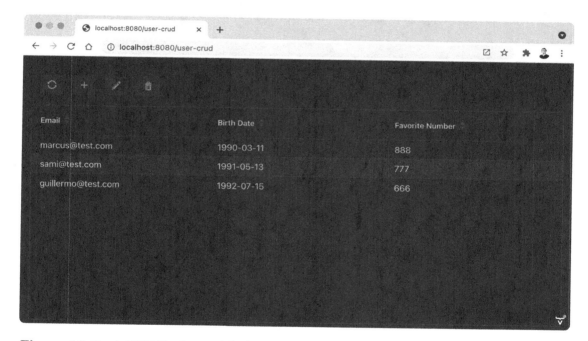

Figure 12-3. *A CRUD view with database connectivity*

The add-on includes many other useful features. You can activate Jakarta Bean Validation, change the layout, add action buttons, and more. To illustrate one of the features, see how the edit form is visualized by default in Figure 12-4.

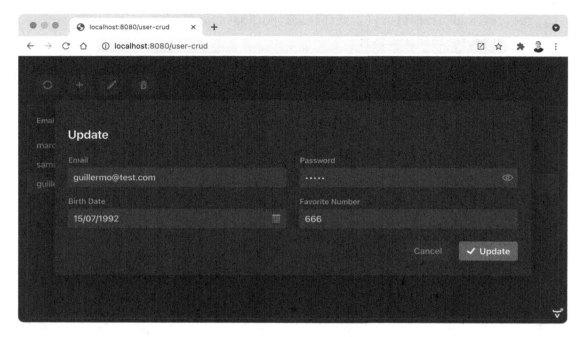

Figure 12-4. *An update form in a CRUD view*

We can easily change the layout to show the edit and new forms on the left next to the Grid by setting a new CrudFormFactory implementation. The Crud-UI add-on includes several alternatives. For example:

```
var crud = new GridCrud<>(User.class,
    new HorizontalSplitCrudLayout());
```

See the result of this change in Figure 12-5.

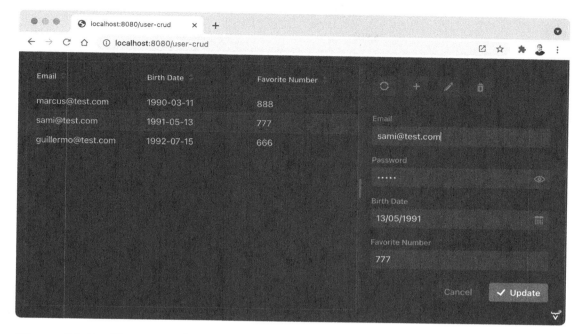

Figure 12-5. *Changing the default layout of a Crud-UI component*

Summary

This chapter got you started with Spring Boot and database connectivity. You saw how to create a new MySQL database and how to configure the connection using JDBC and JPA through Spring. You learned what an Entity is and how to map it to a database table. You saw how easy it is to create a repository class to read and write data and how to use inversion of control and Dependency Injection to connect objects in a Spring application. Finally, you saw how simple it could be to create Vaadin applications when you use the add-ons available in the Vaadin Directory.

The next chapter uses a similar approach than the one used here to explain another powerful technology: Jakarta EE.

CHAPTER 13

Jakarta EE

Jakarta EE (formerly Java Enterprise Edition) is a set of specifications that help developers implement enterprise software with Java. We have already used Jakarta Servlet, Jakarta Bean Validation, and Jakarta Persistence in previous chapters. All these specifications are part of Jakarta EE. To get a better perspective, take a quick look at all the specifications at *https://jakarta.ee/specifications*.

Jakarta EE offers a runtime environment for your Java applications with a programming model based on the concept of *container*. A container envelops your code to add functionality to it by intercepting calls to or from methods in your classes. Examples of this kind of functionality are securing a method call according to user roles, executing code in a transactional context to treat the execution as a unit, asynchronous invocation of methods, and injection of dependencies required by a class.

The Jakarta EE environment is available as an application server in which you deploy your application. You can package the runtime alongside your application code in the same artifact (Uber JAR) or separate the application code from the runtime in a WAR file.

Creating a New Jakarta EE Project

There are several compatible implementations of Jakarta EE:

- Eclipse GlassFish
- Apache Tomcat
- Apache TomEE
- Jetty
- Payara Platform
- Open Liberty

© Alejandro Duarte 2021
A. Duarte, *Practical Vaadin*, https://doi.org/10.1007/978-1-4842-7179-7_13

- WildFly

- Piranha Micro

- Eclipse Jersey

At the time of writing this book, Vaadin supports Jakarta EE 8 (version 9 being the latest), so this limits our choices a bit. We'll use Apache TomEE as a Maven plugin to ease the development cycle, but you can deploy the example application to any Jakarta EE 8–compliant server.

We can take an existing Vaadin project and add the following dependencies to start using the APIs provided by Jakarta EE:

```
<dependency>
    <groupId>jakarta.platform</groupId>
    <artifactId>jakarta.jakartaee-api</artifactId>
    <version>8.0.0</version>
    <scope>provided</scope>
</dependency>
<dependency>
    <groupId>com.vaadin</groupId>
    <artifactId>vaadin-cdi</artifactId>
</dependency>
```

We need a new *beans.xml* file in the *src/main/webapp/WEB-INF/* directory. This file is required to activate Contexts and Dependency Injection (more on this later). Create it with the following content:

```
<?xml version="1.0" encoding="UTF-8"?>
<beans
        xmlns="http://xmlns.jcp.org/xml/ns/javaee"
        xmlns:xsi="http://www.w3.org/2001/XMLSchema-instance"
        xsi:schemaLocation="http://xmlns.jcp.org/xml/ns/javaee
                    http://xmlns.jcp.org/xml/ns/javaee/beans_1_1.xsd"
        bean-discovery-mode="all">
</beans>
```

Instead of installing a Jakarta EE server, we can run the application with Maven adding the Apache TomEE plugin as follows (this is equivalent to installing an application server, only that the server is managed via Maven):

```
<plugin>
    <groupId>org.apache.tomee.maven</groupId>
    <artifactId>tomee-maven-plugin</artifactId>
    <version>8.0.7</version>
    <configuration>
        <context>ROOT</context>
    </configuration>
</plugin>
```

Note   You can learn more about Apache TomEE at `https://tomee.apache.org`.

Now we can add a Vaadin view to check that everything works:

```
@Route("hello-jakarta-ee")
public class HelloJakartaEEView extends Composite<Component> {

  @Override
  protected Component initContent() {
    return new VerticalLayout(new Text("Hello Jakarta EE!"));
  }

}
```

You can build the application using `mvn package` and deploy the WAR file to any Jakarta EE runtime or simply run the application using `mvn tomee:run`. Figure 13-1 shows the result.

Figure 13-1. *A Jakarta EE Vaadin application running on Apache TomEE*

Creating a New Database

As in the previous chapter, before establishing a connection, we need the database server running. Make sure you have MySQL installed and connect to the server with a username and a password.

Note You can download the free MySQL Community Server at *https://dev.mysql.com/downloads*.

I'm going to use the default user (root):

```
mysql -u root -p
```

After introducing the password, create a new database for this chapter's example application:

```
CREATE DATABASE jakarta_ee_example;
```

In this database, let's create a new table to store information about users:

```
USE jakarta_ee_example;

CREATE TABLE users(
  id INT NOT NULL AUTO_INCREMENT,
  email VARCHAR(255),
  user_password VARCHAR(255),
  birth_date DATE,
  favorite_number INT,
  PRIMARY KEY (id)
);
```

Finally, we can insert some initial data in this table:

```
INSERT INTO users(email, user_password, birth_date,
  favorite_number)
VALUES ("marcus@test.com", "pass1", "1990-03-11", 888);
INSERT INTO users(email, user_password, birth_date,
  favorite_number)
VALUES ("sami@test.com", "pass2", "1991-05-13", 777);
```

```
INSERT INTO users(email, user_password, birth_date,
    favorite_number)
VALUES ("guillermo@test.com", "pass3", "1992-07-15", 666);
```

Check that you have some rows in the table:

```
SELECT * FROM users;
```

Configuring the Database Connection

If you remember from the previous chapter, Java applications connect to specific database systems through JDBC drivers. A database connection is something that depends on the environment in which the application runs. For example, when you are developing an application, you probably have a database server running in the same development machine. When you deploy the application to a production server, the application doesn't connect to your development machine but to a production-ready machine. For this reason, database connections are better configured in the environment in which the application runs rather than in the application code.

A Jakarta EE environment allows you to define resources such as database connections in configuration files. Since we are using the Apache TomEE Maven plugin, our runtime environment resides in the same machine we are working and even in the project we are coding. In this case, we can define the details of the connection in files that are inside the project. However, when you deploy the application to a production environment, you won't use the Maven plugin. Instead, you have to define the database connection in the production environment. The application code can reference the database connection resource by a name that we can establish. For now, we'll skip production setups and configure the database connection resource for the Apache TomEE Maven plugin.

First, we need to add the JDBC driver, again, to the runtime (Apache TomEE) defined in the *pom.xml* file. All we need to do is update the Apache TomEE plugin declaration to include the MySQL JDBC driver:

```
<plugin>
    <groupId>org.apache.tomee.maven</groupId>
    <artifactId>tomee-maven-plugin</artifactId>
    <version>8.0.7</version>
```

```
    <configuration>
        <context>ROOT</context>
        <libs>
            <lib>mysql:mysql-connector-java:8.0.25</lib>
        </libs>
    </configuration>
</plugin>
```

Now the JAR file containing the JDBC driver is available during runtime. If you want to deploy the application to an external standalone server, you'll have to add the JAR file there as well.

Now we can configure the database connection details. We can set this up in a new file called *tomee.xml* placed in the *src/main/tomee/conf/* directory:

```
<tomee>
  <Resource id="mysqlDatasource" type="DataSource">
    JdbcDriver com.mysql.cj.jdbc.Driver
    JdbcUrl jdbc:mysql://localhost:3306/jakarta_ee_example
    UserName root
    Password password
  </Resource>
</tomee>
```

Pay atttention to the `id` we used (`mysqlDatasource`). We'll be referencing this data source from the application code using this name. This allows us to decouple the connection details from the runtime environment. A production server could define the data source as a connection to an Oracle database, for example, and we wouldn't have to make any changes to the application code.

Jakarta EE will set up a connection pool to connect to the configured database.

Note   A *connection pool* is a set of connections to the database that are available by the application. Instead of creating connections as transactions happen, the connections in the pool are reused to avoid wasting computing resources. This happens automatically, and you don't need to worry about it for now.

Implementing an Entity

Jakarta EE includes JPA, so we can add the same Entity we coded in the previous chapter, this time using explicit column names in all of the properties and adding Jakarta Bean Validation annotations:

```
@Entity
@Table(name = "users")
public class User {

  @Id
  @GeneratedValue(strategy = GenerationType.IDENTITY)
  @Column(name = "id")
  @NotNull
  private Integer id;

  @Column(name = "email")
  @NotNull
  @NotBlank
  @Email
  private String email;

  @Column(name = "user_password")
  @NotNull
  @NotBlank
  @Size(min = 5)
  private String password;

  @Column(name = "birth_date")
  @Past
  private LocalDate birthDate;

  @Column(name = "favorite_number")
  @PositiveOrZero
  private Integer favoriteNumber;
```

```
@Override
public int hashCode() {
  return Objects.hash(id);
}

@Override
public boolean equals(Object obj) {
  if (this == obj)
    return true;
  if (obj == null)
    return false;
  if (getClass() != obj.getClass())
    return false;
  User other = (User) obj;
  return Objects.equals(id, other.id);
}

... getters and setters ...

}
```

Note   Apache TomEE uses Apache OpenJPA as the JPA implementation. The way
OpenJPA matches the names of the properties with SQL columns is different than
with Hibernate. OpenJPA uses the exact names of the classes and properties to
look for the corresponding tables and columns in the database.

When using JPA in Jakarta EE applications, we need to define a *persistence unit*.
A persistence unit defines the Entities and the data source to use with them. To define
a persistence unit, we need to create a new file named *persistence.xml* in the *src/main/
resources/META-INF/* directory:

```
<persistence xmlns="http://java.sun.com/xml/ns/persistence"
      version="1.0">

    <persistence-unit name="jakarta-ee-example-pu"
          transaction-type="RESOURCE_LOCAL">
          <jta-data-source>mysqlDatasource</jta-data-source>
```

```
    <class>com.apress.practicalvaadin.ch13.User</class>
  </persistence-unit>
</persistence>
```

As you can see, we are using the name of the data source we defined in the Jakarta EE runtime (Apache TomEE). This file is part of the application code, but it doesn't contain any database connection details. As pointed out before, the connection details live in the runtime. Notice also how we added the User class as a managed Entity. If we need more Entities, we can list them there. If we have more than one database, we can define more persistence units and add the corresponding Entities to it.

Adding a Repository

Jakarta EE doesn't itself include functionality for declarative repository implementation. However, it does include mechanisms for extension, and the Apache DeltaSpike (https://deltaspike.apache.org) project includes a library to create this kind of repository classes. We need to add the Apache DeltaSpike Bill of Materials (BOM) in the <dependencyManagement> section of the *pom.xml* file:

```
<dependency>
    <groupId>org.apache.deltaspike.distribution</groupId>
    <artifactId>distributions-bom</artifactId>
    <version>1.9.4     </version>
    <type>pom</type>
    <scope>import</scope>
</dependency>
```

And we need to add the Apache DeltaSpike Data module in the <dependencies> section:

```
<dependency>
    <groupId>org.apache.deltaspike.core</groupId>
    <artifactId>deltaspike-core-api</artifactId>
    <scope>compile</scope>
</dependency>
```

```
<dependency>
      <groupId>org.apache.deltaspike.core</groupId>
      <artifactId>deltaspike-core-impl</artifactId>
      <scope>runtime</scope>
</dependency>
<dependency>
      <groupId>org.apache.deltaspike.modules</groupId>
      <artifactId>deltaspike-data-module-api</artifactId>
      <scope>compile</scope>
</dependency>
<dependency>
      <groupId>org.apache.deltaspike.modules</groupId>
      <artifactId>deltaspike-data-module-impl</artifactId>
      <scope>runtime</scope>
</dependency>
```

Apache DeltaSpike Data requires an `EntityManager`. The way the library looks for this object is through a *CDI producer*. Don't worry too much about these terms for now, and think of the `EntityManager` class as a helper class that serves as the interface to JPA and that Apache DeltaSpike Data uses internally. The CDI producer is simply a factory that produces instances of `EntityManager`:

```
@ApplicationScoped
public class EntityManagerProducer {

  @PersistenceUnit(unitName = "jakarta-ee-example-pu")
  private EntityManagerFactory emf;

  @Produces
  public EntityManager create() {
    return emf.createEntityManager();
  }

  public void close(@Disposes EntityManager em) {
    if (em.isOpen()) {
      em.close();
    }
  }
}
```

The Jakarta EE runtime will automatically create a single instance of this class that Apache DeltaSpike can use later to communicate with the database via JPA. We are declaring the name of the persistence unit to use in the @PersistenceUnit annotation. Now we see how the persistence logic is connected to the data source through this persistence unit and the data source defined in the application server.

With this in place, we can define a repository interface:

```
@Repository
public interface UserRepository
    extends EntityRepository<User, Integer> {

}
```

As with Spring, we don't need to implement this interface.

Contexts and Dependency Injection

Jakarta EE and Vaadin are integrated through a Contexts and Dependency Injection (CDI) library that we already added as a dependency when we were configuring the project. CDI is a Jakarta EE specification that allows to decouple instances of your classes. To understand how it works, let's review the EntityManagerProducer class that we implemented in the previous section:

```
@ApplicationScoped
public class EntityManagerProducer {

  @PersistenceUnit(unitName = "jakarta-ee-example-pu")
  private EntityManagerFactory emf;

  ...

}
```

The CDI runtime will see that the EntityManagerProducer class is annotated with @ApplicationScoped and creates a new instance of this class. This instance is going to be shared by all possible clients of the class in the application. Before creating the instance, however, the CDI runtime sees that an EntityManagerFactory is required since there's a property of this type annotated with @PersistenceUnit. CDI asks JPA to prepare an instance of this class. JPA uses the name of the persistence unit (jakarta-ee-example-pu) to locate the configuration and create the appropriate object. CDI takes this object and "injects" it into the `EntityManagerProducer` instance that it is creating. This is dependency injection in action!

We can use this mechanism to inject instances of classes or interfaces that we added to the application code. In fact, Vaadin views are created via CDI, which means that we can inject CDI beans (other objects created and managed by the CDI runtime) into Vaadin views. For example, we can inject an instance of type UserRepository and call its methods as follows:

```
@Route("user-count")
public class UserCountView extends Composite<Component> {

  private final UserRepository userRepository;

  @Inject
  public UserCountView(UserRepository userRepository) {
    this.userRepository = userRepository;
  }

  @Override
  protected Component initContent() {
    long count = userRepository.count();
    return new VerticalLayout(new H1("How many users?"),
        new Text(count + " users found."));
  }

}
```

As you can see, we are marking the constructor with `@Inject`. This marks an injection point that CDI detects before creating an instance of the Vaadin view.

With a Vaadin view in place, we can run the application using the `tomee:run` Maven goal to test that everything works as expected. Figure 13-2 shows a screenshot of the view.

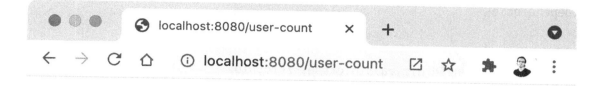

How many users?

3 users found.

Figure 13-2. *A Vaadin view that consumes an SQL database*

Implementing a CRUD

Once again, you should have a clear idea of how to combine the knowledge you have acquired throughout the book to connect Vaadin UI components with repository classes using the Binder class. In this section, we'll implement a fully functional CRUD using my Crud-UI add-on for Vaadin available at *https://vaadin.com/directory/component/crud-ui-add-on*.

To start, let's add the Crud-UI add-on to the pom.xml file:

```
<repositories>
    <repository>
        <id>vaadin-addons</id>
        <url>https://maven.vaadin.com/vaadin-addons</url>
    </repository>
</repositories>
```

```
<dependencies>
        ...
      <dependency>
            <groupId>org.vaadin.crudui</groupId>
            <artifactId>crudui</artifactId>
            <version>4.4.1</version>
      </dependency>
<dependencies>
```

In the previous chapter, you saw how to use this add-on. This time, let's configure the CRUD component in a different way to support Jakarta Bean Validation and make the UX a bit better. Here's the full implementation of the view:

```
@Route("user-crud")
public class UserCrudView extends Composite<Component> {

  private final UserRepository userRepository;

  @Inject
  public UserCrudView(UserRepository userRepository) {
    this.userRepository = userRepository;
  }

  @Override
  protected Component initContent() {
    var crud = new GridCrud<>(User.class,
        new VerticalCrudLayout());
    crud.setSizeFull();
    crud.getGrid().setHeightByRows(true);
    crud.getCrudFormFactory().setUseBeanValidation(true);
    crud.setClickRowToUpdate(true);
    crud.setUpdateOperationVisible(false);

    crud.getGrid().setColumns("email", "birthDate",
        "favoriteNumber");
    crud.getCrudFormFactory().setVisibleProperties("email",
        "password", "birthDate", "favoriteNumber");
```

```
crud.getCrudFormFactory().setFieldType("password",
    PasswordField.class);
crud.setFindAllOperation(userRepository::findAll);
crud.setAddOperation(userRepository::save);
crud.setUpdateOperation(userRepository::save);
crud.setDeleteOperation(userRepository::remove);

VerticalLayout layout = new VerticalLayout(crud);
layout.setSizeFull();
return layout;
  }

}
```

This implementation is similar to the one we used in the previous chapter, but it includes several differences:

- We are using a `VerticalCrudLayout` to visualize the form on the bottom of the page instead of to the right.

- We are setting the CRUD and the layout that contains it to be full size.

- We are configuring the Grid to use as much space vertically to visualize all the contained rows by calling the `setHeightByRows(true)` method.

- We are activating Jakarta Bean Validation in the add and update forms.

- We are activating an option to make the form editable when the user clicks a row in the `Grid` by calling the `setClickRowToUpdate(boolean)` method.

- We are hiding the update button from the UI since it's not required anymore (due to the previous point).

You can see a screenshot of the application in Figure 13-3.

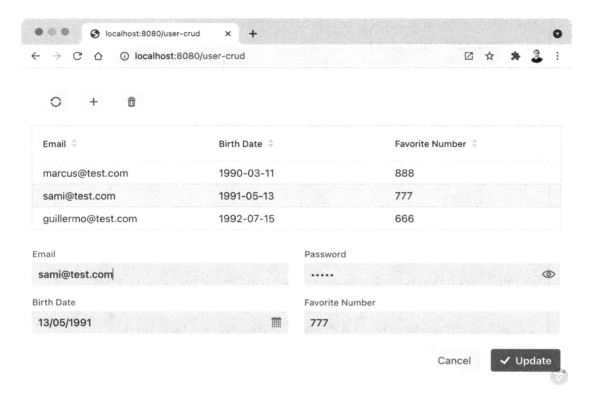

Figure 13-3. *A CRUD with database connectivity*

The CRUD shows error messages if you introduce invalid values in the input fields. Figure 13-4 shows an example.

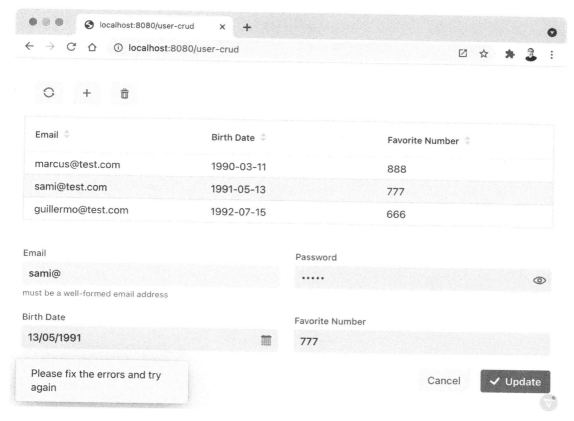

Figure 13-4. *A CRUD view showing Jakarta Bean Validation error messages*

Summary

This chapter got you started with Jakarta EE and database connectivity using Apache DeltaSpike Data. You saw how to configure a database connection using JDBC and JPA. You learned how easy it is to create a repository class to read and write data and how to use dependency injection to connect objects in a Jakarta EE application. Finally, you saw how simple it could be to create Vaadin applications when you use the add-ons available in the Vaadin Directory.

This book ends where it started. The Crud-UI add-on has always been the perfect reminder of why Vaadin is so powerful and fun to use. Implementing graphical web user interfaces using the power of the Java programming language, the Java virtual machine, and the Java ecosystem is luxurious. I hope you continue your journey through modern web development with Vaadin and Java. Happy coding!

Index

A

accept(T) method, 223
access(Command) method, 198–200, 202
addEventData(String) method, 224
AdminView component, 169
AppLayout, 69

B

beforeLeave(BeforeLeaveEvent)
    method, 184
Binder class, 299
bindInstanceFields(Object) method, 125
Breakpoint, 41

C

Cascading Style Sheets (CSS), 10
    built-in themes
        component variants, 239
        material, 236
        Vaadin, 235
        variants, 237, 238
    classes to UI components, 246,
        248–250
    importing files, 241, 242
    Lunimo theme, 243, 244
    shadow DOM, 250, 251
Checkbox class, 77, 78
ComboBox class, 84

Comma-separated values file (CSV)
    Anchor component, 158
    Book class, 160
    Book instances, 159
    pom.xml file, 159
    StatefulBeanToCsvBuilder, 159
    StreamResources, 158, 159
    toString() method, 160
Common Gateway Interface (CGI), 18
Component composition
    alignment, 60, 62
    component, 52
    composite, 51
    CompositionView class, 51, 52
    grow property, 59
    height, 58
    justify-content mode, 62, 64
    margin, 55
    padding, 55
    padding margin/spacing, 55, 56
    primary axis, 62
    scrolling, 64–66
    secondary axis, 60
    sizing, 57, 58
    spacing, 55
    UI components, 53
    VerticalLayout, 49, 50
    width, 58
Components tree, 50, 54
Connection pool, 310

323

© Alejandro Duarte 2021
A. Duarte, *Practical Vaadin*, https://doi.org/10.1007/978-1-4842-7179-7

Printed in the United States
by Baker & Taylor Publisher Services